The Illustrated History of
WEAPONRY

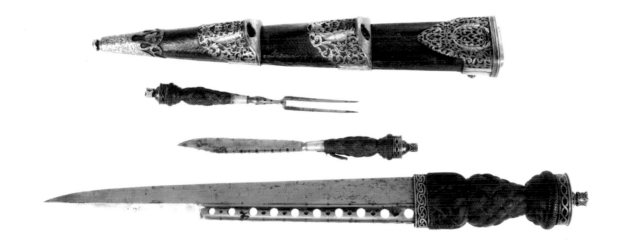

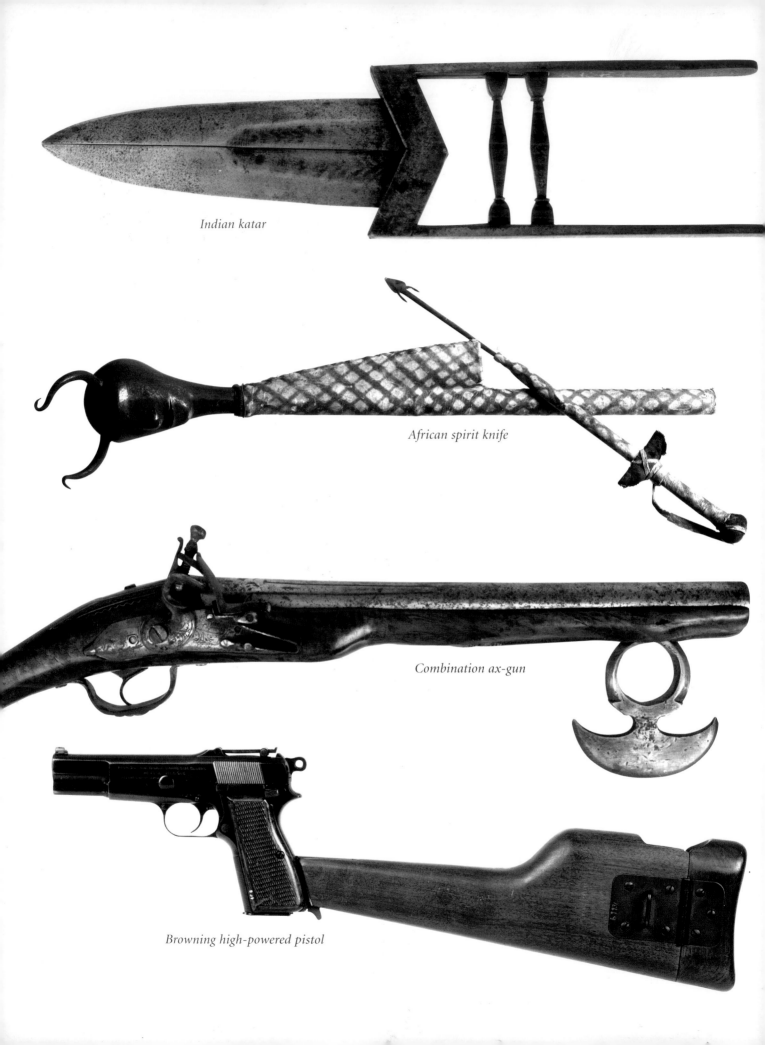

Indian katar

African spirit knife

Combination ax-gun

Browning high-powered pistol

The Illustrated History of
WEAPONRY

From Flint Axes to Automatic Weapons

Chuck Wills

In Association with the Berman Museum of World Art

HYLAS
PUBLISHING

Hylas Publishing
129 Main Street, Suite C
Irvington, New York 10533
www.hylaspublishing.com

Hylas Publishing
Publisher: Sean Moore
Publishing Director: Karen Prince
COO/Photographer: ƒ-stop fitzgerald
Art Director/Designer: Gus Yoo
Editorial Director: Gail Greiner
Production Managers: Sarah Reilly, Wayne Ellis
Editor: Suzanne Lander
Assistant Editor: Jessica Smith
Assistant Designer: Erika Lubowicki

Additional photography by Richard McCaffrey
Indexing by Liss Index

Library of Congress Cataloging-in-Publication Data

Wills, Chuck.
The illustrated history of weaponry : from flint axes to automatic weapons / by Chuck Wills
in association with the Berman Museum of World Art. p. cm.
Includes bibliographical references and index.
ISBN 1-59258-127-7
1. Weapons—History—Catalogs. 2. Berman Museum (Anniston, Ala.)—Catalogs.
I. Berman Museum (Anniston, Ala.) II. Title.
U804.U62A55 2006
623.4074'76163—dc22
2006006042

Printed and bound in China
Distributed in the U.S. by National Book Network
Represented in Canada by Kate Walker Ltd.
Distributed in Canada by The Jaguar Book Group

First American Edition published in 2006

2 4 6 8 10 9 7 5 3 1

"A sword is never a killer, it is a tool in the killer's hands."
—Seneca

"The greatest joy a man can know is to conquer his enemies and drive them before him. To ride their horses and take away their possessions. To see the faces of those who were dear to them bedewed with tears, and to clasp their wives and daughters in his arms."
—Genghis Khan

"The root of the evil is not the construction of new, more dreadful weapons. It is the spirit of conquest."
—Ludwig von Mises

"Political power grows out of the barrel of a gun."
—Mao Zedong

Bali kris holder

CONTENTS

FOREWORD 8

PART I. **PREHISTORIC AND ANCIENT WEAPONS** 13
   Stone Weapons 16
   The Bronze Age 20
   Weapons of the Americas & Australasia 22
   Bows & Crossbows .26
   Feature: The Hundred Years War 30

PART II. **CHANGING WAYS OF WARFARE** 33
   Maces & Flails 36
   Feature: The Crusades 38
   Pole Arms & Axes .40
   Armor 46
   Daggers & Fighting Knives 50
   Feature: The Introduction of Gunpowder 64

PART III. **REVOLUTIONARY TIMES** 67
   The First Firearms: From Handcannon to Flintlock . . .70
   From Matchlock to Flintlock 72
   The Flintlock Pistol 78
   The European Sword 84
   Swords of Asia & Africa 90
   Dueling Pistols .100
   The Blunderbuss .102
   Feature: Naval Weapons 104

PART IV. **FROM NAPOLEON TO 1914** 107
   Weapons of the Napoleonic War 110
   From Flintlock to Percussion Caps 114
   The Nineteenth-Century Sword 120
   Pepperboxes & Derringers 126
   Colt's Revolvers .130
   Colt's Competitors 134
   Feature: The U.S. Civil War 138
   Union Weapons of the Civil War 140
   Confederate Weapons of the Civil War 142

   Weapons of the American West 144
   Bolt-Action Rifles 148
   The Automatic Pistol 152
   Personal Defense Weapons 156
   Combination Weapons 164
   Feature: Alarm, Trap, and Special-Purpose Guns 170

PART V. **WORLD WAR I** 173
   Edged Weapons 176
   Pistols 178
   Infantry Rifles .180
   Machine Guns 182
   Feature: Trench Warfare 184
   Guns of the U.S. Roaring Twenties 186

PART VI. **WORLD WAR II AND BEYOND** 189
   Edged Weapons of World War II 192
   Axis Pistols 194
   Allied Pistols 196
   Rifles 198
   Ceremonial Weapons 202
   Machine Guns 206
   Submachine Guns .208
   Specialized Weapons 210
   Weapons of Espionage 212
   Feature: Germ Warfare 214
   Weapons after the World Wars 216

APPENDICES 221
Glossary 222
Bibliography 226
About the Berman 229
Index 230
Acknowledgments 240

FOREWORD

From the rock first held in the hands of Paleolithic man to the twenty-first century assault rifle, weapons have been an integral component in human history. As early humans evolved, so did their technology. Small rocks became specialized tools and weapons. These early innovations helped man in his quest for food, and eventually in protecting both family and territory. Stone technology gave way to metallurgy and as humans passed through each period of history—copper, bronze, and iron—their use and development of weapons increased. With the advent of agriculture and animal domestication, the reliance on weapons shifted from hunting food to protection from wild animals and other humans. Newly acquired possessions—food, animals, and shelter—carried intrinsic wealth and brought status. Humans used weapons to protect both.

Turkish ax head

Early weapons were effective only in hand-to-hand combat. The introduction of gunpowder into Europe brought radical change in weaponry and warfare. Its military use was first recorded in 919 C.E., and by the eleventh century explosive bombs filled with gunpowder were fired from catapults in China. Europe's initial use of gunpowder in the thirteenth century was recorded by the English philosopher Roger Bacon, and cannons were made in Florence, Italy, around 1326 with technology used by bell makers. By the later fourteenth century, hand-held firearms made an appearance. When metal projectiles could pierce armor, chain mail became a necessity, yet often was a poor defense against gunpowder and lead. Soon hand-to-hand combat was used only as a last means of defense.

The design of new weaponry was not left to the military. Leonardo da Vinci, the great Renaissance artist and inventor who hated war was, however, fascinated by structure and

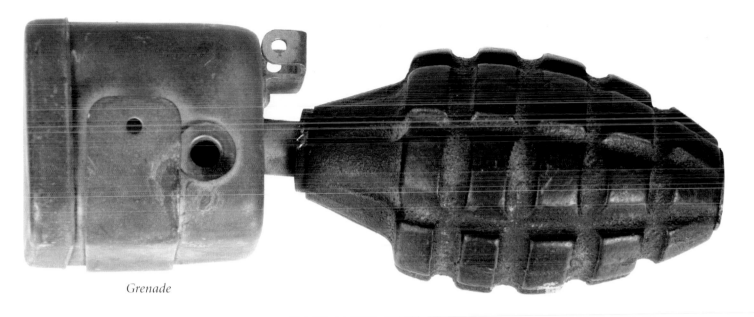

Grenade

function and the beauty of design and utility. This must have been why his great genius was used in inventing numerous weapons, including missiles, multi-barreled machine guns, grenades, mortars, and even a modern-style tank. As deadly as these early weapons were, it would be several centuries before technological advances allowed hand guns to fire more than one projectile at a time. Guns did not cause the obsolescence of other weapons; knives, swords, and other implements were still needed in combat. To overcome the deficiency of single-fire weapons, combination weapons—those that could perform more than one function—were developed. Single-fire guns were fitted with bayonets, and the fighting ax contained a gun in the handle. If the shot missed the target, its user had an alternate defense source. Combination weapons continue to be manufactured today. A recent example would be a cellular phone that contains a small .22 caliber pistol that could be used for assassinations or easily smuggled through security screening by terrorists.

"Guns did not cause the obsolescence of other weapons; knives, swords, and other implements were still needed"

Multishot weapons appeared in the nineteenth century. Early examples called "pepperboxes" shot from five to twenty times. Perhaps the most

Thompson sub-machine gun

famous multishot weapon was the Gatling gun, capable of firing up to 800 rounds per minute, which—had it been introduced earlier—might have meant an earlier triumph by the Union Army during the U.S. Civil War. The twentieth century saw its share of multi-shot weapons; one of the best known was the Thompson sub-machine gun used by the likes of Roaring Twenties gangsters Dillinger and Bonnie and Clyde. Once it was adopted by the military, the multishooting machine gun changed warfare. With one-shot guns, advancement toward an enemy could be accomplished during reloading. With machine guns, movement on an open battlefield became more deadly, and gunplay was performed from entrenchments and behind barricades. Technology changes were required to protect battlefield soldiers. Tanks and other armored vehicles were developed in the early twentieth century to reduce battle casualties by protecting soldiers as they advanced across an open battlefield.

In the modern era, technology continues to change the way weapons function in society, yet today's weapons technology has not made firearms obsolete. The military use of precision guided missiles has changed the way modern armies accomplish their goals and objectives. Yet, firearms and knives still play an important role in warfare.

In addition to their intrinsic value as property and the worth of the materials of which they were composed (the Persian scimitar owned by both Abbas I and Catherine the Great being a case in point), weapons throughout history have represented status in society, communicating one's prosperity and power. Many early weapons were costly, affordable only to the wealthy. Rulers in Europe and Asia had weapons constructed of gold or silver and encrusted with precious stones to flaunt their wealth, not only in their own society, but to those visiting their country. Many beautiful weapons come from the area around Persia—what is present-day Iran—and the Near East. Gold inlay, called damascene, embellished steel blades; hilts were decorated with rubies, emeralds, and other precious stones. Today, weapons reveal the status of their buyer, but in a different way. The country with the most weapons or the largest arsenal has the most military power, and military power symbolizes superior world status.

Aside from practical use, weapons have a unique appeal for collectors and museums because of their technology, materials, craftsmanship, and beauty. The most ordinary weapons tell the story of time and the society in which they were made and used. Though they served and continue to serve deadly purposes, weapons allow a glimpse into human history.

Robert P. Lindley

Robert Lindley
Collections Manager
Berman Museum of World History
Anniston, Alabama
March 2006

Persian scimitar owned by Abbas I and Catherine the Great

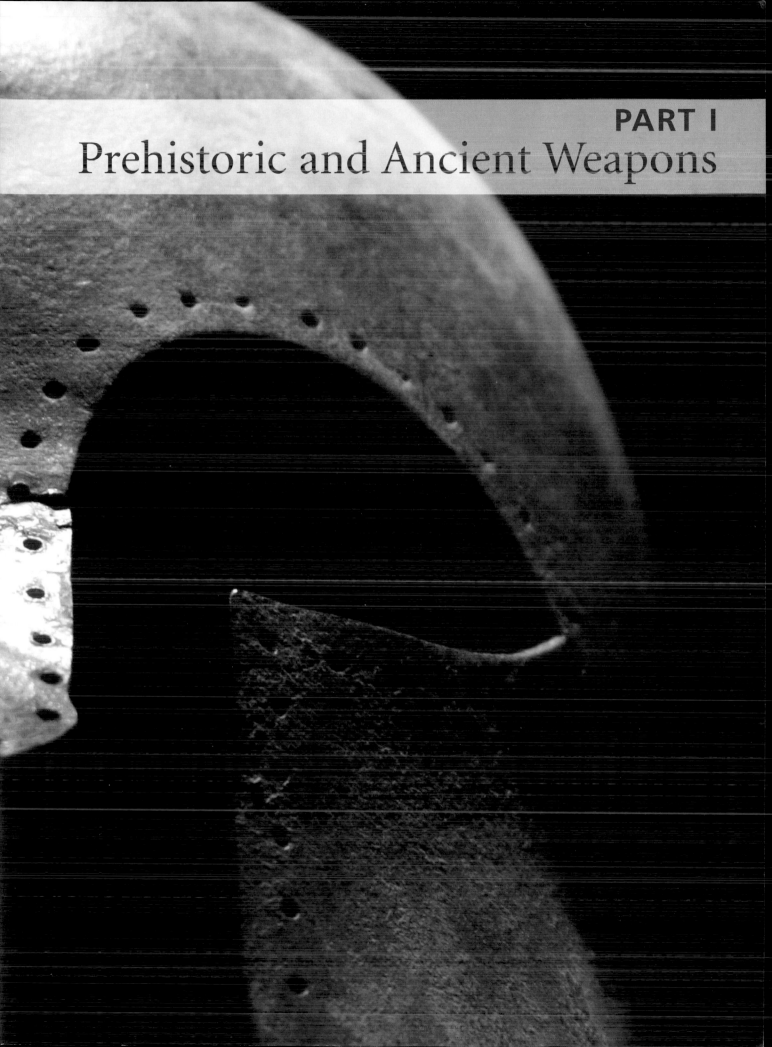

PART I

Prehistoric and Ancient Weapons

"Permit me not to languish
	out my days,
But make the best exchange
	of life for praise.
This arm, this lance, can
	well dispute the prize;
And the blood follows,
	where the weapon flies."

—Virgil, from *The Æneid*

The story of weapons begins with creation of the the first crude stone implements by early hominids, perhaps as long as 5 million years ago. Sometime between 15,000 and 10,000 BCE, early modern humans refined the toolmaking process to craft effective axes, knives, and spear points, and toward the end of this period came the development of the bow and arrow and the knife. These early weapons, along with the atlatl (spear thrower) and specialized devices like the bola, were used in hunting; just when and where humans turned such weapons on each other in a way that we would recognize as warfare is still a matter of debate.

The next great advance in weapons technology came when humans discovered how to smelt mineral ore to produce metal—first copper, then bronze, and finally iron and steel, allowing the creation of ever more durable blades and projectiles.

STONE WEAPONS

Between 5 million and 1.5 million years ago, the early hominids *Australopithecus* lived in Africa's Olduvai Gorge. At some point, one of them chipped a small rock against another to create a crude cutting edge—the first tool. This modest event was the "big bang" for human technology—including weaponry.

TOOLS OF THE AGE

Over millions of years the first hominids evolved through successive stages into *Homo sapiens sapiens*— modern humans. (Another group, the Neanderthals, also appeared and eventually became extinct, but whether they were ancestors of modern humans or a completely different species is still debated.) Around 3 million years ago, the Stone Age began, as people learned to fashion tools of stone.

The term "Stone Age" is broad and imprecise; it ended in different parts of the world at different times as stone tools gave way to metal implements, and in remote parts of the world, indigenous peoples remained at Stone Age level, in technological terms, into our own era.

It's difficult to make generalizations, and archeological evidence is often fragmentary or contradictory, but the next great advances in tool-making technology came between 600,000 and 100,000 BCE, when multipurpose stone tools like the hand-ax replaced cruder implements. At the later scale of that time frame, humans developed sophisticated techniques to "flake" blades from stone. Flint was the preferred material, and there's evidence that early people in Europe traveled up to 100 miles/160km to reach good sources of flint. These flint tools were used for a variety of purposes, from digging up edible roots to scraping animal hides.

In this pre-agricultural time, procuring a steady food supply was the main priority. Fruit, nuts, and roots could be gathered, but animals had to be hunted. Spears were the earliest weapons used to hunt mammals, and by 250,000-100,000 BCE hunters learned to harden the wooden tips of spears in a fire or to tip them with heads of edged stone. The development of the atlatl, or spear thrower (see p 19), greatly increased the spear's range and power, while spears of bone or antler could be carved with barbs to stick in an animal's flesh. The bow and arrow came on the scene around 10,000 BCE, as did the knife in its modern form.

FROM HUNTING TO WAR

How and when these hunting weapons began to be used against humans rather than animals, and when warfare as an organized activity developed, are controversial questions. In anthropological circles, no subject is more hotly debated than whether human aggression toward other humans is "hardwired" in our DNA or if it is imparted culturally. But it's likely that prehistoric peoples fought over hunting territory, especially as the climatic changes that occurred throughout the period transformed landscapes.

In 1964, archaeologists found the bodies of more than fifty people—both men and women—at Jebel Sahaba, a site in what is now Egypt near the Sudanese border dating from between 12000 and 5000 BCE. They had been killed with stone-bladed weapons. To some archaeologists and historians, the number of bodies and the manner of their deaths seemed to be evidence that prehistoric warfare went beyond mere raiding and territorial clashes. Others contend the evidence is inconclusive.

By this time humans had begun to make the transition from a hunter-gatherer existence to agriculture and to live in settled communities. Two of these early towns—Jericho (in present-day Israel) and Çatal Hüyük (in present-day Turkey), both first occupied around 7000– 6000 BCE—were built with stout walls, suggesting their inhabitants feared attack, and making them perhaps the first fortified settlements. As with Jebel Sahaba, the excavations at Jericho and Çatal Hüyük have led many historians to believe that warfare in the modern sense began much earlier than previously thought.

Over time the switch to agriculture led to the rise of city-states, and then to empires with armies of professional with weapons made expressly for killing humans. In fact, most of the weapons used by European armies until the coming of firearms—and for centuries afterward, in other parts of the world—like the bow, the spear, and the sword (an evolution of the knife) had their prototypes in prehistory.

STEATITE HOE

A hoe blade is made from steatite, a variety of soapstone with a high chalk content. Being fairly easy to shape, steatite was used for tools, decorative objects, and weapons by many early people. This example comes from the Mississippian Native American culture (c. 1000–1500 CE) in what is now the southeastern United States.

GREENSTONE CELT

Archaeologists use the term celt (from the late Latin *celtis*, meaning "chisel") to describe the stone (and later bronze) ax- and adze-heads used by early peoples. These celts, from North America, are made from greenstone. A very hard rock found in riverbeds, greenstone is hard to work, but its durability is similar to that of iron. While these celts were used as woodworking tools, they and similar blades are the early ancestors of weapons like the battle-ax (see p 40).

BOLA
Like the atlatl, the bola or bolas (from the Spanish *boleadros*, or "balls") was a simple but elegant and highly effective weapon. First used by indigenous peoples of South America to hunt animals like guanaco, the bola, such as the one shown here, consisted of round weights—usually three, sometimes more—attached to cords. The user whirled the cords overhead and then launched the bola at the animal to entangle its legs. The bola's ability to immobilize an animal without wounding or killing it led to its later adoption by South American gauchos (cowboys) for rounding up cattle.

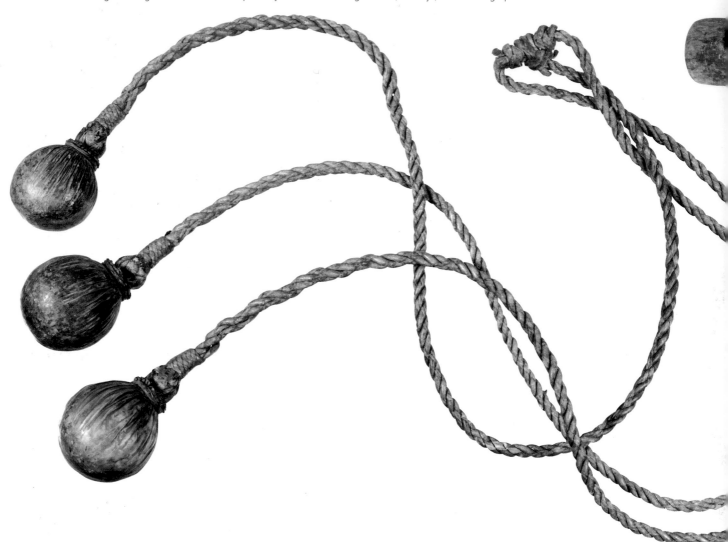

"The party endeavours to get as close as possible to the herd […] Each man carries four or five pair of the bolas."

—Charles Darwin, describing the gauchos hunting wild cattle in *The Voyage of the Beagle*, volume 29

ATLATL

One of the most effective early weapons was the atlatl, or spear thrower. The atlatl consisted of a grooved shaft, into which the user placed a spear or dart; a hook-like projection at the end of the shaft held the projectile in place until the user was ready to "fire" by thrusting the atlatl toward the target. The additional force provided by the atlatl sent the spear flying with much more speed than if it had been thrown by hand, and thus increased its impact on the target. A refinement to the basic design added a small weight, or banner stone (like the one shown above) to increase resistance. Atlatls were in use in various parts of the world from 18000 BCE onward; in the hands of a skilled user, atlatl-thrown darts could achieve ranges of up to 230ft/70m and bring down the largest game—including woolly mammoths. The bow and arrow (see pp 26–27) eventually supplanted the atlatl in many cultures, but for some peoples, like the Aztecs of Mexico, the atlatl became a weapon of war. (The name "atlatl" comes from the Aztecs' language, Nahuatl.) When Hernan Cortes and his Spanish conquistadors invaded the Aztec Empire in 1519, they were shocked to find that atlatl darts were capable of piercing their armor.

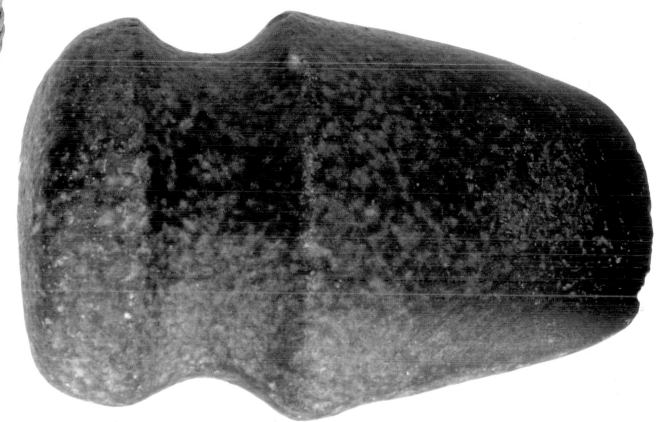

AX HEAD

A full-grooved ax head dating from between 1000 and 1500 CE. The groove allowed the head to be mounted on a wooden handle.

THE BRONZE AGE

The Bronze Age was a huge technological advance for humankind. During this period, people first learned how to create tools—and weapons—by refining, smelting, and casting metal ores. The term "Bronze Age" is elastic, because different cultures developed metalwork at different times. It is also something of a misnomer, because in its earliest phase, copper rather than true bronze (an alloy of about 90 percent copper and 10 percent tin) was used. This period is sometimes sub-categorized as the Chalcolithic Age. Copper metallurgy was known in China and the Eastern Mediterranean by 3500–3000 BCE, and over the next millennium or so the use of copper and, later, bronze spread into Europe and also developed independently in South America.

COPPER, BRONZE... IRON AND STEEL

Copper and especially bronze weapons offered vast advantages in strength, sharpness, and durability over stone weapons. So significant were these metals that historians credit their development with spurring the growth of urban civilizations by creating a class of skilled metalworkers, and with greater contact between scattered peoples as traders traveled far abroad in search of copper and tin deposits.

Bronze and copper weapons also helped ancient armies overwhelm opponents who had not mastered the new technology. Bronze, however, had some disadvantages—chiefly that while copper was a fairly common ore, tin deposits were concentrated in a few locations, like Britain and Central Europe.

An alternative appeared in the form of iron, another abundant ore. Once metalsmiths had figured out how to achieve the high temperatures needed to smelt iron ore by using charcoal, and

how to temper iron implements by alternately hammering and tempering them in water, iron weapons began to replace those of copper and bronze. As with the earlier minerals, the process developed at different times in different parts of the world, but historians generally date the start of the Iron Age to between 1200 and 1000 BCE. Around a thousand years later, Indian and Chinese metalsmiths learned how to combine iron with carbon to create an even better metal—steel.

SPEARHEAD
This is a modern replica of a late Bronze Age spearhead from the Mycenaean Era—a period named for the Greek city-state that dominated much of the Mediterranean world from 3000 to about 1000 BCE. It has a fluted, leaf-shaped blade and an overall length of 27.5in/70cm.

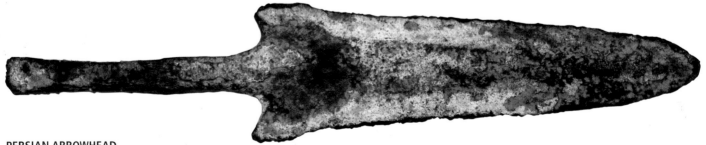

PERSIAN ARROWHEAD
Made of solid bronze, this arrowhead was found in the Luristan Mountains of Persia (modern Iran) and dates from sometime between 1800 and 700 BCE. Exactly who made this weapon and similar objects is debated; they may have been brought to the site by nomadic tribes from what is now Russia, or created locally.

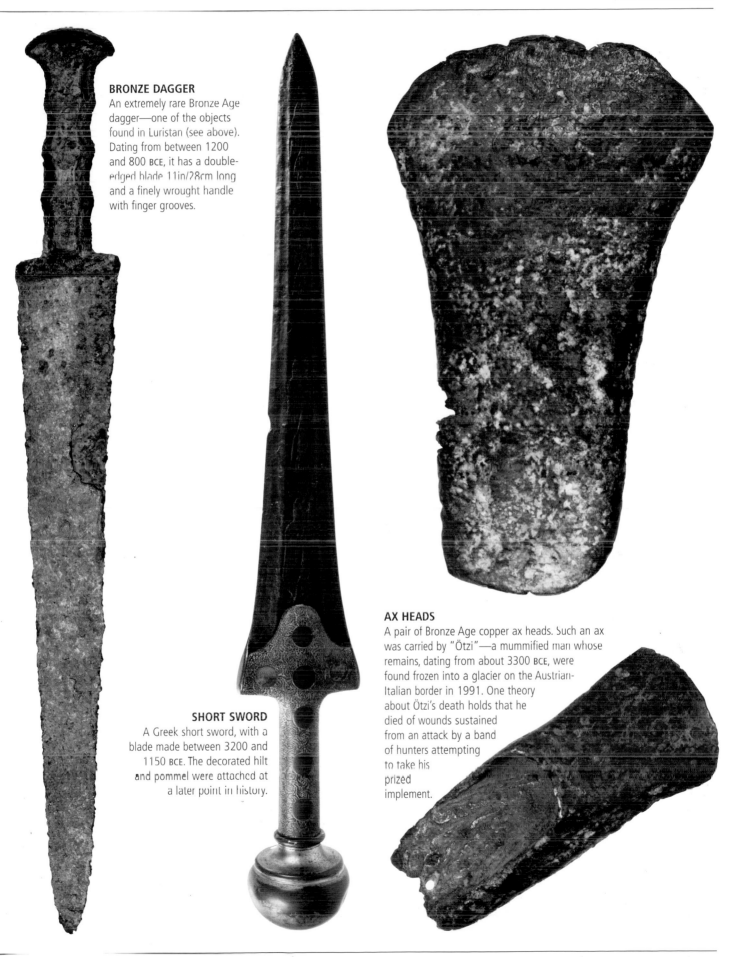

BRONZE DAGGER
An extremely rare Bronze Age dagger—one of the objects found in Luristan (see above). Dating from between 1200 and 800 BCE, it has a double-edged blade 11in/28cm long and a finely wrought handle with finger grooves.

SHORT SWORD
A Greek short sword, with a blade made between 3200 and 1150 BCE. The decorated hilt and pommel were attached at a later point in history.

AX HEADS
A pair of Bronze Age copper ax heads. Such an ax was carried by "Ötzi"—a mummified man whose remains, dating from about 3300 BCE, were found frozen into a glacier on the Austrian-Italian border in 1991. One theory about Ötzi's death holds that he died of wounds sustained from an attack by a band of hunters attempting to take his prized implement.

WEAPONS OF THE AMERICAS AND AUSTRALASIA

For many of the indigenous peoples of what Europeans dubbed the "New World"—the Americas and the islands of the Pacific—warfare was a way of life. In some cultures, every neighboring people who weren't explicitly allies were considered enemies, and no young male was considered fully a man until he'd been tested in battle. At the same time, however, warfare in these areas differed in concept from what historian Victor Davis Hanson termed "the Western Way of War," in which the annihilation of the enemy was the goal.

USE OF "TRADITIONAL" WEAPONS

In many indigenous societies, the warrior's priorities were to prove his personal courage (thus elevating his social status) or to seize loot or to capture the enemy for enslavement or (as in the Aztec Empire in Mexico) for ritual sacrifice. Combat was often highly ritualized and subject to strict rules—in parts of Polynesia, for example, the use of the bow and arrow was apparently forbidden in warfare but permitted in ceremonial competitions.

The club, the bow and arrow, and the spear were the chief weapons of warriors in these areas, and their use persisted among some peoples even after European and American traders arrived with guns to sell, because using the traditional weapons—which required the user to get close to his opponent—brought more honor to the warrior. Still, the effectiveness of firearms wasn't lost on indigenous peoples—especially as they lost their lives and lands to the white newcomers. A

British sailor who encountered the Tlingit people of Alaska in the 1790s summed up that tragic development: "Their former weapons, Bows and Arrows, Spears and Clubs are now thrown aside & Forgotten. At Nootka…everyone had his musket. Thus they are supplied with weapons which they no sooner possess than they turn against their donors. Few ships have been on the coast that have not been attack'd.…and in general many lives…lost on both sides."

NORTHWEST INDIAN CLUBS

The war club was a common weapon among many North American peoples; shown here are two distinct examples from the Pacific Northwest. The carving and decoration on the upper one indicate it might have been for ceremonial use.

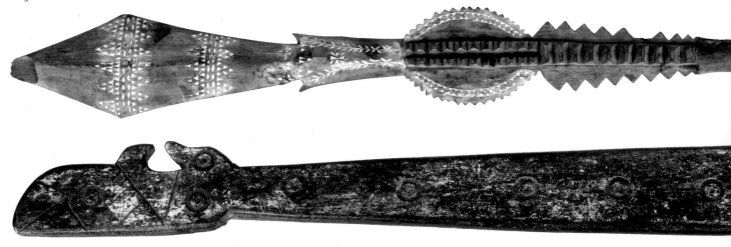

AMAZON SPEAR

A ceremonial spear of the Caraja people, who live on the banks of the Araguaia River, deep in the Brazilian rainforest. These spears are usually adorned with the feathers of birds like eagles and macaws.

TLINGIT CLUB & DRUM

A ceremonial war club [above] and drum [at right] of the Tlingit people of southern Alaska. Tlingit clubs were made of a variety of materials, including ivory and bone, and a special type of club was used to ritually kill enemy captives taken in battle.

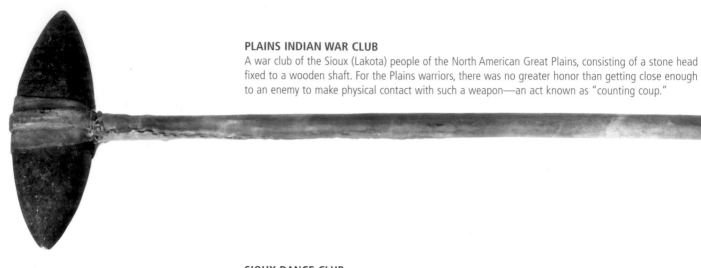

PLAINS INDIAN WAR CLUB

A war club of the Sioux (Lakota) people of the North American Great Plains, consisting of a stone head fixed to a wooden shaft. For the Plains warriors, there was no greater honor than getting close enough to an enemy to make physical contact with such a weapon—an act known as "counting coup."

SIOUX DANCE CLUB

Ritual music and dance played a major role in the spiritual life of many North American indigenous peoples, including the Sioux; the beaded club shown here was used in these ceremonies.

MAORI PATU

The short-handled war club, or patu, was the principal weapon of the Maori people of New Zealand. They could be carved from the wood of the kauri tree, whalebone, or jade, as in the example shown here. The hole in the handle would have accommodated a leather thong attaching the weapon to the warrior's wrist.

FIJIAN WAR CLUB
A Polynesian war club, made of wood and with blue decoration. In some areas, especially the Hawaiian Islands, such clubs were edged with shark's teeth.

FIJIAN CALACULA
A Fijian *calacula*, or club, with a saw-tooth "blade." Fijian warriors used a wide variety of clubs and sometimes decorated them with teeth taken from slain enemies.

BOWS AND CROSSBOWS

The bow and arrow date back to at least the Mesolithic Era (c. 8000–2700 BCE) and the weapon is common to peoples in every part of the world. By providing a means of killing at a distance, the bow and arrow was a huge advance in hunting—and in warfare, especially after composite bows came into use around 3000 BCE. Composite bows used layers of sinew and horn to reinforce the wooden bow, giving it greater strength, flexibility, and overall effectiveness. The development of the recurved bow, in which the tips of the bow face in the opposite direction from the user when firing, was another technical advance: Recurving allowed a more efficient application of energy and, because recurved bows were shorter and more compact than "straight" bows, they were more suited to use on horseback.

ARMIES OF ARCHERS

Mounted archers, often fighting from chariots, were an important component of the armies of empires like the Assyrians and Egyptians in ancient times. The Greeks and Romans, however, preferred the sword and spear, and the proportion of archers to infantry fell in European armies. The use of the bow revived in Europe during the medieval era in the form of the longbow and crossbow (see below).

East of the Mediterranean, however, the bow and arrow remained the primary weapon of the nomadic "horse peoples" of Central Asia. Perhaps the greatest masters of the art of bow-and-arrow warfare were the Mongols who, starting in the early thirteenth century, conquered vast stretches of Asia and made inroads into Europe and the Middle East. Each Mongol horseman carried a short, composite recurved bow with an effective range of 1000ft/305m and a variety of specialized arrows—some for long-range targets, some for close-in fighting, and some for use against horses.

THE LONGBOW AND CROSSBOW

Originally developed in Wales, the longbow was adopted by the English and used to deadly effect against the French in the battles of the Hundred Years War (1337–1453). Made of elm or yew and generally about 6ft/1.8m long, the weapon had a range of up to 600ft/183m. It was not always aimed directly at single targets; English longbowmen mastered the tactic of sending swarms of arrows raining down on the enemy from above. This proved so devastating to French knights that one wrote that before the Battle of Agincourt in 1415, "The French were boasting that they would cut off the three fingers of the right hand of all the archers that should be taken prisoners [so] neither man nor horse should ever again be killed with their arrows." The longbow's disadvantages were that it required considerable strength and training to use effectively.

The crossbow, chiefly used in Continental Europe, had a short bow attached at right angles to a wooden (sometimes metal) stock. It fired either arrows or metal bolts, known as quarrels, at a range of up to 1000ft/305m. Prior to the introduction of firearms, the crossbow was the most technically advanced weapon in European warfare—and one of the most feared, because its bolts could pierce even plate armor. The Church, in fact, tried to ban its use (at least by Christians against Christians) in 1139. It had a slow rate of fire, however, as drawing back the bowstring either with a winch-like device or by placing a foot on a "stirrup" fixed to the stock and pulling the weapon upward required considerable time and effort.

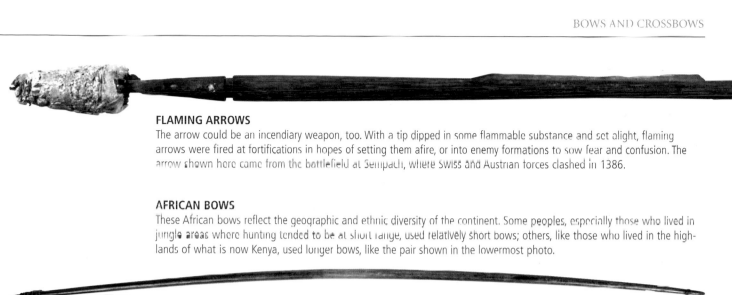

FLAMING ARROWS

The arrow could be an incendiary weapon, too. With a tip dipped in some flammable substance and set alight, flaming arrows were fired at fortifications in hopes of setting them afire, or into enemy formations to sow fear and confusion. The arrow shown here came from the battlefield at Sempach, where Swiss and Austrian forces clashed in 1386.

AFRICAN BOWS

These African bows reflect the geographic and ethnic diversity of the continent. Some peoples, especially those who lived in jungle areas where hunting tended to be at short range, used relatively short bows; others, like those who lived in the highlands of what is now Kenya, used longer bows, like the pair shown in the lowermost photo.

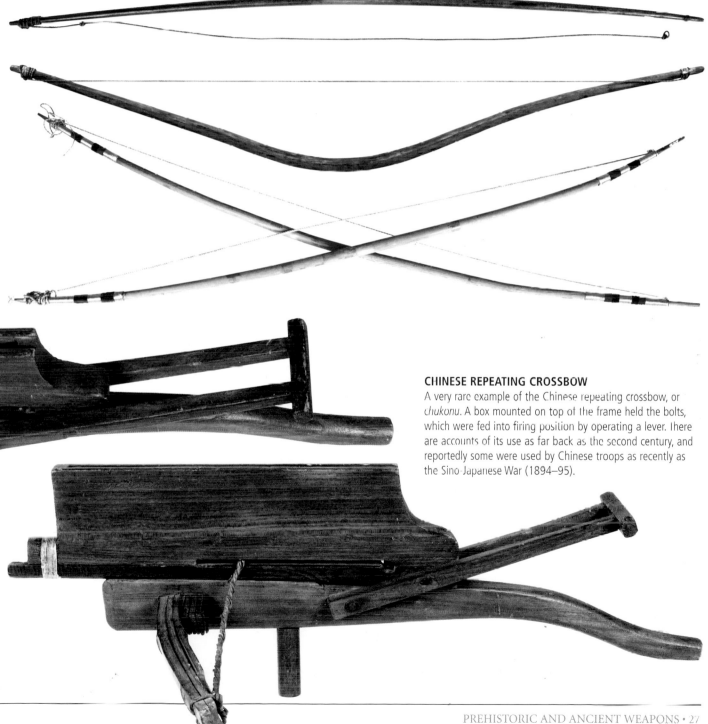

CHINESE REPEATING CROSSBOW

A very rare example of the Chinese repeating crossbow, or *chukonu*. A box mounted on top of the frame held the bolts, which were fed into firing position by operating a lever. There are accounts of its use as far back as the second century, and reportedly some were used by Chinese troops as recently as the Sino-Japanese War (1894–95).

AFRICAN ARROWS
A variety of arrows used by the Wellengulu people of Kenya's Aberderes Mountains.

CHILD'S CROSSBOW
A seventeenth-century toy crossbow.

CROSSBOW
A seventeenth-century sporting crossbow such as the one pictured proved excellent for shooting game or targets. The crossbow is still viable for military usage today, as a weapon for silent killing by special forces.

INDO-PERSIAN
A eighteenth-century Indo-Persian bow, shown unstrung.

JAPANESE SIGNAL ARROWS
Arrows have been used not only as combat projectiles but for signaling as well. These eighteenth-century Japanese arrows had a small cloth flag wound around the shaft, which opened upon firing.

CENTRAL AMERICAN INDIAN BOW
The indigenous peoples of Central and South America made graceful bows for use in hunting, fishing, and warfare; arrows were often tipped with curare or other poisons. The bow shown here is from Panama.

AFRICAN QUIVER
An African quiver (arrow holder) from around 1900. Made of woven wicker and waterproofed with resin, it held both conventional arrows or poison darts.

THE CRUSADES

"Deus Vult!" ("God wills it!") proclaimed Pope Urban II at Clermont, France, in 1095. Instead of fighting each other, the Pope wanted the Christian nobility of Europe to unite to stem the tide of Islamic expansion in the East and to restore the Holy Land to Christian rule. The result was the Crusades—a number of separate conflicts over several hundred years (the term probably derives from *crux*, or *crus*, Latin for "cross," i.e., the cloth cross that European Crusaders wore, and eventually "Crusade" signified any "holy war"). Despite initial successes, the Crusaders ultimately failed to achieve their objectives and fostered a hostility between the Western and Islamic worlds that persists today. However, they also led to a cultural exchange between West and East—an exchange that was reflected in weaponry and warfare.

CRUSADER VS. SARACEN

The invading Crusaders and their Islamic opponents (whom they dubbed "Saracens") had fundamentally different styles of fighting. In the words of British historian John Keegan, "Crusading warfare was a strange contest, which confronted the face-to-face warriors of the north European tradition with the evasive, harrying tactics of the steppe horsemen."

The Saracens drew on the traditions of the "horse peoples" of Central Asia (see p 26), with their highly mobile armies of mounted bowmen and hit-and-run tactics. (Using a composite bow, a horsemen could penetrate chain mail at up to 475ft/145m.)

In contrast, the European forces were still based around knights—heavily loaded down with lances, swords, chain-mail armor, and metal helmets—who considered anything other than close combat with the enemy to be dishonorable, and whose preferred tactic was an all-out charge at the enemy. Eventually the Crusaders realized the value of infantry against their light-cavalry opponents and upped the ratio of foot soldiers—including archers and crossbow-men—in their formations. The English crusader Richard the Lionhearted used these new tactics successfully in battle near Jaffa in 1192, when his force of about 2,000 infantry and 50 knights (less than half of them mounted) defeated 7,000 horsemen led by the great Saladin. For their part, Islamic armies realized that heavy cavalry had some advantages and began to study their opponent's tactics.

SIEGES IN THE HOLY LAND

As another historian put it, pitched battles were "[L]ess typical of crusading warfare than the long, unglamorous grind of a siege." While on the offensive, the Crusaders had to lay siege to cities like Jerusalem, which fell after a relatively brief military onslaught in 1099. Within a century, however, Jerusalem had been recaptured and the Crusaders driven into a handful of castles and other fortified positions on the Mediterranean coast. Now it was their turn to endure siege.

The Saracens were adept at this kind of warfare—both as attackers and defenders, and particularly in their use of incendiary (flame-producing) weapons. They used inflammable compounds—some apparently similar to Greek Fire (see p 104)—to set fire to the siege towers used by Crusaders in attempts to scale castle walls or tunnel underneath them. On the offensive, they used trebuchets and other siege engines to hurl incendiaries into Crusader fortifications.

The greatest threats to those under siege were not fire or projectiles but hunger, thirst, and disease. Not to mention treachery: The Crusaders' capture of Antioch in 1098, for example, was facilitated by a deal struck with one of the city's defenders. If a castle or city fell, the fate of its inhabitants was often grim: In one of many such episodes, the Christian Crusaders celebrated the capture of Jerusalem by slaughtering much of the city's Jewish and Muslim population.

"Valiant and tried, ready
this day to die
For me their king, each with
his weapon grasped,
Each skillful in the field."

—*The Bhagavad-Gita*, lines 24–26

Weapons technology remained relatively stagnant in the West in the hundreds of years after the fall of the Roman Empire. The adoption of the stirrup in Europe, roughly between the nineth and eleventh centuries, led (along with many other factors) to the dominance of mounted knights, armed with lances and swords, on European battlefields, supported by infantry carrying a variety of arms, from crude clubs, farm implements, and spears to more sophisticated weapons like flails, maces, and halberds. Personal armor developed in parallel, with chain mail eventually giving way to suits of plate armor. Even the heavily armored knights of the Middle Ages were vulnerable to two innovations, the longbow and the crossbow. Elsewhere in the world, horsemen armed with the composite bow helped the Mongols dominate much of Asia, while Persian, Indian, Chinese, and Japanese craftsmen produced weapons of great beauty—and deadliness.

Maces and Flails

The mace—a heavy club with a broad head often studded with spikes or knobs—has its roots in prehistory; the first known examples date from the Bronze Age (see pp 20–21) and the earliest depiction of its use in battle comes from the ancient Egyptian Narmer Palette dating from around 3100 BCE. While the use of mace-type weapons in the "Old World" declined in the Classical Era, they gained a new lease on life in Medieval Europe thanks to their effectiveness against armor. A variation on the mace was the flail, which had a head attached to a shaft by a chain; it probably derived from an agricultural tool used to separate chaff from grain.

THE MEDIEVAL MACE

The Medieval revival of the mace came in response to the increasing use of chain mail and, later, plate armor in warfare—not only in Europe, but also in Northern Africa and the Indian Subcontinent. The mace (now typically of iron or steel construction) didn't necessarily have to penetrate armor; a strong blow was often enough to break an opponent's limb or skull or otherwise stun or incapacitate him. Between the eleventh and thirteenth century, however, flanged maces appeared; these had heads with bladelike metal ridges that could penetrate armor. Other versions had spikes, which also had armor-piercing qualities.

Maces were most commonly used by foot soldiers, but shorter versions, more suited to mounted use, were often carried by knights. Cheap to make and simple to use, the mace was also a favorite weapon of peasant revolutionaries, like the Hussites (followers of the religious and political reformer Jan Hus) in early fifteenth-century Bohemia (now the Czech Republic).

THE CEREMONIAL MACE

The mace was also a favorite weapon of fighting clergy, because unlike a sword or other edged weapon, it could wound or kill without shedding blood, which was forbidden by the canonical law of the Roman Catholic Church. (Modern historians, however, dispute whether the mace and similar weapons were used to any significant extent by Medieval churchmen—although the Bayeux Tapestry, which chronicles the Norman invasion of England in 1066, depicts Bishop Odo of Bayeux wielding a large mace.)

Like the halberd (see pp 40–45), over time the mace went from being a combat weapon to a ceremonial object and a symbol of authority. In England and Scotland, elaborately decorated maces have long been carried in civic and academic processions by "sergeants at arms," mayors, and other worthies. In the British Parliament's House of Commons, for example, a mace lies on the table in front of the Speaker during debates.

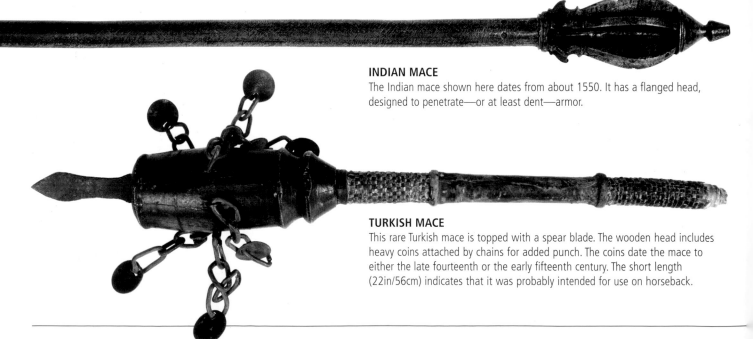

INDIAN MACE
The Indian mace shown here dates from about 1550. It has a flanged head, designed to penetrate—or at least dent—armor.

TURKISH MACE
This rare Turkish mace is topped with a spear blade. The wooden head includes heavy coins attached by chains for added punch. The coins date the mace to either the late fourteenth or the early fifteenth century. The short length (22in/56cm) indicates that it was probably intended for use on horseback.

ENGLISH FLAIL

An English flail from the time of King Henry VII (r. 1485–1509). While similar to the morgenstern in design, flails usually had several lengths of chain or spiked balls attached to a shaft, although this example has only one. A major advantage of the morgenstern and the flail was that they could be swung over or around a knight's shield.

MORGENSTERN

One of the most common types of sixteenth-century European maces was the morgenstern, which had a spiked head attached to the shaft. The morgenstern was used extensively by the Habsburgs, and the name comes from either the German for "morning star," likely a reference to its sunlike spiked head, or as a grim joke based on the fact that the weapon was often used in dawn raids on enemy encampments.

SOME CURIOSITIES

CROSS DAGGER

This fifteenth-century wooden cross from France conceals a deadly surprise: a dagger with a 9.5in/24cm scalloped blade.

CHASTITY BELT

The history of the chastity belt is a contentious one. Some modern historians argue that such devices had a purely symbolic use, with men giving them to their wives or lovers as a reminder of the importance of fidelity. Others assert that most surviving examples are hoaxes. However, references to them in Medieval literature include a 1405 book on weaponry that describes "breeches of iron" worn by women of Florence. In popular legend, chastity belts were fitted to the wives of knights going off to crusade (see pp 30–31), but this is highly unlikely, if only for sanitary reasons. If used to any extent, the belt was probably not a means of preserving "virtue," but rather a woman's defense against rape when traveling through bandit-ridden areas. This particular chastity belt dates from the seventeenth century.

THUMBSCREWS

A Spanish thumbscrew proved a nasty torture device; a simple vice, it squeezed the victim's thumbs or other fingers or even toes, breaking the bones and crushing the flesh. Like the mace, thumbscrews such as these late fifteenth-century ones were supposedly favored by the Inquisition (the agency of the Roman Catholic Church charged with rooting out heresy). This is because their use for extracting confessions didn't violate the Church's law against the shedding of blood by clergy.

THE HUNDRED YEARS WAR

The Hundred Years War between France and England was actually a series of conflicts that lasted 116 years—from 1337 to 1453. Its causes were dynastic and territorial. Starting with Edward III (r. 1327–1377), English kings asserted their right to the throne of France on the basis of their descent from the Normans who had conquered England in 1066, and they also sought direct rule of the French province of Aquitaine. The long struggle was highly significant in the development of weaponry and warfare. Historians view it as marking the end of the medieval way of war. It saw the use of devastating weapons like the longbow (see p 26), and it was the first European conflict in which firearms, in the form of artillery, played a role. Also, by fueling nationalist sentiment and contributing to the rise of the centralized state in both countries, it led to the development of professional armies, replacing the earlier ad hoc mix of noble "men at arms" and peasant recruits and conscripts.

CRÉCY AND POITIERS

At the beginning the sides seemed unevenly matched. In 1337, France had a population of 14 million, against England's 2 million, and the French enjoyed a reputation as being among Europe's best warriors. The French, however, still organized their forces in the old-school fashion—around heavily armored mounted knights. The English had greater tactical flexibility, less chivalrous notions of warfare—and the longbow.

In the first decisive battle of the war, fought at Crécy on August 26, 1346, French knights on horseback repeatedly charged Edward III's army, only to be cut down by volleys of arrows from English and Welsh longbowmen and hammered by English knights fighting on foot. The French King Philip VI (r. 1328–1350) hoped to counter the longbowmen with mercenary troops from Italy armed with crossbows (see pp 26–28), but the longbow's far higher rate of fire prevailed.

Casualty figures for medieval battles are notoriously unreliable, but the French probably lost at least 10,000 men at Crécy, including many nobles. Edward III moved on to capture the French port of Calais and, in the words of the French chronicler Jean Froissart, "The realm of France was afterward much weakened in honor, strength, and counsel."

Major hostilities lagged as plague ravaged Europe, but in 1356, Edward III's son, Edward, "the Black Prince," invaded France. After ravaging much of northern France, Edward's forces were surrounded by a much larger French army near Poitiers. On September 19, 1356, the French attacked Edward. Not having learned the lessons of Crécy, Poitiers was something of a replay of the earlier battle. It ended in a huge defeat for the French, with the French King John II (r. 1350–1364) captured. A subsequent treaty yielded a third of French territory to the English.

AGINCOURT TO CASTILLON

Despite the English victory, French fortunes ultimately revived, resulting in a regain of much lost territory in the late fourteenth century, although conflicting claimants to the French crown threw the country into virtual civil war. Taking advantage of the situation, King Henry V (r. 1413–1422) crossed the channel in 1415 and—in a sign of things to come—battered the port of Harfleur into surrender with twelve cannon. Although his force was outnumbered, beset by sickness, and low on supplies, Henry defeated a French army at Agincourt on October 24, in one of history's best known battles—thanks in large part to Shakespeare's play *Henry V*.

Despite the English victories, the war ultimately went against them. The English threat united the often-fractious French nobility and inspired ordinary people—including the charismatic woman warrior Jeanne d'Arc (Joan of Arc)—to resist the invaders. And while cannon had been used earlier in the war, it now began to play an important part on the battlefield. At the Battle of Formigny (April 15, 1450), the French deployed cannon to disperse the English longbowmen who had been so formidable at Crécy, Poitiers, and Agincourt. In the last major battle of the war (Castillon, July 17, 1453) the French used about 300 cannon to defeat an English force—the first battle, in the opinion of many historians, in which artillery was the deciding factor. In the end, the English retained only their bastion at Calais, which ultimately fell to France in 1588.

POLE ARMS AND AXES

A pole arm is a weapon with a blade or pointed tip attached to a long shaft. While pole arms have existed in various forms since prehistoric times, they gained prominence in the Medieval and Renaissance eras in Europe and elsewhere as a means of dealing with cavalry; the length of pole arms like the halberd extended the foot soldier's "reach" by providing the means of attacking a mounted opponent while staying out of range of sword thrusts. The battle-axe was another ancient weapon that found a new usefulness when pitted against armored warriors. The introduction of firearms and the subsequent decline in the battlefield prominence of heavily armored horsemen downgraded pole arms to ceremonial use in the West, though the pike retained its usefulness—as a means of protecting firearm-equipped infantry—well into the gunpowder era.

THE HALBERD AND THE PIKE

While there were many different types of European pole arms, the "classic models" were the halberd and the pike.

First appearing in the fourteenth century and usually about 5ft/1.5m long, the halberd was a triple-threat weapon; it was topped with a spiky point to keep mounted opponents at bay; a hook that could be used to pull an opponent out of the saddle; and an ax-head that could penetrate armor.

The pike—a simple, spear-like weapon consisting of a metal head attached to a wooden shaft—came into widespread use in the twelfth century, and was originally used as a defensive weapon against cavalry. The Swiss, however, turned the pike into a formidable offensive weapon, arming phalanx-like infantry formations called Gewalthaufen with pikes as long as 22ft/6.7m.

POLE ARMS AROUND THE WORLD

Warriors in other cultures also made extensive use of pole arms, for the same reasons as Europeans: Besides their effectiveness against cavalry, they were relatively simple to manufacture and didn't require lengthy training to use. While the Samurai of Medieval Japan, for example, are popularly associated with the sword (see pp 96–97), they were supported by foot soldiers who wielded *yari* (spears).

The spear—whether used as a thrown weapon or as a stabbing implement in close combat— remained a mainstay of warriors in many cultures until the spread of firearms around the world. Perhaps the greatest spearmen in history are the Zulu warriors of Southern Africa: Formed into units called impis and armed with the short assegai spear, they conquered much of the region in the early nineteenth century.

The following five pages show an interesting sampling of polearms and axes spanning the globe and dating from the sixteenth through nineteenth centuries.

ENGLISH HALBERD
A fine example of the halberd, this one dates from the sixteenth century and is probably of English origin.

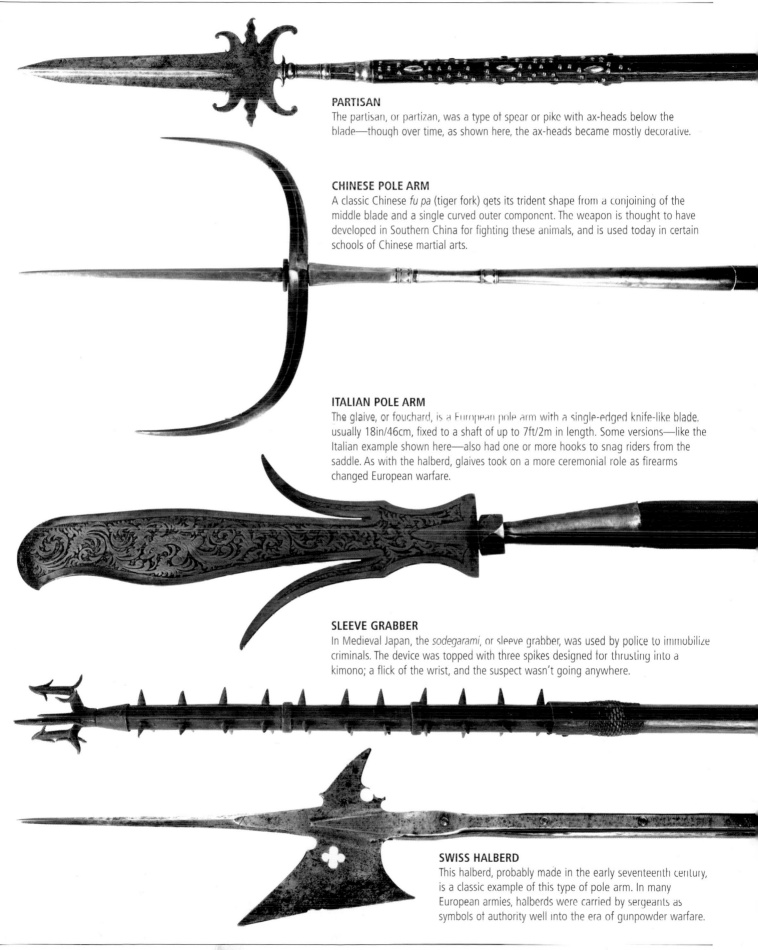

PARTISAN
The partisan, or partizan, was a type of spear or pike with ax-heads below the blade—though over time, as shown here, the ax-heads became mostly decorative.

CHINESE POLE ARM
A classic Chinese *fu pa* (tiger fork) gets its trident shape from a conjoining of the middle blade and a single curved outer component. The weapon is thought to have developed in Southern China for fighting these animals, and is used today in certain schools of Chinese martial arts.

ITALIAN POLE ARM
The glaive, or fouchard, is a European pole arm with a single-edged knife-like blade, usually 18in/46cm, fixed to a shaft of up to 7ft/2m in length. Some versions—like the Italian example shown here—also had one or more hooks to snag riders from the saddle. As with the halberd, glaives took on a more ceremonial role as firearms changed European warfare.

SLEEVE GRABBER
In Medieval Japan, the *sodegarami*, or sleeve grabber, was used by police to immobilize criminals. The device was topped with three spikes designed for thrusting into a kimono; a flick of the wrist, and the suspect wasn't going anywhere.

SWISS HALBERD
This halberd, probably made in the early seventeenth century, is a classic example of this type of pole arm. In many European armies, halberds were carried by sergeants as symbols of authority well into the era of gunpowder warfare.

ENGLISH POLE ARMS
Here are two examples of the English pike. While the introduction of the bayonet led to the decline of the pike in land battle, they were used in boarding actions in naval warfare into the nineteenth century.

INDO-PERSIAN LANCE HEAD, BATTLE-AX
A twin-bladed Indo-Persian lance head, used during the Qajar Dynasty (1794–1925). An eighteenth-century Indo-Persian battle-ax designed for mounted use.

BOAR SPEAR
This European spear was used for hunting wild boar, a favorite pastime of the European nobility: A 1547 inventory of arms at the Tower of London lists a number of "Boar speres" owned by King Henry VIII of England. They were also used occasionally on the battlefield.

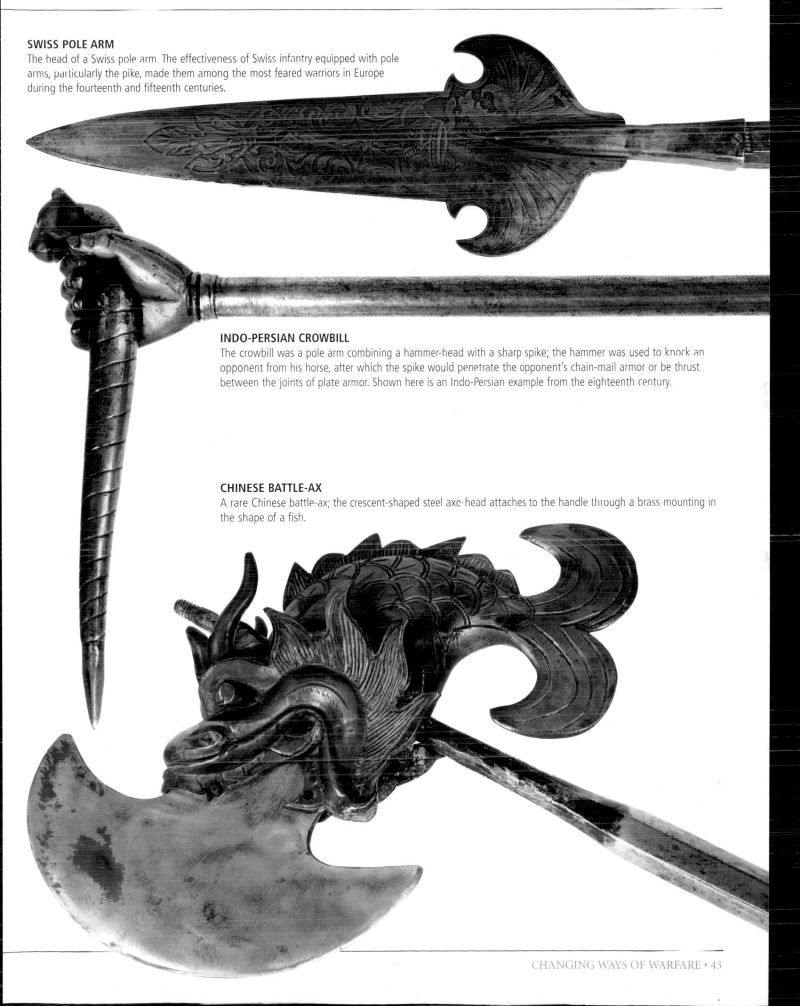

SWISS POLE ARM
The head of a Swiss pole arm. The effectiveness of Swiss infantry equipped with pole arms, particularly the pike, made them among the most feared warriors in Europe during the fourteenth and fifteenth centuries.

INDO-PERSIAN CROWBILL
The crowbill was a pole arm combining a hammer-head with a sharp spike; the hammer was used to knock an opponent from his horse, after which the spike would penetrate the opponent's chain-mail armor or be thrust between the joints of plate armor. Shown here is an Indo-Persian example from the eighteenth century.

CHINESE BATTLE-AX
A rare Chinese battle-ax; the crescent-shaped steel axe-head attaches to the handle through a brass mounting in the shape of a fish.

JAPANESE SPEAR

The head of a Japanese spear (*yari*) from the eighteenth century. The weapon first came into widespread use in the fourteenth century, and several variations subsequently developed. Generally, Japanese infantry used a long version, which could be up to 20ft/6m in length, while Samurai carried a shorter model.

INDIAN BATTLE-AX

Eighteenth-century Indian battle-ax with decorative etched blade and spike tip.

ZULU SPEAR

A Zulu *umKhonto* (spear). The most famous Zulu spear was the assegai. The decision by great Zulu leader Shaka (1787–1828) to equip his warriors with these stabbing spears—replacing longer throwing spears that weren't very lethal—helped the Zulu forge a vast empire in the region.

CHINESE YANYUE DAO

The name of this spear is the Chinese for "crescent moon," which the blade resembles. This specimen dates from the middle part of the Qing Dynasty (c. 1840).

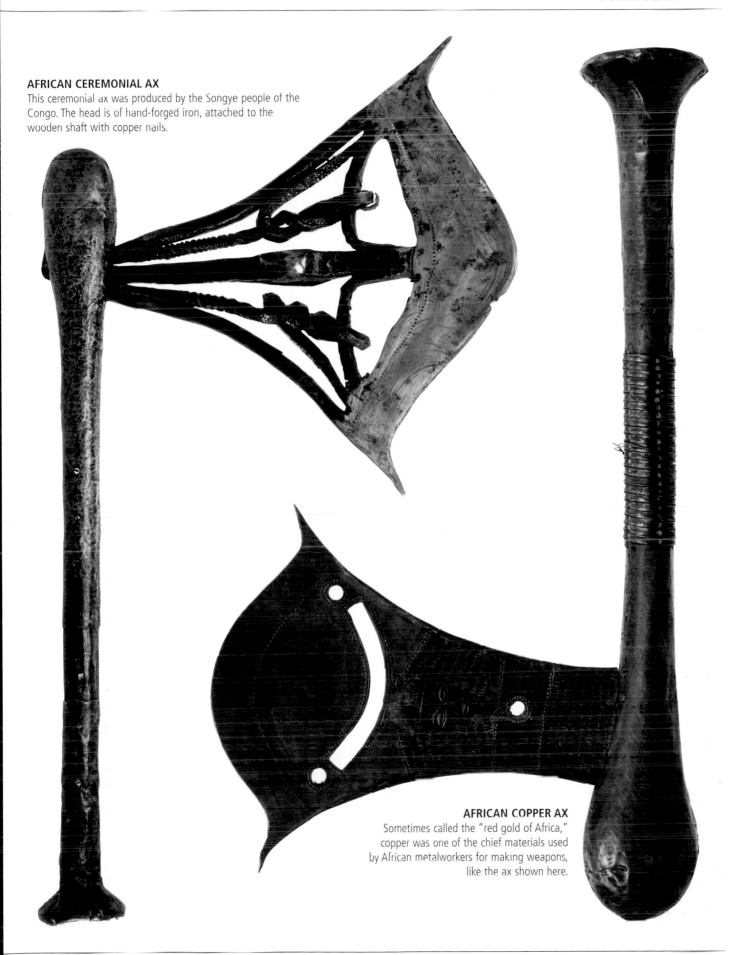

AFRICAN CEREMONIAL AX
This ceremonial ax was produced by the Songye people of the Congo. The head is of hand-forged iron, attached to the wooden shaft with copper nails.

AFRICAN COPPER AX
Sometimes called the "red gold of Africa," copper was one of the chief materials used by African metalworkers for making weapons, like the ax shown here.

ARMOR

The use of special clothing to protect the wearer from projectiles and blades goes back at least 10,000 years, when Chinese soldiers wore cloaks of rhinoceros hide, but warriors were probably wearing protective garments of leather and other materials long before this. Metal armor—first chain mail, and later plate armor—was used widely in Europe from ancient times into the late medieval period (and later, in other parts of the world), until the growing effectiveness of firearms led to its decline. In more recent times, the introduction of new synthetic materials has led to a revival in body armor.

HOPLITES TO KNIGHTS

Ancient Greek infantry (hoplites) went into battle protected by a cuirass made of bronze, which protected the torso, as well as a helmet and greaves (shin protectors) of the same metal. The soldiers of Ancient Rome's legions also wore a cuirass, although their version consisted of a sort of leather vest covered in iron hoops, and they wore iron helmets.

Starting around the ninth century, European knights began to wear coats of chain mail—thousands of small iron rings riveted or welded together. Because chain mail by itself was often insufficient to deflect an arrowhead or spear point, coats of mail were usually worn over a leather tunic. Helmets came in a variety of styles, from simple conical iron affairs to more sophisticated models with articulated visors.

Chain mail was hardly lightweight (a typical coat weighed 30lb/13.5kg), but it offered the wearer relative freedom of movement. In the late medieval era, however, the introduction of weapons like the longbow and crossbow (see pp 26–29), whose arrows and bolts could penetrate mail, led European warriors to adopt armor made of overlapping plates of iron or steel. At their most sophisticated, suits of plate armor afforded the wearer full-body protection. The trade-off was their heavy weight, which put a knight knocked off his feet or his horse in a vulnerable position.

AROUND THE WORLD

Variations on chain mail—usually consisting of overlapping metal plates—were used by warriors in many nations, from Persia and India to China and Japan. The suits of armor worn by the samurai of medieval Japan were particularly fine and, like the best of European plate-armor suits, were magnificent examples of craftsmanship. As in Europe, in many cultures the wearing of armor was largely limited to the warrior elite (they were the only ones able to afford these expensive items, for one thing), but in India and elsewhere foot soldiers used garments of leather or heavily padded fabric for protection.

One of the most interesting non-metal forms of armor was the raw silk shirts worn by Mongol horsemen. Because of silk's strength, if an enemy arrow pierced the horseman's body, the silk would be driven into the wound along with the arrowhead, allowing the arrow to be more easily removed than if it had torn through another type of material.

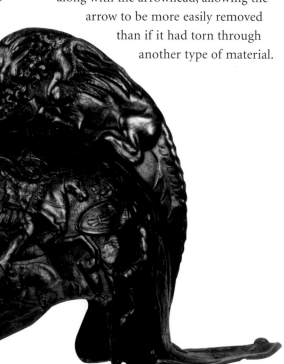

ITALIAN PARADE HELMET
This highly embossed bronze helmet, from sixteenth-century Italy, was probably made for purely ceremonial use.

INDO-PERSIAN HELMET
A beautifully made Indo-Persian kulah khud (helmet), topped with a spike and fringed with chain mail.

ENGLISH HELMET
The first forged-steel helmets appeared in Europe in the tenth century. The sixteenth-century English helmet shown here is of a type known as a *burgonet*, which—while it did not offer the protection of earlier helmets that covered the entire head or face—gave the wearer greater visibility and freedom of movement.

ITALIAN SHIELD
A heart-shaped Italian shield from the sixteenth century, beautifully decorated with the coat of arms of three families that had inter-married. Shields of this type were not used in combat, but rather were heraldic objects made to commemorate a noble family's history of military prowess.

SPANISH ARMOR
Probably made around 1580, this armor—consisting of a breast and back plate—was worn by a Spanish conquistador in South America. It was found in Bolivia during the 1950s.

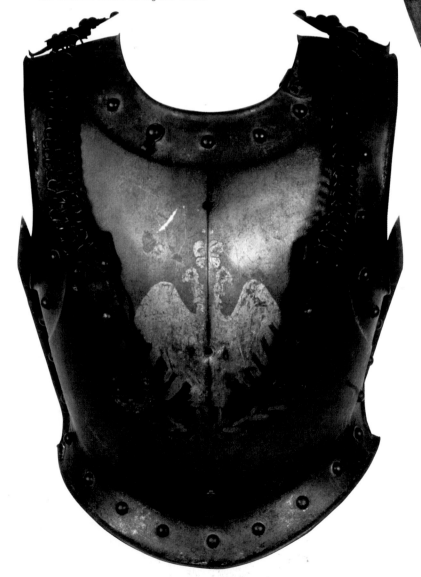

SPIKE SHIELD
A sixteenth-century European shield with a spike in its center. During the Medieval Era, large shields gave way to the smaller, lighter buckler (apparently from an Old French word meaning "fist of metal"), which could be used to parry an opponent's sword or mace blow (see pp 36–37).

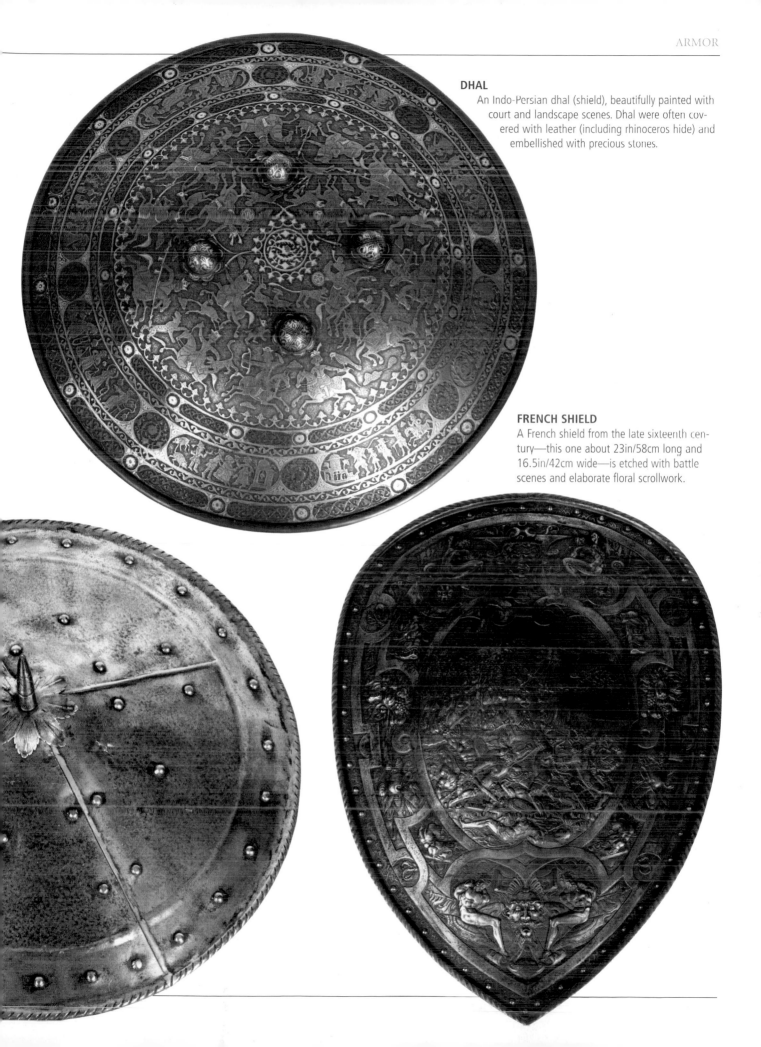

DHAL

An Indo-Persian dhal (shield), beautifully painted with court and landscape scenes. Dhal were often covered with leather (including rhinoceros hide) and embellished with precious stones.

FRENCH SHIELD

A French shield from the late sixteenth century—this one about 23in/58cm long and 16.5in/42cm wide—is etched with battle scenes and elaborate floral scrollwork.

DAGGERS AND FIGHTING KNIVES

A dagger is simply a short-bladed knife, held in one hand and intended for stabbing. The name may come from the ancient Roman province of Dacia (now Romania) and originally meant "Dacian knife." Daggerlike weapons have certainly been in use since prehistoric times; they predate the sword, and versions are found in cultures around the world. The dagger's small size limited its usefulness in warfare, but that same attribute—and its concealability—made it a favorite of both criminals and assassins. In addition to daggers, many cultures have adopted knives of an intermediate size between the dagger and sword; these weapons are generally known as fighting knives.

THE DAGGER IN THE WEST

In Medieval and Renaissance times, the dagger served a special function—penetrating armor where plates joined together or in other openings, like a helmet visor. Knocked off his horse or otherwise disabled, a knight became easy prey to a mere foot soldier with a dagger. One of the most famous types of dagger, the narrow-bladed Italian stiletto, was developed specifically for this purpose.

In the sixteenth century, a new style of sword fighting gained popularity in Europe, in which a dagger was held in the left hand and the sword in the right hand, with the dagger being used to parry the opponent's sword thrusts.

The growing popularity of the pistol as a personal defense (or offense) weapon in the 1700s led to a decline in the dagger's use, although some nations' military officers and members of paramilitary and political groups continued to wear them for ceremonial purposes. Fighting knives had a resurgence during the trench warfare of World War I (see pp 176–177) and later by special forces—for "silent elimination" of sentries, for example (see p 193).

BLADES AROUND THE WORLD

In many traditional societies, daggers and knives fulfilled multiple roles—as weapons, tools, and symbols of an owner's wealth and power. The kukri of the Ghurkha people of Nepal, for example, is justly famous as a weapon, but also was used for mundane tasks like skinning animals or chopping wood, while the finely wrought and richly decorated knives made by many Sub-Saharan African peoples were used in combat and also as a token of social standing.

In addition to these roles, knives are objects of great cultural significance in many societies and are often considered to be endowed with spiritual power; a classical example is the Southeast Asian kris.

DAGGER CANE

Stylish canes concealing swords and daggers enjoyed a vogue in eighteenth- and nineteenth-century Europe. This English dagger cane from around the turn of the nineteenth century and has a 10in/25cm blade encased in a Malacca cane; the ivory handle is carved in the shape of a dog's head with diamond clusters for eyes and a "collar" of emeralds, rubies, and sapphires.

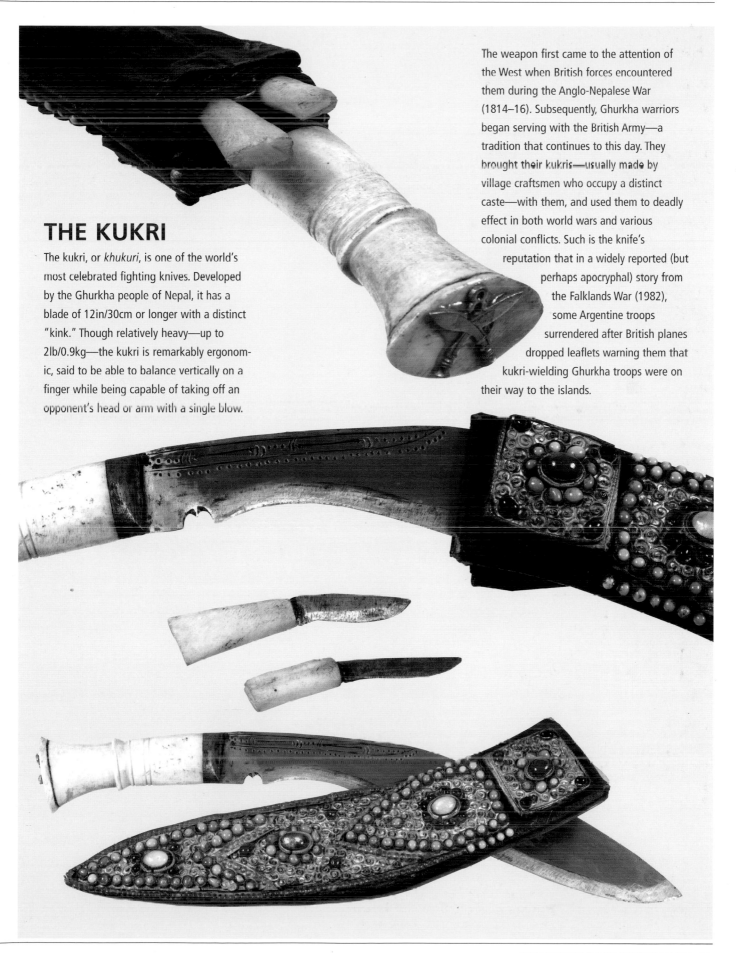

THE KUKRI

The kukri, or *khukuri*, is one of the world's most celebrated fighting knives. Developed by the Ghurkha people of Nepal, it has a blade of 12in/30cm or longer with a distinct "kink." Though relatively heavy—up to 2lb/0.9kg—the kukri is remarkably ergonomic, said to be able to balance vertically on a finger while being capable of taking off an opponent's head or arm with a single blow.

The weapon first came to the attention of the West when British forces encountered them during the Anglo-Nepalese War (1814–16). Subsequently, Ghurkha warriors began serving with the British Army—a tradition that continues to this day. They brought their kukris—usually made by village craftsmen who occupy a distinct caste—with them, and used them to deadly effect in both world wars and various colonial conflicts. Such is the knife's reputation that in a widely reported (but perhaps apocryphal) story from the Falklands War (1982), some Argentine troops surrendered after British planes dropped leaflets warning them that kukri-wielding Ghurkha troops were on their way to the islands.

NAVAL DIRK
A relatively long knife, the Scottish dirk (the word probably comes from the Gaelic *sgian dearg*, or "red knife") was often used in conjunction with the claymore broadsword (see pp 84–87). This example, with a gilt brass handle with ivory grips, is a British naval model from about 1770.

LEFT-HANDED DAGGER
A left-handed dagger, designed to be used in conjunction with a sword. These daggers, like the eighteenth-century French one shown, sometimes had substantial down-curved quillions which could be used to trap the opponent's blade long enough to get in a sword thrust.

MAIN GAUCHE
Another main gauche, or left-handed dagger, this one from seventeenth-century Spain. The weapon has a 13.5in/34cm blade with a cutout near the hilt to trap an opponent's blade. The wire-wound grip is short, as the user's thumb would be extended to the blade itself, though the hand would be fairly protected by the large guard.

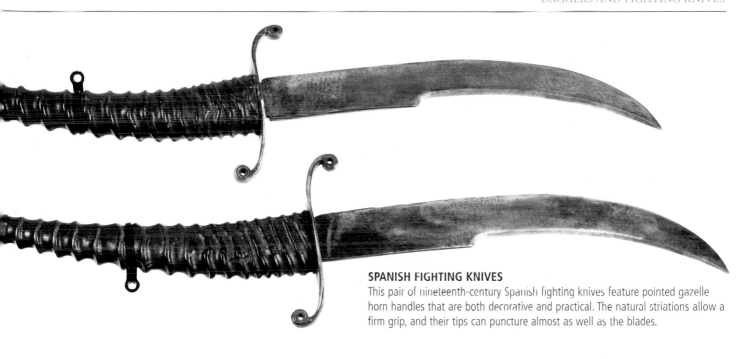

SPANISH FIGHTING KNIVES

This pair of nineteenth-century Spanish fighting knives feature pointed gazelle horn handles that are both decorative and practical. The natural striations allow a firm grip, and their tips can puncture almost as well as the blades.

COSSACK KINDJAL

Sometimes called the "Circassian dagger," from its origin with the Circassian people of the Caucasus Mountains, the *kindjal* was adopted by the Cossacks of the Russian Empire from the eighteenth century onward. This nineteenth-century example has a 14in/36cm blade and a hilt inlaid with semiprecious stones. In the hands of Cossack warriors, it was used in conjunction with the *shashka* sword.

SYRIAN DAGGER

A set of three Syrian daggers, each with a blade that measures 5.25in/13cm; two have curved blades and one, a straight blade. The three bone-hilted knives fit into a sheath of crocodile skin.

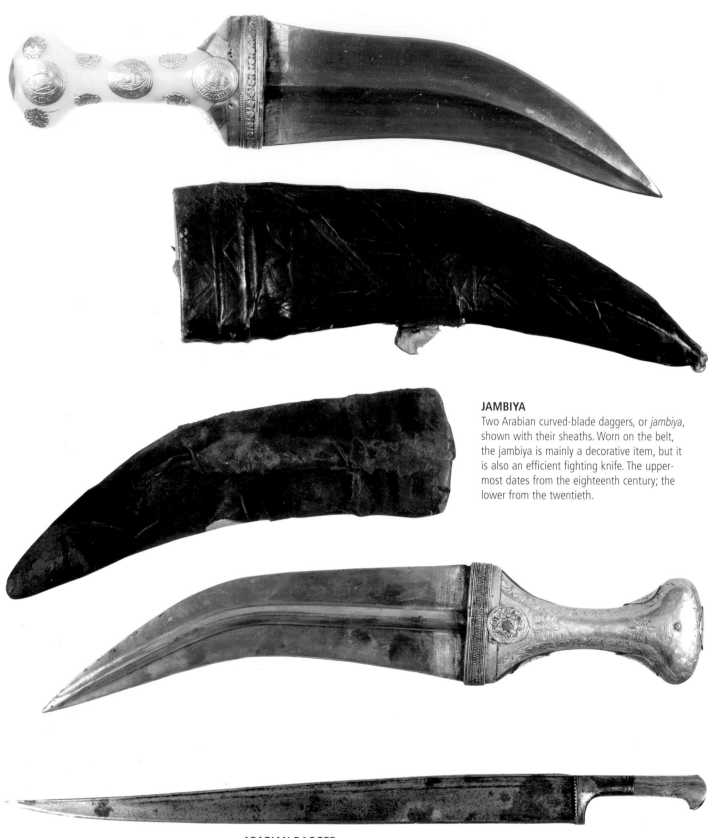

JAMBIYA

Two Arabian curved-blade daggers, or *jambiya*, shown with their sheaths. Worn on the belt, the jambiya is mainly a decorative item, but it is also an efficient fighting knife. The uppermost dates from the eighteenth century; the lower from the twentieth.

ARABIAN DAGGER

Another Arabian dagger, this one made in Tunis (capital of the modern nation of Tunis) in the nineteenth century.

YATAGHAN

Named for a town in present-day Turkey, the yataghan was a major edged weapon of the Ottoman Empire from the fifteenth through the nineteenth centuries, especially in the hands of the Janissaries, the "slave-soldiers" who formed the bulwark of the Ottoman military. With blades of up to 31in/80cm in length, they are really more short sword than knife, but their relatively compact form allowed them to be carried on the waist by infantry. The yataghan design spread to much of Central Asia. The two shown here are Turkish models from the eighteenth [upper] and nineteenth [lower] centuries.

PESH KABZ

With its curved T-sectioned blade tapering to a slender point, the Indo-Persian pesh kabz was ideal for penetrating chain-mail armor; its effectiveness at this task led the design to spread from Persia and Northern India throughout Central Asia, the Indian Subcontinent, and the Middle East. This example is from Egypt.

AFRICAN SWORD

A Masai *seme*, or lion knife, from Eastern Africa with its leather sheath dyed the traditional red. With its double-edged blade that widens from the hilt until almost the tip, this item dates from the late nineteenth century.

AFGHAN

This eighteenth-century pesh kabz from Afghanistan features gold inlay on the blade.

INDO-PERSIAN DAGGER

This rare and unusual Indo-Persian knife has a three-piece blade. While it appeared to be an ordinary knife to a sword-wielding attacker, the user separated the blades by means of a spring-loaded hinge in hopes of catching the attacker's sword blade between the main blade and one of the auxiliary blades. Twisting the knife would then immobilize (or, even better, break) the sword blade, allowing the defender to use his own sword on his opponent.

PERSIAN 3-BLADE DAGGERS

Persian three-bladed daggers—in these examples, the blade is made up of three leafs that spring apart when the weapon is pulled from its sheath. The blades are decorated with silver and gold damascening.

NIMCHA

Common in North Africa, the curved-blade nimcha had a blade of varying lengths and could be either a long dagger or a short sword. Similar to the Arab saif, the nimcha's most notable feature is its distinctively shaped hilt.

NORTH AFRICAN DAGGER

A nineteenth-century North African dagger with a sinuous blade.

AFRICAN RITUAL KNIFE

This African knife, probably made early in the twentieth century, was used in ceremonial rituals. Its hilt is decorated with a tuft of animal hair.

AFRICAN FIGHTING KNIVES
This pair of North African fighting knives have handles of ebony.

SCISSORS DAGGER
An Indo-Persian scissor dagger, with 6.5in/17cm blades. This was a particularly nasty weapon; the attacker thrust it into his victim's body, and the blades sprang apart during withdrawal to do maximum damage.

FIGHTING BRACELET
A very rare iron fighting bracelet, dating back to the fifteenth or sixteenth century and made in what is now Nigeria. Fighting with bracelets like these was a form of martial art among some Sub-Saharan African cultures.

THROWING KNIFE
Many African peoples made use of knives specially designed for throwing. Most had multiple blades to increase the chances of hitting an opponent; they were usually thrown horizontally, from right to left. According to some accounts, a skilled warrior could use such a weapon to take off an opponent's limb at ranges of up to 65ft/20m. This example comes from the Somali people of East Africa.

INDIAN FIGHTING IMPLEMENTS

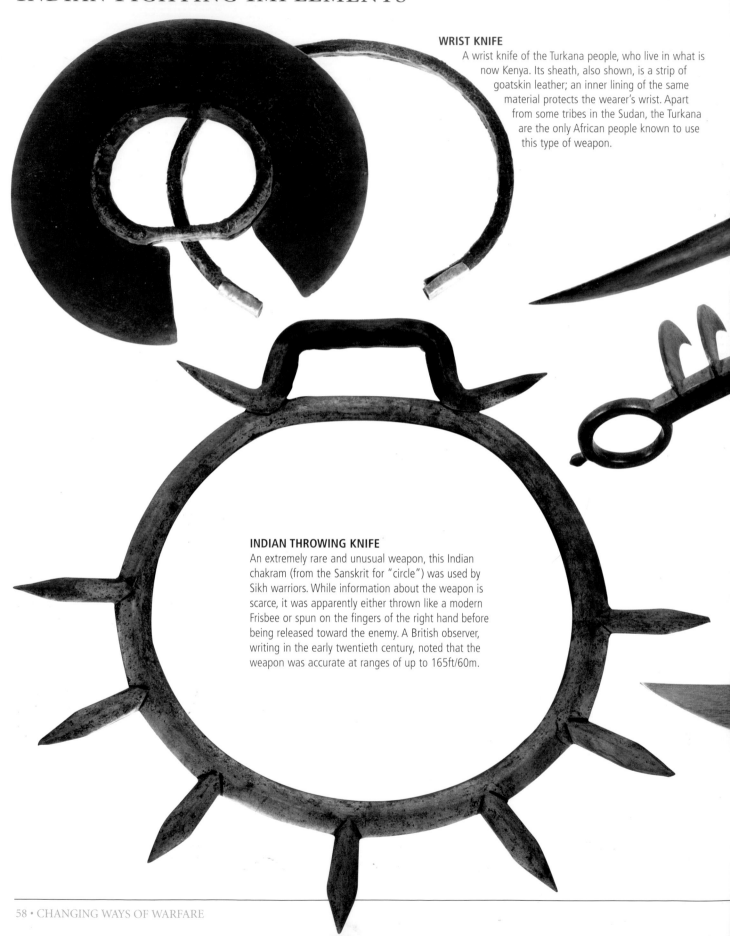

WRIST KNIFE

A wrist knife of the Turkana people, who live in what is now Kenya. Its sheath, also shown, is a strip of goatskin leather; an inner lining of the same material protects the wearer's wrist. Apart from some tribes in the Sudan, the Turkana are the only African people known to use this type of weapon.

INDIAN THROWING KNIFE

An extremely rare and unusual weapon, this Indian chakram (from the Sanskrit for "circle") was used by Sikh warriors. While information about the weapon is scarce, it was apparently either thrown like a modern Frisbee or spun on the fingers of the right hand before being released toward the enemy. A British observer, writing in the early twentieth century, noted that the weapon was accurate at ranges of up to 165ft/60m.

INDIAN CLAW DAGGERS

The *bagh nakh*, or "tiger claw," was another unusual Indian fighting knife. In addition to the dagger blade, they had from three to five curved blades protruding from the handle, which had rings accommodating the user's index and little fingers; these were designed to rake an opponent's throat. The name comes from the fact that they caused wounds similar to those inflicted by a tiger, and these implements were handy for assassins, who would take the victim out into the wild, where the attack would occur. Both of the examples shown here date from the nineteenth century.

FINGER KNIFE
Another traditional Turkana weapon—a finger knife.

PIHA KAETTA

The traditional knife of Sri Lanka (now Ceylon), the *piha kaetta* (from the Sinhalese for "resplendent") was mainly a ceremonial weapon; as such, these weapons were often elaborately decorated, with carved hilts of bone or even coral, as in this example.

THE KRIS

KRIS SCABBARD
The sheath is topped with an attractively grained, curved block of wood, known in Malay as a *wranga*. The wranga is said to symbolize a boat, representing the sea-faring history of the Malay people.

KRIS
A Balinese or Malay kris with a 15in/38cm blade, the hilt is carved in the form of a demon and inlaid with semiprecious stones [see detail above].

KRIS

Also known as a *keris*, the kris is the traditional knife of what are now the nations of Malaysia and Indonesia, although the design spread to neighboring regions of Southeast Asia like the Philippines. Intended for stabbing, the blade is of variable length and can be either straight or curvy, as in the example shown here; in a curved blade kris, each bend is called a *luk*.

KRIS STAND

A Balinese kris in its stand, which is carved in the figure of a dancer. In Malay and other cultures, the kris was considered to be a living thing, with the power to bring good or bad luck, or even to operate on its own.

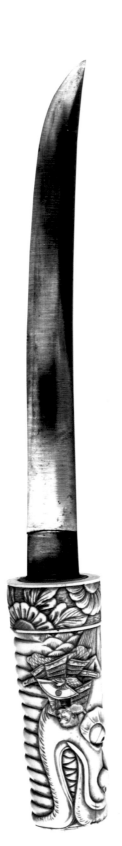

TANTO
Here are two nineteenth-century examples of the Japanese tanto, or dagger. While often carried by samurai (see pp 96–97), the tanto later became identified with the modern yakuza, criminal gangs which (though this is subject to debate) have existed in various forms in Japan for centuries.

CHINESE DAGGER
A nineteenth-century Chinese dagger, with a typically curved blade and a beautifully carved bone sheath.

CHINESE EXPORT DAGGERS
During the nineteenth and early twentieth centuries, skilled Chinese craftsmen produced vast numbers of knives for export to the West; most were put to no more lethal use than opening letters. Two examples shown here [top] have cloisonné hilts and sheaths; the third [bottom] has a cloisonné sheath and a jade hilt.

THE GUNPOWDER REVOLUTION

The term "gunpowder," or "black powder," refers to an explosive compound of charcoal, potassium nitrate (saltpeter), and sulfur. Its introduction into warfare—which, as best as can be determined, took place in fourteenth-century Europe—represented a huge advance in military technology: For the first time, energy to drive a projectile could be stored in chemical form, rather than in the form of human muscle power or by mechanical means. The so-called "Gunpowder Revolution" didn't happen overnight; it would take many years to develop truly effective gunpowder weapons and to figure out how to deploy them to optimum effect in battle, but the revolution's effects would be profoundly felt throughout the world.

FROM FIREWORKS TO FIREARMS

There are various theories about where and when black explosive powder was first "discovered" and how it was first applied to weaponry. Most historians agree that the substance was known in China as early as the tenth century, where it was apparently used in Taoist religious rituals, and later as fireworks and possibly as a means of signaling. Whether the Chinese made use of black-powder weapons over the next few centuries is still debated. Other's assert that Arab scientists may have made black powder during approximately the same period, or that Medieval European alchemists stumbled across the formula in their neverending quest to "transmute" base metals like lead into gold. It's also possible that explosive powder developed simultaneously in several societies over the course of a few centuries.

Sometime between the tenth and fourteenth centuries, came the discovery that black powder could propel a projec tile from a tube. The earliest dated image of a gunpowder weapon in use appears in an illuminated European manuscript of 1326. It depicts a soldier touching a bar of heated iron to the base of a vase-shaped vessel, which discharges an arrow-like projectile.

Out of primitive weapons like this developed the cannon—an iron tube banded to a wooden frame, firing balls of iron or carved stone. Given the primitive metallurgy and chemistry of the time (a truly stable and storable version of gunpowder would not be developed until the seventeenth century), these early artillery pieces burst easily and were often more dangerous to the firer than to the target.

CASTLES UNDER SIEGE

The first use of cannon in battle is also debated. An account of the Battle of Crecy (1346) in the Hundred Years War between England and France describes the English army using "bombards" against the French, and cannon were also present at the Battle of Agincourt in 1415. Given the poor accuracy of these early cannon, their effectiveness on the battlefield was probably more psychological than anything else; belching smoke and flame with ear-splitting noise, a cannon hurling a projectile could knock a mounted knight off his horse or tear through an infantry formation (with a very lucky shot). These new weapons were terrifying to soldiers who had never before seen anything like them.

The most significant use of early artillery, however, was as siege weapons to batter down the castle walls and other fortifications. By the end of the fifteenth century, French and Italian gunmakers had developed relatively sturdy and easily transportable guns, and rulers like Louis XI of France (1423–1483) and his successor Charles VII (1470–1498) skillfully exploited artillery both to consolidate their authority at home and conquer territory abroad.

While improvements in fortification eventually stymied the effectiveness of siege cannon, to an extent these weapons played an important role in facilitating the rise of the centralized nation-state in Europe. In the same era, the Ottoman Turkish Empire used massive siege guns—some so big they had to be manufactured on-site—to help destroy the walls of Constantinople (now Istanbul) in 1453, ending the thousand-year-old Byzantine Empire.

Around the turn of the fifteenth century, firearms intended for infantry troops began to appear on battlefields. Originally called hand cannons or hand gonnes (see pp 70–71), they were later known by a variety of terms, including the arquebus and, eventually, the musket, the latter term probably coming from the French *mosquette*. These muskets used the matchlock firing system, which was unreliable in damp conditions; as muzzle-loaders, they had a slow rate of fire; and as smoothbore weapons, they were accurate only at short distances, typically no more than 900ft/75m. The introduction of the flintlock firing system in the seventeenth century increased the musket's reliability, but the problems of slow firing and relative inaccuracy wouldn't be solved until the advent of breach-loading weapons and the widespread adoption of rifling in the nineteenth century.

"The main foundations of every state, new states as well as ancient or composite ones, are good laws and good arms—you cannot have good laws without good arms, and where there are good arms, good laws inevitably follow."

—Niccolo Machiavelli, from *The Prince*

Gunpowder's origins are somewhat mysterious. Cannon and bombs may have been used in Chinese warfare as early as the twelfth century, and their first reported use in Europe came around two centuries. Often firing balls of carved stone, early cannon were crude and dangerous to operate, but they were effective against fortifications and their use on battlefields must have had a powerful psychological effect. The development of handheld firearms had profound consequences, giving the infantry the upper hand in battle and ultimately ending the era of the mounted knight. By the eighteenth century, firearms technology had advanced from the matchlock arquebus to the flintlock musket, which—in the hands of drilled, disciplined, professional armies—came to dominate the battlefield. The "Gunpowder Revolution" also gave European soldiers an advantage over indigenous peoples as the Western powers built empires in what they called "the New World."

FROM HAND CANNON TO MATCHLOCK

Handheld gunpowder weapons—usually called hand cannons or hand gonnes—developed in parallel with artillery. They first appeared in Europe during the mid-fifteenth century and were basically just miniature cannons, held under a soldier's arm or braced against his shoulder—and often supported by a stake—with a second soldier firing the weapon by means of a slow match (see below). The introduction of the matchlock firing system (see pp 64–65) led to the development of lighter, less awkward handheld guns that could be loaded and fired by one man, including the arquebus and its successor, the musket. In the next century, infantry equipped with matchlock-equipped guns would become a major component of armies in both Europe and Asia.

THE MATCHLOCK

The "match" in matchlock was actually a length of cord soaked in a chemical compound (usually potassium nitrate, aka saltpeter) to make it burn slowly. The match was held in an S-shaped lever (the serpentine) over a pan of priming powder. Pulling the trigger lowered the match, igniting the priming powder, which then (by means of a touch-hole) ignited the main powder charge in the barrel and fired the projectile. A later, spring-loaded variation, the snap lock, "snapped" the serpentine down into the pan.

Shoulder-fired matchlock guns—variously known as arquebuses, hackbuts, calivers, culverins, and eventually muskets—had many drawbacks, most notably their unreliability in wet weather and the fact that the smoldering match could betray the firer's position to the enemy. Despite their deficiencies, matchlock firearms proved remarkably enduring—largely because they were inexpensive to manufacture and simple to use.

CHINESE SIGNAL GUN

While the Chinese probably made the first use of gunpowder (see pp 64–65) as early as the tenth century, just when they applied gunpowder to weaponry is debated. The Chinese certainly made use of gunpowder for ceremonial purposes, for firecrackers, and for signaling purposes early on; shown here is a Chinese hand cannon, probably used for signaling, from the eighteenth century. It is made of bronze and decorated with a dragon stretching from breech to muzzle.

INDIAN TORADOR

The torador was a type of matchlock musket used in India for hundreds of years. This model, from the eighteenth or early nineteenth century, has a 46in/117cm barrel ending in a muzzle chiseled in the form of a leopard's head; the breach and muzzle feature koftgari decoration—a form of inlaying gold and steel.

SPANISH HAND CANNON

While hand cannons were usually braced against the chest or shoulder or held under the arm, this sixteenth-century Spanish weapon, just 5.5in/20cm in overall length, was fired literally from the hand—making it an early pistol. Made of bronze, the handle is in the form of a seated lion.

JAPANESE PISTOL

An eighteenth-century Japanese matchlock pistol. The first firearms came to Japan by way of Portuguese traders in the 1540s and were soon copied by native craftsmen. The Japanese took quickly to guns, with competing feudal lords equipping their soldiers with matchlock muskets (tanegashima). After the establishment of the Tokugawa Dynasty in 1603, however, production and possession of firearms was severely restricted in Japan.

BATTLE OF MORAT GUN

This hand cannon—which hints at the form factor of the later pistol—was captured by Swiss troops after the Battle of Morat, fought near Bern on June 22, 1476. The battle saw the outnumbered Swiss defeat the forces of Charles the Bold, the Duke of Burgundy. The battle was notable in being one of the first in which large numbers of handheld firearms were used; as many as 10,000 on both sides combined, according to some sources.

FRENCH HAND GONNE

An early French hand cannon, with a 1in/2.5cm barrel attached to a rough wooden stock with iron bands. This weapon eventually wound up in Morocco, North Africa.

RIFLING

As early as the fifteenth century, European gunsmiths began boring grooves on the inside of gun barrels—a process that would become known as rifling. The initial purpose was probably to reduce the buildup of gunpowder residue in the barrel, but it was discovered that a barrel with spiral grooves gave stability to a bullet in flight, greatly increasing its accuracy. Rifling, however, was a difficult process until the improvements in technology brought by the Industrial Revolution. Although rifles were used in hunting and carried by specialist military units, most firearms remained smoothbore (i.e., nonrifled) until well into the nineteenth century.

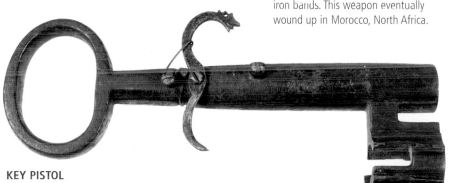

KEY PISTOL

Shown here is a highly unusual adaptation of the matchlock mechanism: A combination gate key and matchlock pistol from eighteenth-century Scotland. The key operated the gate of a castle; the gatekeeper carried the weapon in case an intruder attempted to break into the castle while the gate was being unlocked.

FROM MATCHLOCK TO FLINTLOCK

Despite its remarkable longevity, the matchlock's deficiencies (see pp 70–71) led gunsmiths to experiment with better firing systems for handheld weapons. The next major advance in this field came with the introduction of the wheel-lock mechanism in the early sixteenth century, but this system was later supplanted by the flintlock mechanism. Widely adopted in Europe in the seventeenth century, the flintlock remained standard in much of the world until the introduction of the percussion cap system in the nineteenth century (see p 114).

THE WHEEL LOCK

The wheel lock combined a spring-loaded, serrated metal wheel and a dog, or cock—a pair of metal jaws that held a piece of iron pyrite. The wheel was wound up (usually with a key) to put tension on the spring. When the trigger was pulled, the cock struck against the rotating wheel, striking sparks to fire the weapon. Various conflicting theories abound of when, where, and how the wheel-lock gun developed, but it was likely inspired by the handheld tinder-lighters in use at the time.

The introduction of the wheel lock spurred the development of the pistol. (The term "pistol" may derive from the arms-producing city of Pistoia in Italy, although there are other theories; early pistols were often called dags, which probably derives from an old French word for "dagger.") Pistols put firepower into the hands of mounted troops; as concealable weapons, criminals and assassins also quickly adopted them. In 1584, a wheel-lock pistol was employed to murder the Dutch leader William the Silent in the world's first political assassination by pistol.

THE FLINTLOCK

The wheel lock's heyday was brief. By the mid- to late sixteenth century, Northern Europe saw the development of the snaphance, or snaphaunce, lock. (The term came from a Dutch word for "pecking bird.") In the snaphance, the cock held a piece of flint, which sprang forward on the trigger-pull to strike a piece of steel (the frizzen), sending sparks into the priming pan. A similar type of lock, the miquelet, appeared around the same time in Southern Europe. Technical refinements to both eventually led to the introduction of the true flintlock early in the seventeenth century.

GERMAN WHEEL-LOCK RIFLE
A German wheel-lock rifle, probably made in Nuremberg in 1597. The stock is inlaid with ivory carvings of deer and fowl. Wheel-lock muskets and rifles were expensive, so they enjoyed much popularity as hunting weapons for the aristocracy and the rich.

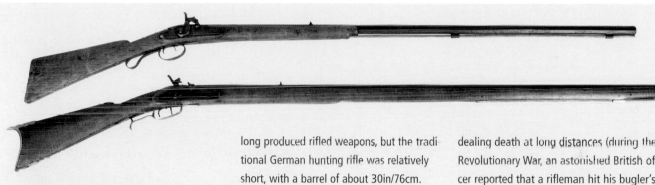

THE KENTUCKY RIFLE

A weapon steeped in American history and folklore, the Kentucky rifle (or long rifle) was first produced by immigrant German gunsmiths in Pennsylvania, Virginia, and other colonies in the mid-eighteenth century. (The designation "Kentucky rifle" was popularized in a song, "The Hunters of Kentucky," which celebrated the marksmanship of volunteers from that state in the Battle of New Orleans on January 8, 1815.) German gunsmiths had long produced rifled weapons, but the traditional German hunting rifle was relatively short, with a barrel of about 30in/76cm.

In America, gunsmiths began lengthening the barrel to between 40in/101cm and 46in/117cm, greatly increasing its accuracy. The resulting weapon, typically .50, proved ideal for hunting in the North American wilderness. They were handsome weapons as well, usually with stocks of curly maple and often beautifully decorated. Formations of riflemen recruited from the frontier fought against the British in the Revolutionary War and in the War of 1812. Although capable of dealing death at long distances (during the Revolutionary War, an astonished British officer reported that a rifleman hit his bugler's horse at a range of 400yd/366m), the long rifle was even slower to reload than the smoothbore musket, a fact that limited its effectiveness in conventional battle.

Originally flintlock, many long rifles were later converted to percussion (see pp 118–119), including the two examples shown here; the lower one was made by the Lemans of Lancaster County, Pennsylvania, a family of prominent gunsmiths active from the mid-1700s to around 1875.

"For 'tis not often here you see A hunter from Kentucky."

—lyrics from "The Hunters of Kentucky," 1824

RAMPART GUN

A wheel-lock European rampart gun from about 1600. Rampart guns were mounted on the walls of castles and fortifications (and, at sea, on ship's rails) for defense; this .76 model was designed so that it could be fired by "remote control" by means of a string.

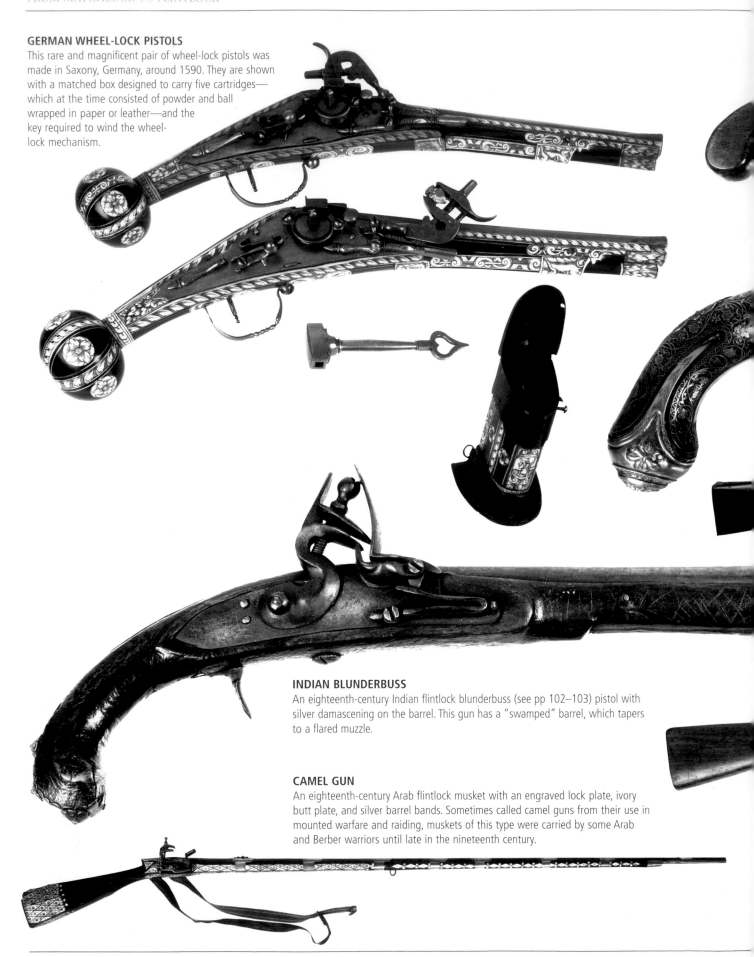

GERMAN WHEEL-LOCK PISTOLS

This rare and magnificent pair of wheel-lock pistols was made in Saxony, Germany, around 1590. They are shown with a matched box designed to carry five cartridges—which at the time consisted of powder and ball wrapped in paper or leather—and the key required to wind the wheel-lock mechanism.

INDIAN BLUNDERBUSS

An eighteenth-century Indian flintlock blunderbuss (see pp 102–103) pistol with silver damascening on the barrel. This gun has a "swamped" barrel, which tapers to a flared muzzle.

CAMEL GUN

An eighteenth-century Arab flintlock musket with an engraved lock plate, ivory butt plate, and silver barrel bands. Sometimes called camel guns from their use in mounted warfare and raiding, muskets of this type were carried by some Arab and Berber warriors until late in the nineteenth century.

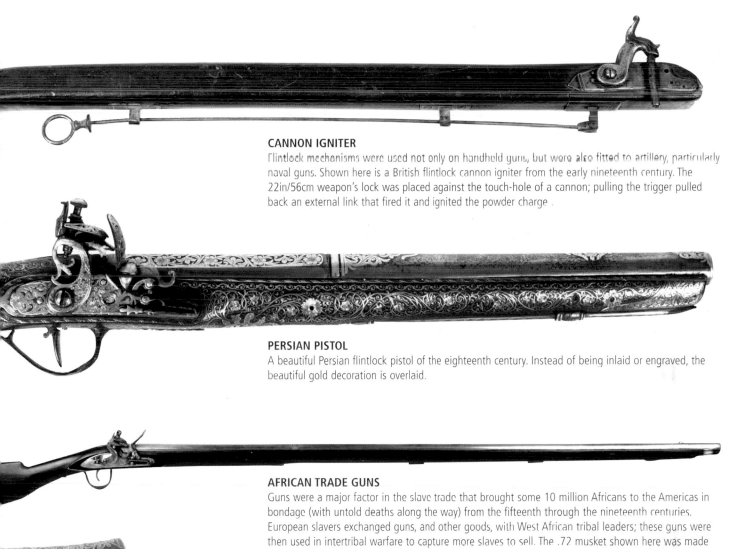

CANNON IGNITER
Flintlock mechanisms were used not only on handheld guns, but were also fitted to artillery, particularly naval guns. Shown here is a British flintlock cannon igniter from the early nineteenth century. The 22in/56cm weapon's lock was placed against the touch-hole of a cannon; pulling the trigger pulled back an external link that fired it and ignited the powder charge .

PERSIAN PISTOL
A beautiful Persian flintlock pistol of the eighteenth century. Instead of being inlaid or engraved, the beautiful gold decoration is overlaid.

AFRICAN TRADE GUNS
Guns were a major factor in the slave trade that brought some 10 million Africans to the Americas in bondage (with untold deaths along the way) from the fifteenth through the nineteenth centuries. European slavers exchanged guns, and other goods, with West African tribal leaders; these guns were then used in intertribal warfare to capture more slaves to sell. The .72 musket shown here was made for African export in the eighteenth century, although the barrel was apparently manufactured in Italy much earlier.

FRENCH MUSKET
This French military musket made in 1813 and shown with its bayonet, is typical of the last generation of smoothbore flintlock long arms. Within a couple of decades they would be replaced by rifled weapons using the percussion-cap (see p 114) firing system.

GERMAN WHEEL-LOCK MUSKET
Another finely made example of a wheel lock weapon.

SUNDIAL GUN

Made in 1788, this "gun" uses the
heat of the sun's rays, rather than any type of
lock, to fire. The purpose of these so-called sundial guns
was to announce the arrival of noon. Aligned on a north-south
axis, the lens was adjusted, according to the season, to focus the
sun's rays on a powder charge, which discharged a small gun when the
sun was directly overhead—i.e., at noon.

This implement was mostly used shipboard, as the sound carried well
over the water, but the sundial gun had its detractors. In an edition of Poor
Richard's Almanac, Ben Franklin found this contraption an attractive target:
"How to make a STRIKING SUNDIAL, by which not only a Man's own
Family, but all his Neighbours for ten Miles round, may know what o'Clock
it is, when the Sun shines, without seeing the Dial. [. . .] Note also, That the
chief Expence will be the Powder, for the Cannon once bought, will, with
Care, last 100 Years. Note moreover, That there will be a great Saving of
Powder in cloudy Days. Kind Reader, Methinks I hear thee say, That it is
indeed a good Thing to know how the Time passes."

COEHORN MORTAR

A mortar is a short-barrelled cannon that fires projectiles in an arching
trajectory—"plunging fire," in military terminology, as opposed to the
"direct fire" of conventional cannon. They were ideal for siege warfare
because they could lob an exploding shell (a hollow projectile filled with
gunpowder and fitted with a fuse before firing) over the walls of a castle or
fort. Early mortars were often massive and crude weapons, but in the late
seventeenth century the Dutch military engineer Menno van Coehorn
(1641–1704) invented a compact, lightweight mortar that could be carried
close to the target by a crew of two to four men. Mortars of the Coehorn
type remained in use well into the nineteenth century; shown here is an
English example from the early eighteenth century. The Coehorn is the
ancestor of the mortars used for infantry support in all contemporary armies.

ARAB MIQUELET

An Arab flintlock gun using a snaphance-style mechanism. The stock is inlaid with silver wire and, as with many guns from North Africa and the Middle East, the buttstock is of finely carved ivory.

VOLLEY GUN

Volley guns—weapons with multiple barrels, all of which discharged simultaneously—were used in close in naval fighting to repel boarders. The most famous of these guns is probably the Nock volley gun shown here. (While the famous British gunsmith Henry Nock made the weapon, he was apparently not the designer.) First appearing around 1780, the flintlock gun had seven 20in/51cm .50 rifled barrels. Some 600 were produced for the Royal Navy. While obviously a formidable weapon, it had its downside: The recoil was said to be severe enough to break the firer's shoulder, and the muzzle blast sometimes set sails and rigging on fire. The weapon is familiar to modern readers of Bernard Cornwell's popular series of historical novels set during the Napoleonic Wars, in which it is carried (on land) by one of the main characters.

DEATH BATTERY

Known as "death organs," or "organ guns," because their rows of barrels resemble a rack of organ pipes, weapons like the one shown here—which dates from the seventeenth century—were an early form of multishot firearm. This example has 15 barrels, each 17.5in/44cm long fixed to a wooden base. Organ guns evolved into battery guns, which were used to defend bridges and other vulnerable locations in conflicts up until the American Civil War.

THE FLINTLOCK PISTOL

The adoption of the flintlock firing mechanism (see p 72) led to a proliferation of pistols. Despite their considerable drawbacks—ineffectiveness at any but close ranges, slow loading by the muzzle, vulnerability to inclement weather—these guns gave individuals a potent weapon for self-defense, which was no small thing in an era without the benefit of any organized police forces, and in which robbers lurked after dark on the streets of towns and cities and highwaymen haunted rural roads.

COAT, HOLSTER, AND BELT PISTOLS

Generally, pistols of the flintlock era fall into three types:

The first were coat pistols, also known as traveler's pistols. As the name implies, these were personal-defense weapons compact enough to be carried in the pockets of the overcoats worn by men of the time; very short-barreled versions could also be carried in a waistcoat pocket or elsewhere on one's person.

The second type were holster, or horse pistols—relatively long-barreled weapons intended to be worn in a holster attached to a horse's saddle.

The third type were belt pistols. Of an intermediate size and caliber between coat and holster pistols, they were usually fitted with a hook, which could be attached to the belt.

TURN-OFFS AND TURN-OVERS

While a majority of flintlock pistols were muzzle-loaders, like their long-arm counterparts, the so-called turn-off, or screw-off pistol appeared in the mid-seventeenth century. These weapons had a cannon-shaped barrel (see the example on p 82) that could be unscrewed, loaded with a bullet, and replaced; the powder charge went into a compartment in the breech. In contrast to the mostly smoothbore pistols of the time, turn-offs often had rifled barrels, greatly increasing accuracy. During the English Civil Wars (1642–51), Prince Rupert, commander of the Royalist cavalry, is said to

have used such a weapon to hit the weathervane atop a church at a distance about 300ft/91m; he then repeated the shot to prove the first was not a fluke.

There were also multiple-barreled pistols. One type had two side-by-side barrels, each fired by a separate lock; another, the turn-over pistol, had two or more barrels that were loaded individually and rotated into place to be fired by a single lock. Gunsmiths also tried flintlock pepperboxes and even revolvers (see pp 128–29, 114); however, most multiple-shot flintlock pistols tended to be unreliable and prone to accidental firing. An exception was the duckfoot pistol (see the example below), which had several barrels in a horizontal configuration designed for simultaneous firing.

This fascinating selection of flintlocks features both rare and significant items from the fifteenth through nineteenth centuries.

BALKAN AX-PISTOL

Another ax-pistol combination, this one made in the Balkans in the 18th century. The stock is inlaid with silver wire in traditional Balkan designs.

TINDER LIGHTER

Though not a gun, this tinder lighter}s design was based on the flintlock mechanism and was used to start fires with wood shavings or chips. The sparks were created by the friction of the flint against metal. Made around 1820, this item predates the match.

PISTOL-SWORD
A rare sword-pistol combination from the mid-eighteenth century. Weapons like these were apparently used mainly by marines and naval officers in boarding engagements at sea (see pp 104–5).

GERMAN AX-PISTOL
Made in the Central European region of Silesia in the seventeenth century, this weapon combines a flintlock pistol with a battle-ax. Its decorative elements include an elephant stamped into the lock and a stock inlaid with bone.

BALKAN DRESS PISTOL
Also from the Balkans, this interesting pistol is not a weapon at all—while it resembles a typical locally made pistol, right down to its elaborate decoration and "rat-tail" butt, it lacks a functioning lock. Balkan nobles and warriors of the sixteenth and seventeenth centuries were required by custom to carry pistols, but this led to a spate of assassinations. As a compromise, non-functioning pistols like the one shown here were worn at meetings and on ceremonial occasions: They satisfied dress requirements, but put no one in danger.

DUCKFOOT PISTOL
"Duckfoot" pistols—like the four-barreled version shown here, made by the London shop of Goodwin & Co.—were multiple-barreled weapons, so called because the angled barrels resembled a duck's web. In popular legend, at least, they were favorites of sea captains and prison warders, because they could be used to keep a mutinous crew or rioting prisoners at bay.

COAT PISTOL
A short-barreled coat pistol, probably made in France around the turn of the nineteenth century.

DOG HEAD PISTOL
Another French coat pistol, this one with a butt carved in the form of a fierce dog's head.

DUBLIN CASTLE PISTOL
This walnut-stocked, brass-finished .65 pistol was made in Dublin, Ireland, and bears the royal cipher of King George III (1738–1820). Ireland was a British colony at the time, and the armory at Dublin Castle was—together with the armories at Birmingham and at the Tower of London in England—a principal supplier of arms to the British army and navy.

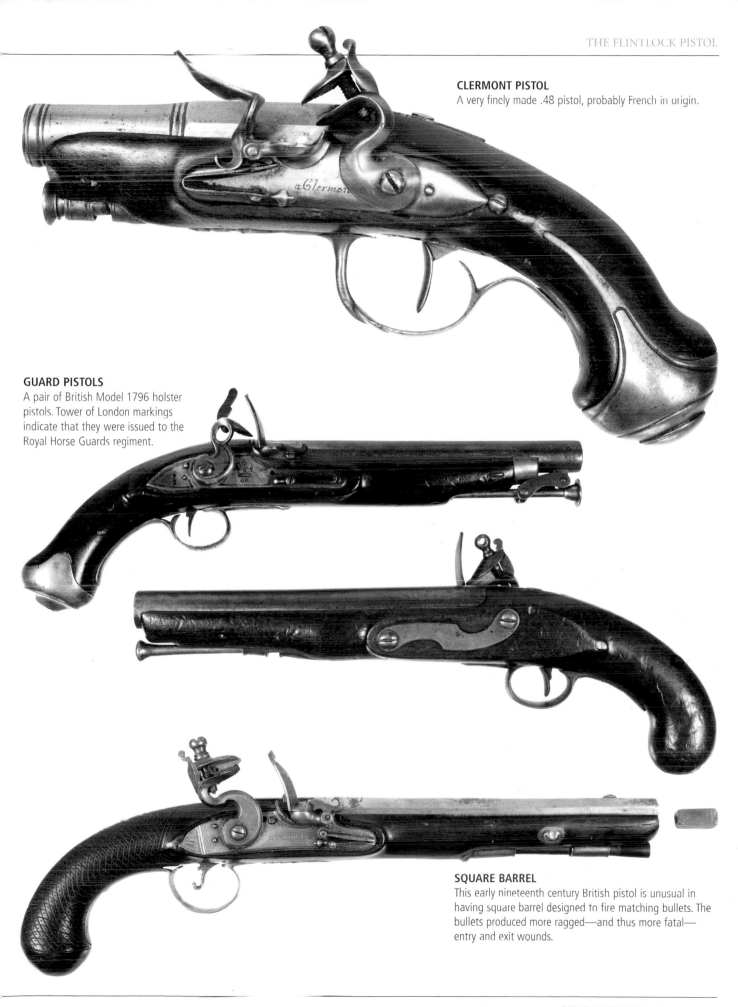

CLERMONT PISTOL
A very finely made .48 pistol, probably French in origin.

GUARD PISTOLS
A pair of British Model 1796 holster pistols. Tower of London markings indicate that they were issued to the Royal Horse Guards regiment.

SQUARE BARREL
This early nineteenth century British pistol is unusual in having square barrel designed to fire matching bullets. The bullets produced more ragged—and thus more fatal—entry and exit wounds.

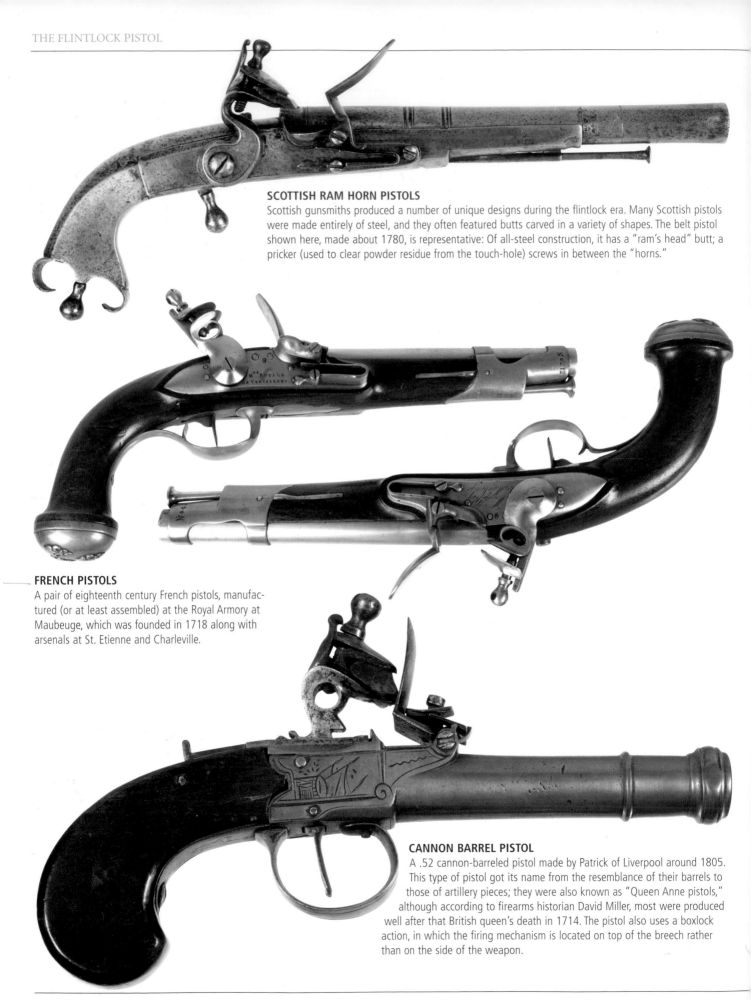

SCOTTISH RAM HORN PISTOLS

Scottish gunsmiths produced a number of unique designs during the flintlock era. Many Scottish pistols were made entirely of steel, and they often featured butts carved in a variety of shapes. The belt pistol shown here, made about 1780, is representative: Of all-steel construction, it has a "ram's head" butt; a pricker (used to clear powder residue from the touch-hole) screws in between the "horns."

FRENCH PISTOLS

A pair of eighteenth century French pistols, manufactured (or at least assembled) at the Royal Armory at Maubeuge, which was founded in 1718 along with arsenals at St. Etienne and Charleville.

CANNON BARREL PISTOL

A .52 cannon-barreled pistol made by Patrick of Liverpool around 1805. This type of pistol got its name from the resemblance of their barrels to those of artillery pieces; they were also known as "Queen Anne pistols," although according to firearms historian David Miller, most were produced well after that British queen's death in 1714. The pistol also uses a boxlock action, in which the firing mechanism is located on top of the breech rather than on the side of the weapon.

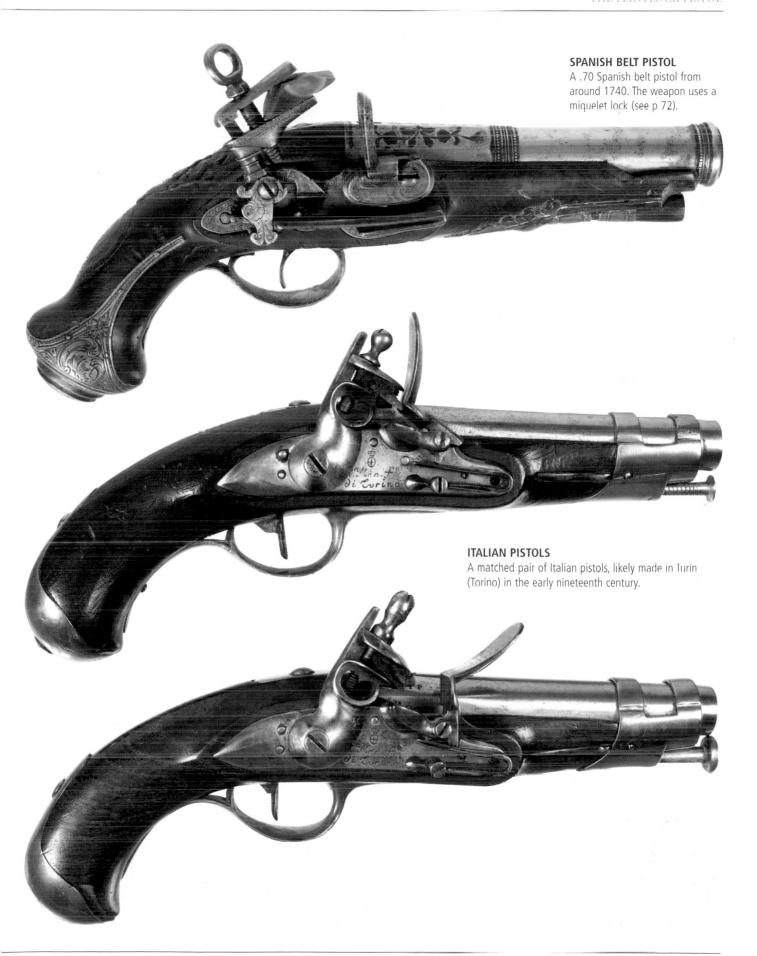

SPANISH BELT PISTOL
A .70 Spanish belt pistol from around 1740. The weapon uses a miquelet lock (see p 72).

ITALIAN PISTOLS
A matched pair of Italian pistols, likely made in Turin (Torino) in the early nineteenth century.

THE EUROPEAN SWORD, C. 1500–1800

While the advent of firearms (see pp 70–71) would transform European (and later world-wide) warfare, this transformation didn't happen overnight, and the sword remained part of the warrior's arsenal, especially among mounted knights and mercenary infantry. By the late seventeenth century, however, firearms technology and tactics had advanced to a point at which the sword's battlefield usefulness was limited—but swords continued to enjoy a vogue among European men, both for dueling and as a status symbol.

BIGGER AND LONGER

Sword design closely followed changes in armor (see pp 46-49) during this period. By the turn of the sixteenth century, heavy plate armor had largely replaced the chain-mail armor formerly worn by knights and other warriors. This led to a movement away from shorter cutting swords, which could penetrate mail, to much longer and heavier swords—generically known as longswords—with enlarged grips to permit two-handed use. The ultimate example of this type is probably the zweihänder, which could be up to 6ft/183cm in length.

While the longsword was devastating, it still lacked the ability to actually pierce plate armor, so swordsmiths developed the weapon variously known as the *estoc* (in France), the tuck (in England), and the *panzerstecher* (in German-speaking Europe). These swords had blades of varying lengths, but all ended in a cutting point. While these swords might not pierce plate armor, they could be thrust into the joints between plates with deadly effect.

THE SWORD AS STATUS SYMBOL

With firearms replacing edged weapons on the battlefield, the sword increasingly became a civilian weapon, used for self-defense, or for dueling. The narrow-bladed rapier, which evolved from the sixteenth-century Spanish *espada ropera*, became an especially popular dueling sword, and in turn evolved into the épée used in the modern sport of fencing.

By the eighteenth century, a sword was an essential fashion accessory for all European gentlemen—or those who wanted to look like one. The most common type of sword for everyday wear was the small sword, a lightweight thrusting weapon that first appeared in France late in the seventeenth century.

The ubiquity of the sword in the eighteenth century is evidenced by a newspaper advertisement for the first performance of G. W. Handel's oratorio *Messiah* in Dublin, Ireland, in 1742; the notice politely requested gentlemen to not wear their swords to the concert in order to increase seating space in the hall. (Handel, by the way, had fought a bloodless sword duel with a fellow composer some years earlier.)

By the turn of the nineteenth century, however, swords had fallen out of fashion, largely replaced by dueling pistols (see pp 100–101). These six pages display a scintillating selection of blades.

KNIGHT'S LONG SWORD
A knight's longsword from the fifthteenth century. A slashing weapon wielded with both hands, these swords were known as *langes schwert* ("long swords") in German and *spadone* ("big sword") in Italian.

LANDSKNECHT
The longest of all European swords of the Renaissance were those used by the *landsknechts*—mercenary soldiers recruited mostly from the Holy Roman Empire, which comprised much of modern-day Germany. Their swords, which could be as long as 6ft/183cm, were known as *zweihänder*—"two-handers"—and they were used not only as antipersonnel weapons, but also to strike aside enemy pikes and halberds to break up infantry formations. This German example dates from the sixteenth century.

THE BLADES OF TOLEDO

The city of Toledo in central Spain has long been famous for its high-quality swords and other edged weapons—a tradition that dates back at least to the fifth century BCE, when local swordsmiths produced a type of sword that would later be called the falcata. The first reference to Toledan weapons comes from the first century BCE, in a work by the Roman writer Grattius. The swordsmiths of Toledo used an excellent form of steel that was arguably better than Damascus steel (see pp 92); the resulting swords were prized by warriors across Europe, and according to some sources at least, some Japanese samurai may have used Toledo blades. In his book *Guns, Germs, and Steel*, historian Jared Diamond contends that weapons of Toledo steel were instrumental in the Spanish conquest of the Americas— the steel swords and other weapons of the sixteenth-century Spanish conquistadores were far superior to those wielded by the soldiers of the Aztec and Inca empires.

A Spanish small sword with Fabrica de Toledo ("Made in Toledo") etched on the blade.

GERMAN LONG SWORD

Despite the progress of democracy in Europe in the 18th and 19th centuries, army officers still tended to be drawn from the aristocracy, and swords became family heirlooms. This Bavarian sword bears an aristocratic coat-of-arms and a family motto—"In firm faith."

ROYAL COMPANY OF ARCHERS SHORT SWORD

Originally founded in the 1670s, the Scots Royal Company of Archers was designated the "King's Body Guard for Scotland" in the early nineteenth century. Members carried this short sword, with a 16.75/42.6cm blade etched with both the Royal Arms of Great Britain and the thistle, a traditional symbol of Scotland. The beautifully decorated hilt is cast bronze.

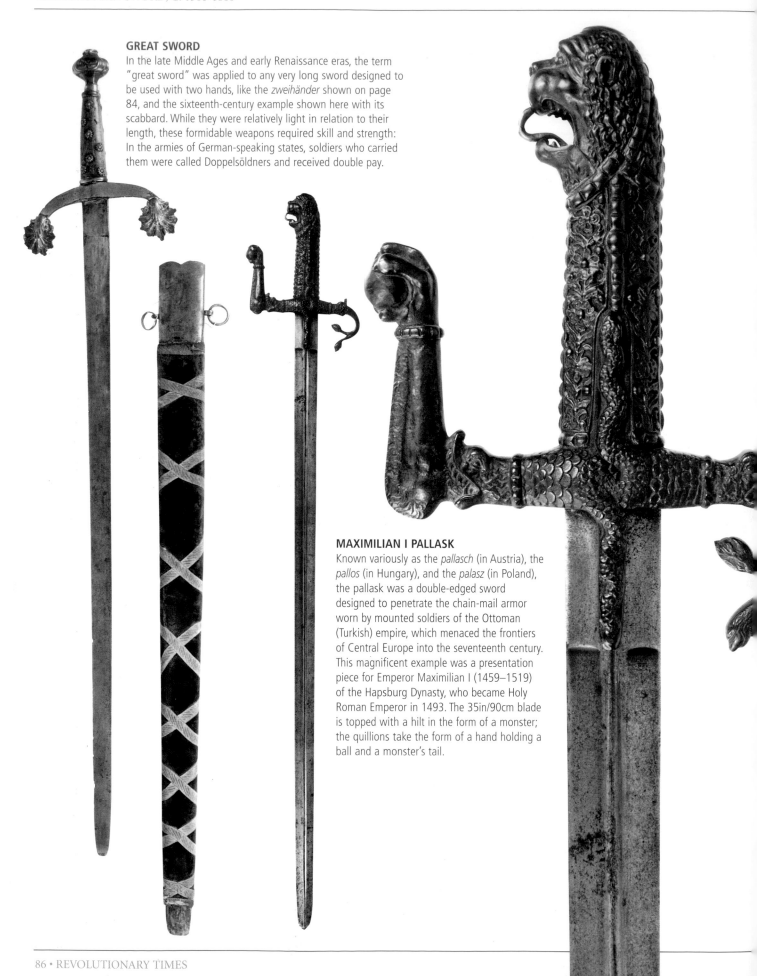

GREAT SWORD

In the late Middle Ages and early Renaissance eras, the term "great sword" was applied to any very long sword designed to be used with two hands, like the *zweihänder* shown on page 84, and the sixteenth-century example shown here with its scabbard. While they were relatively light in relation to their length, these formidable weapons required skill and strength: In the armies of German-speaking states, soldiers who carried them were called Doppelsöldners and received double pay.

MAXIMILIAN I PALLASK

Known variously as the *pallasch* (in Austria), the *pallos* (in Hungary), and the *palasz* (in Poland), the pallask was a double-edged sword designed to penetrate the chain-mail armor worn by mounted soldiers of the Ottoman (Turkish) empire, which menaced the frontiers of Central Europe into the seventeenth century. This magnificent example was a presentation piece for Emperor Maximilian I (1459–1519) of the Hapsburg Dynasty, who became Holy Roman Emperor in 1493. The 35in/90cm blade is topped with a hilt in the form of a monster; the quillions take the form of a hand holding a ball and a monster's tail.

SCOTTISH BROADSWORD

From the middle ages into the eighteenth century, Scots clansmen went into battle (both inter-clan, and against the encroaching English) armed with the fearsome claymore, a double-handed slashing weapon up to 55in/140cm in length. (The name derives from the Gaelic word for sword, claidheamh.) The claymore name was later applied to basket hilted swords like the one shown here, which were carried by officers in Highland Scots regiments of the British Army.

KNIGHTS OF MALTA

Also known as the Knights Hospitaller and the Order of St John of Jerusalem, the Knights of Malta was one of the orders of "warrior monks" founded to protect Christian pilgrims to the Holy Land during the Crusades. A member of the order carried this sword, with a cruciform hilt that echoes the Maltese cross, in the seventeenth century. By this time the order had been driven from the Holy Land to the Mediterranean island of Malta. The 25.5in/65cm blade is etched with a variety of religious symbols.

LOUIS XIII ROYAL GUARD SWORD

This seventeenth-century sword was carried by the King's royal guard during the reign of Louis XIII (1601–1642)

DANISH SHORT SWORD

A Danish short sword from the eighteenth century, with a D-shaped guard and a grip of wire-wrapped leather. This weapon appears to be a Model 1788 hirshfänger.

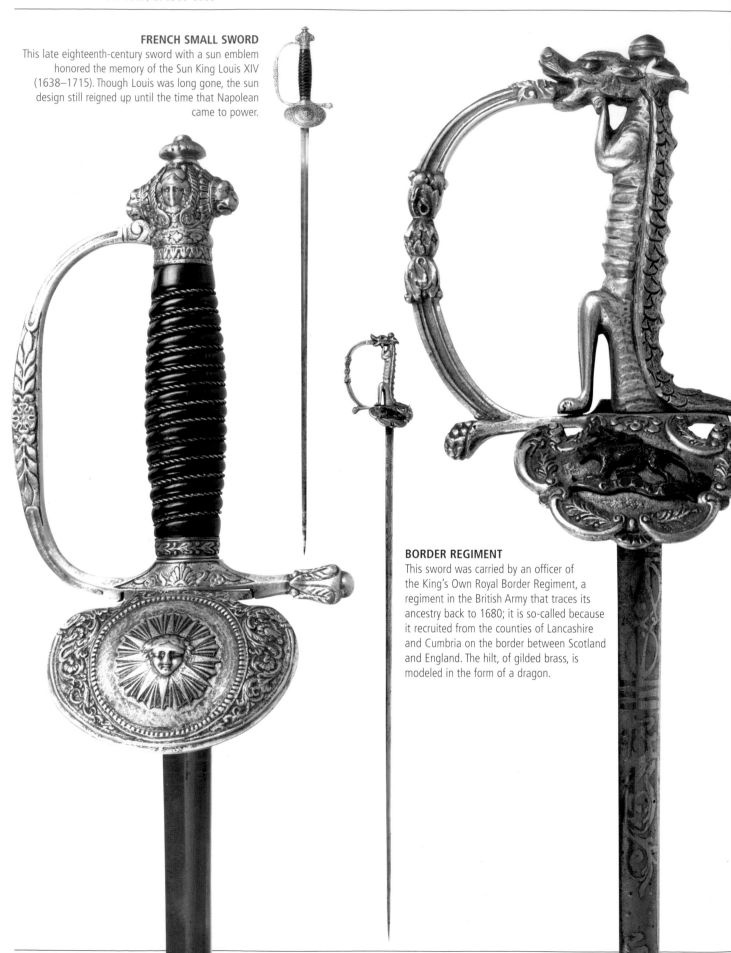

FRENCH SMALL SWORD

This late eighteenth-century sword with a sun emblem honored the memory of the Sun King Louis XIV (1638–1715). Though Louis was long gone, the sun design still reigned up until the time that Napolean came to power.

BORDER REGIMENT

This sword was carried by an officer of the King's Own Royal Border Regiment, a regiment in the British Army that traces its ancestry back to 1680; it is so-called because it recruited from the counties of Lancashire and Cumbria on the border between Scotland and England. The hilt, of gilded brass, is modeled in the form of a dragon.

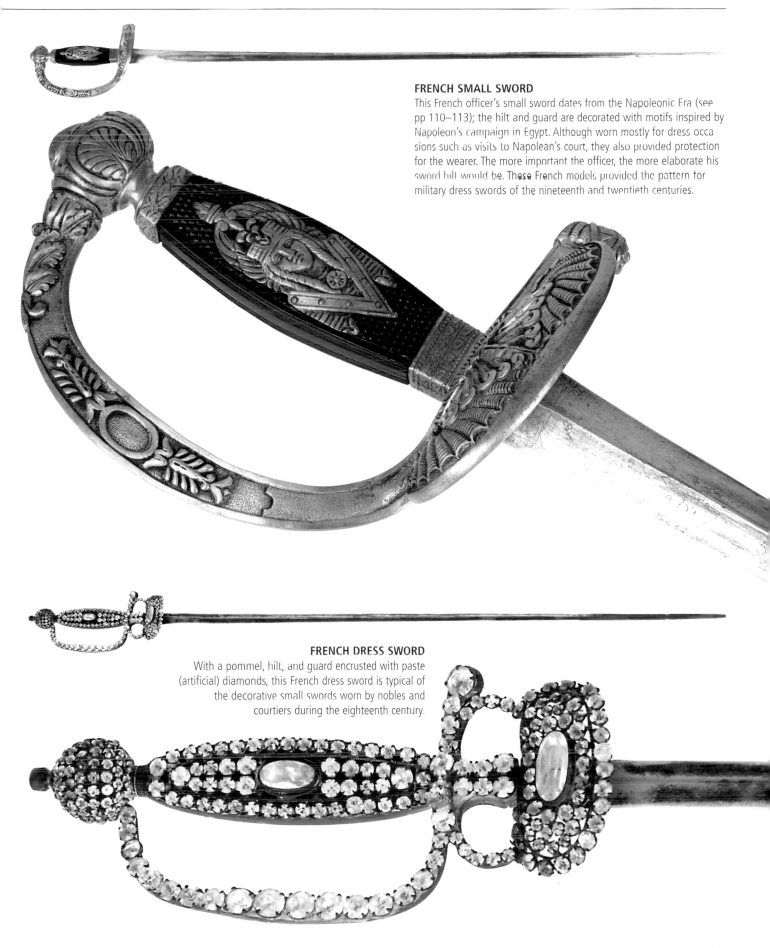

FRENCH SMALL SWORD

This French officer's small sword dates from the Napoleonic Era (see pp 110–113); the hilt and guard are decorated with motifs inspired by Napoleon's campaign in Egypt. Although worn mostly for dress occasions such as visits to Napolean's court, they also provided protection for the wearer. The more important the officer, the more elaborate his sword hilt would be. These French models provided the pattern for military dress swords of the nineteenth and twentieth centuries.

FRENCH DRESS SWORD

With a pommel, hilt, and guard encrusted with paste (artificial) diamonds, this French dress sword is typical of the decorative small swords worn by nobles and courtiers during the eighteenth century.

SWORDS OF AFRICA AND ASIA

The following pages present a variety of swords (and some other edged weapons) from the non-Western world. While European missionaries, explorers, and traders collected most of these weapons in the eighteenth, nineteenth, and twentieth centuries, the construction and design of many are unchanged from swords made centuries or even millennia ago.

THE MONGOL INFLUENCE

From ancient times, swords in the Western world (see pp 84–89) were mainly thrusting weapons, usually single-edged—a design suited to the "Western way of war," in which infantry played the key role in battle. Starting in the early thirteenth century, the mounted armies of the Mongols came out of Central Asia to conquer much of China, India, and what is now known as the Middle East. The Mongol horseman's primary weapon was the bow, but he also carried a curved-bladed, single-edge sword designed for one-handed slashing from horseback.

This weapon, referred to by historians as the Turko-Mongol saber, had a huge influence on the development of the sword throughout much of the world. The offspring of this "parent sword" includes the Arab saif, the Indian tulwar (and its Afghani counterpart, the pulwar), the Persian shamshir, the Turkish kilic, and eventually the European saber. In the West, curved swords of this type became generally known as "scimitars"—a designation that may derive from the Persian shamshir—although this catch-all term doesn't do justice to the wide variety of local adaptations to the original Turko-Mongol saber.

INDIGENOUS SWORDS

Outside the areas of Mongol influence (and European influence, at least until the era of European imperialism began in the fifteenth and sixteenth centuries), indigenous swordmaking flourished: Examples include the tabouka of the Tuareg, a nomadic North African people, and the Sudanese kaskara. Some of the finest swords of Sub-Saharan Africa were the work of the Kuban culture, a coalition of Bantu-speaking peoples living in what is now Congo.

THE CRAFT IN CHINA

Chinese swordmaking has a long and distinguished history, beginning with the bronze swords of the Chou Dynasty (1122–770 BCE). Through the centuries, Chinese swordsmiths progressed from bronze to iron and eventually to steel, and developed techniques—like repeated forging and folding and differential hardening of edges—that influenced swordmaking throughout South and Southeast Asia, particularly in Japan. Some Chinese swordsmiths would leave blades exposed to the open air for years, subjecting them to all kinds of weather and extremes of temperature, as a form of "stress test"; only after blades survived this ordeal were they deemed worthy of completion.

As in Japan, swords had a cultural significance in China that went beyond mere weaponry: In the words of one historian, "Swords went on to assume multiple roles such as decoration, symbols of honor, power, and rank, and articles used in ceremonial or religious rites."

JAPANESE BLADES

In Japan, the sword played a unique and important cultural role. For centuries, sword ownership was restricted to the samurai—members of the warrior class, pledged to follow the code of bushido and bound to serve a lord, or daimyo. Samurai typically carried a katana, a curved single-edged weapon often wielded with both hands, and the wakizashi, a shorter sword; together, the two weapons were known as a daisho, which roughly translates to "big and little."

Although samurai fought primarily with bows and spears in actual battle, the sword was considered "the soul of the warrior," and countless hours were spent mastering it. Swordsmanship was an integral part of Japanese martial-arts traditions that survive today.

Swordsmiths were the most highly respected craftsmen in Medieval Japan; because of the sword's cultural significance, their work was considered as much spiritual as artisanal. The making of a katana was a long and intricate process, involving multiple hammerings and forgings of layers of steel to create blades whose sharpness and strength became legendary.

THE MAMELUKE SWORD

The Turko-Mongol saber also influenced the design of swords used by the Mamluks, or Mamelukes slave-soldiers who formed a major part of Islamic armies from the ninth century on, and who set up dynasties of their own in Egypt and Syria from the thirteenth to sixteenth centuries. The Mamelukes were succeeded by the Ottoman Turks in Egypt. In 1804, an Ottoman official presented a Mameluke-style sword to U.S. Marine Corps Lieutenant Presley O'Bannon in recognition of his leadership of a mixed force of marines and mercenaries in an expedition to the city of Derne (in what is now Libya). There, he and his troops defeated the "Barbary pirates" of the North African coast, who were attacking American and European shipping and enslaving captured crew and passengers. The Commandant of the Marine Corps decreed the adoption of the "Mameluke sword" for marine officers, and marines still proudly wear the sword in the twenty-first century.

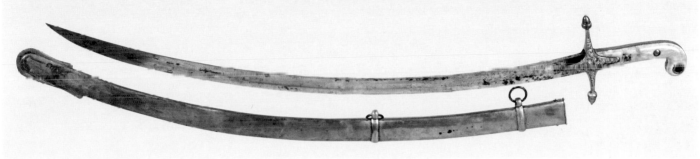

ROYAL PERSIAN SCIMITAR

Certainly one of the most beautiful weapons in existence, this royal Persian court sword was commissioned by Abbas the Great, Shah of Persia (modern-day Iran) from 1588 to 1629. It is decorated with 1,295 rose-cut diamonds, 50 karats worth of rubies, and an 11-karat emerald set in the hilt—all set in 3lb/1.360kg of gold. The sword's history is no less fascinating than its appearance. After the fall of the Safavid Dynasty in the eighteenth century the sword fell into the hands of the Ottoman Turkish government, which then presented it to Empress Catherine the Great (1729-1796) of Russia. It resided in the Czarist Treasury until it disappeared in the chaos of the Russian Revolution of 1917. The sword resurfaced in Europe after World War II and spent some years in a private museum before being purchased by Colonel Farley Berman in 1962. It is now one of the "crown jewels" of the Berman Collection.

DAMASCUS STEEL

A great technological leap in swordmaking came around 900 CE with the introduction of Damascus steel in the Middle East. The term may derive from the Syrian city of Damascus, or from the Arabic word *damas*, which means "watery"—probably a reference to the shimmering appearance of blades made of the material. As with Greek Fire (see p 104), the exact techniques and materials used to produce Damascus Steel are still debated, but the end product was likely the result of a special alloy and a secret forging process. Together, they produced a blade that met the two most important criteria for an effective, reliable sword—hardness, which allowed the blade to be sharpened to a razorlike edge, and flexibility, which kept the blade from breaking when struck against an opponent's weapon. In the mid-eighteenth century, however, the technique of making "true" Damascus steel died out; although later edged weapons (and gun barrels) are sometimes described as being made of Damascus steel, they were actually produced with different methods. In recent years, some weapons historians have contended that original Damascus steel was basically the same as wootz steel, an alloy used in Indian swordsmithing as early as 200 BCE.

PERSIAN SWORD

A Persian sword—this one with a straight blade and dating from the eighteenth century. The hilt features strips of gold in a basket pattern, and the Damascus steel blade is inlaid with gold.

TULWAR

This Indian tulwar from the late eighteenth or early nineteenth century, is of all-steel construction. (Sometimes spelled talwar, the name derives from *taravari*, the Sanskrit word for sword.) The weapon typically had a curved blade of up to 30in/76cm; one of its distinctive features is the disk-shaped pommel. Like the Japanese katana (see pp 96–97), the tulwar was designed to be effective as both a slashing and thrusting weapon.

MUGHAL

An Indian sword of the Mughal Era (1526–1857), when most of the Indian Subcontinent was ruled by a dynasty founded by the Mongol conqueror Babur. The weapon's jade hilt is decorated with two rubies.

INDIAN RITUAL SWORD

This rare ceremonial temple sword originated in Southern India in the early eighteenth century. The steel blade is double edged and peculiarly bent. It's upper edge possesses seven minute holes used for hanging small enclosed bells that would jangle with any movement of the blade.

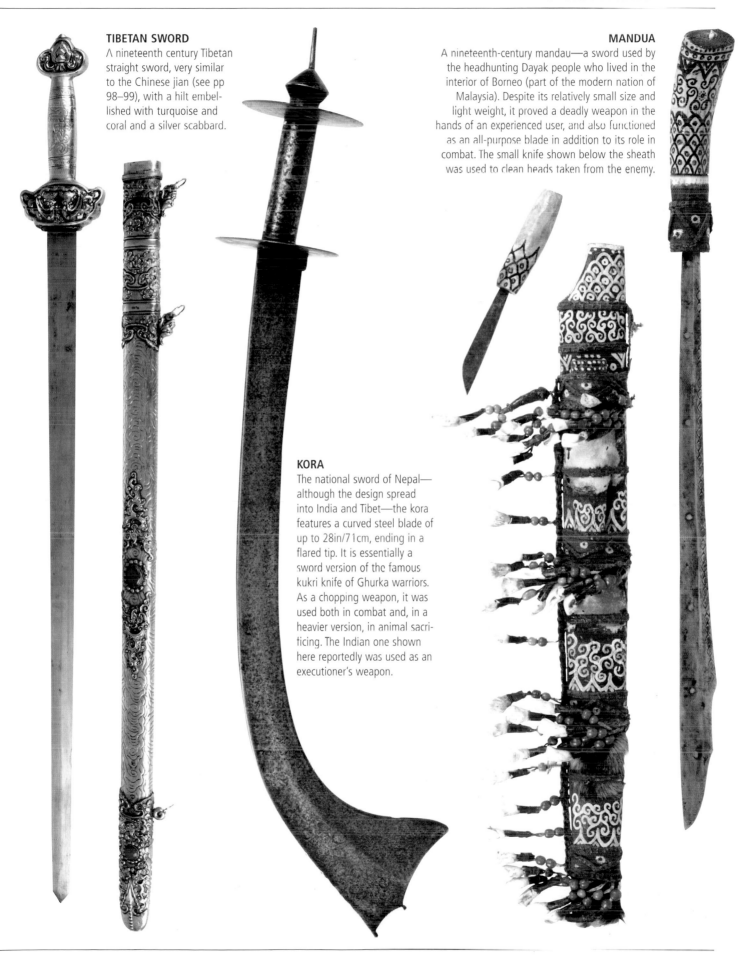

TIBETAN SWORD
A nineteenth century Tibetan straight sword, very similar to the Chinese jian (see pp 98–99), with a hilt embellished with turquoise and coral and a silver scabbard.

MANDUA
A nineteenth-century mandau—a sword used by the headhunting Dayak people who lived in the interior of Borneo (part of the modern nation of Malaysia). Despite its relatively small size and light weight, it proved a deadly weapon in the hands of an experienced user, and also functioned as an all-purpose blade in addition to its role in combat. The small knife shown below the sheath was used to clean heads taken from the enemy.

KORA
The national sword of Nepal—although the design spread into India and Tibet—the kora features a curved steel blade of up to 28in/71cm, ending in a flared tip. It is essentially a sword version of the famous kukri knife of Ghurka warriors. As a chopping weapon, it was used both in combat and, in a heavier version, in animal sacrificing. The Indian one shown here reportedly was used as an executioner's weapon.

ADZE

Not a sword but rather a type of hatchet used (in its utilitarian function) to shape wood, the adze played a ceremonial role in many African cultures. This nineteenth-century ceremonial adze comes from the West African kingdom of Dahomey, which originated in what is now Benin.

KUBAN SWORD

The name of the Kuba people of West Africa translates to "People of Lightning"—an apt description; they were one of the most warlike cultures of the region, and even sent women warriors into battle. They carried beautifully made but deadly weapons like the metal-bladed hardwood-handled sword shown here. The larger the blade, the greater the bearer's social status.

NORTH AFRICAN SWORD

A nineteenth-century North African ceremonial sword [above] with a carved wooden hilt ending in a pommel shaped like a man's head [detail, below]. The guard is unusual in that it includes a thumb-rest.

DHA LWE

The Burmese word dha simply means "blade" or "edged weapon"; a sword is a *dha lwe* and a dagger is a *dha hmyaung*. Shown here with their sheaths are two dha hmyaung, probably from the 19th century; the lower one's blade is inlaid with damascened designs, a typical form of decoration for all kinds of dha. (Damascening is the technique of inlaying decorations on a steel blade.) Carrying a dha was a sign of status for men of cultures like the Hmong, Karen, Mien, and Shah, who lived in Burma (now Myanmar) and other parts of Southeast Asia, including modern-day Thailand and Laos.

AFRICAN SWORDS

A rare pair of African swords, these weapons—with 27in/66cm double-edged blades—have hand-carved hilts with male and female figures as pommels.

SALAMPASU SWORD

An iron-bladed sword used by warriors of the Salampasu people of what is now Zaire in Central Africa. The leather-covered wooden sheath is decorated with strips of cane.

DHA HMYAUNG

An eighteenth-century *dha lwe*, with a highly decorated blade and wooden scabbard. The steel of the blade was typically blued to accentuate the decoration, which was often done in silver wire.

EIGHTEENTH-CENTURY SWORD

This photo shows the *tsuka* (handle) and *kashira* (pommel) of an eighteenth-century katana.

KATANA

A nineteenth-century katana, or sword. Like the tanto, the katana was primarily a slashing weapon, but one that also could be used in a thrusting role. The small needle-like spike is a thrusting knife, used to jab upward into an opponent's heart should the fighter have the opportunity to get close enough.

IVORY TANTO

An nineteenth-century tanto, this one with a hilt and sheath of intricately carved ivory depicting dragons.

SAMURAI SWORD

The wearing of a katana, such as the eighteenth-century one shown here, was initially restricted to the samurai. Very sharp—and dangerous—this sword necessitated a great deal of practice with it to be proficient. It is traditionally worn with its blade edge-up. With the fall of the feudal system, the warrior aristocracy was outlawed in 1868, and sword makers set to work creating their goods for export.

JAPANESE OFFICER SWORD

The swords carried by Japanese officers in the invasion of China in the 1930s and, later, during World War II—like the one shown here—retained the basic katana style, but were made with modern forging techniques instead of traditional Japanese swordsmith's methods.

TANTO WITH CLOISONNÉ SHEATH

Blades like this, were worn with a military uniform for formal occasions. This knife dates from about 1870 and its sheath is an extremely well-done work of cloisonné. This blade was probably owned by an affluent Chinese army officer.

JIN

JIAN
The practitioners of Chinese martial arts know the straight-edged *jian* as "the Gentleman of All Weapons." This nineteenth-century model features cloisonné decoration on the hilt and on the scabbard.

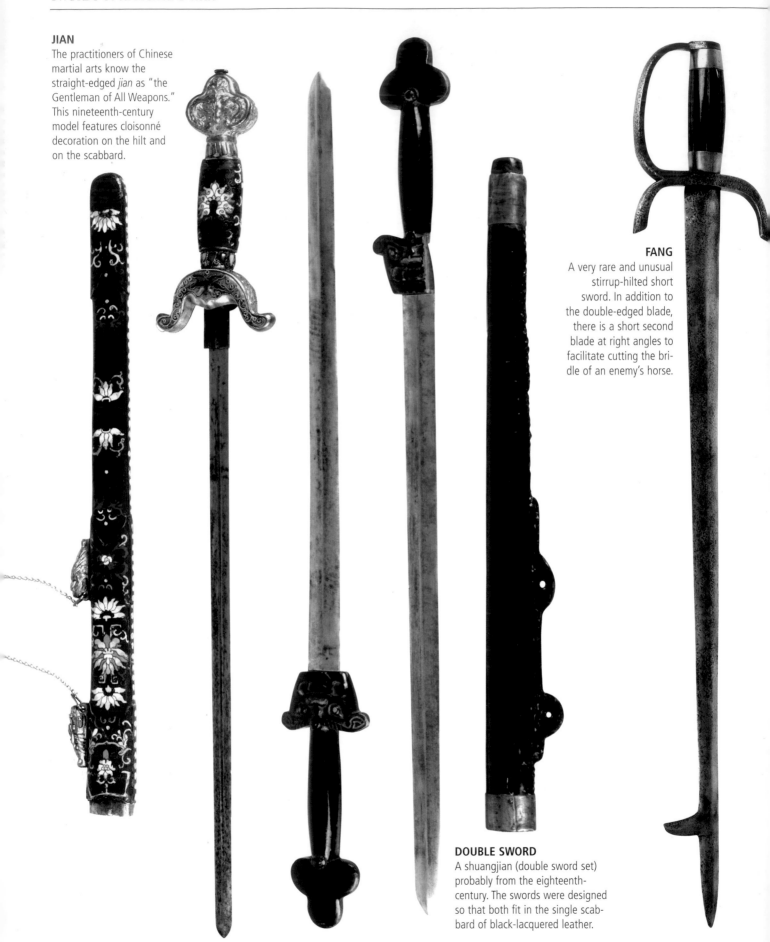

FANG
A very rare and unusual stirrup-hilted short sword. In addition to the double-edged blade, there is a short second blade at right angles to facilitate cutting the bridle of an enemy's horse.

DOUBLE SWORD
A shuangjian (double sword set) probably from the eighteenth-century. The swords were designed so that both fit in the single scabbard of black-lacquered leather.

HELMET BREAKER
This Chinese helmet breaker was used like a club. Made of solid brass, this implement could knock out an opponent in battle even if he wore protective head gear.

SHORT SWORD
A richly decorated short sword with a hilt and scabbard of carved ivory. The carving on the latter depicts a monkey-hunting expedition.

DUELING PISTOLS

Combat between individuals to settle disputes over personal honor is as old as history, but the practice of dueling familiar to us today developed in Southern Europe during the Renaissance, and began to flourish—largely among the upper classes—in Europe and North America in the eighteenth century. Although widely outlawed and denounced (George Washington forbade his officers to fight duels, calling it a "murderous practice"), dueling continued in Britain and America into the early nineteenth century, and somewhat later in Continental Europe. Until the mid-1700s, duelists fought mainly with swords, but the fashion moved to firearms, creating a new class of weapon—the dueling pistol.

THE GREAT GUNSMITHS

Originally, duelists used ordinary pistols, but around 1770, gunsmiths—chiefly in England and France—began producing purpose-built dueling pistols. These were usually made as "cased pairs"—two identical pistols in a box with powder flasks, bullet molds, and other accessories. With dueling mainly an upper-class custom (in Europe at least), owning a costly cased set of dueling pistols was a status symbol—like driving a high-powered sports car today. The pistols produced by the most famous (and expensive) London gunsmiths—like Robert Wogdon and the rival brothers John and Joseph Manton—were, in this sense, the Ferraris and Porsches of their time.

ACCURACY AND RELIABILITY

Most dueling pistols were approximately 15 inches long with 10-inch- barrels; the usual caliber was between .40 and .50. They were extremely accurate at about twenty yards—the usual distance at which duelists fired—although the commonly accepted rules of dueling stipulated smoothbore barrels and only the simplest sights. (Some duelists cheated by rifling all but the last couple of inches of the barrel—a practice known as "blind rifling.")

For maximum accuracy, many dueling pistols featured a "set" or "hair" trigger. The set trigger utilized a mechanism that kept tension on the trigger so that only a slight pressure would fire the weapon. (Conventional triggers required a heavy pull that tended to distort the firer's aim.)

Besides accuracy, reliability was the duelist's paramount concern in a pistol, so all components were finely tooled and fitted. In contrast to many firearms of the era, most dueling pistols had only minimal ornamentation, so that sunlight gleaming off gold or silver inlay wouldn't distract the duelist. Continental gunsmiths, however, did make some richly ornamented dueling pistols, and elaborately inlaid and engraved cased pairs were often produced as presentation pieces not intended for actual use on the "field of honor."

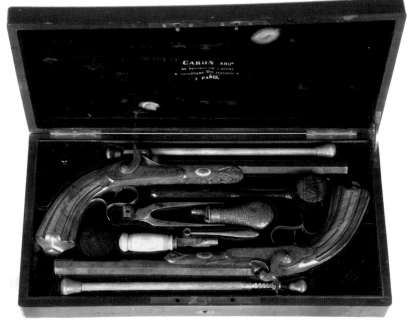

CARON'S CASE

France's royal gunmaker, Alphonse Caron of Paris, made this cased set of pistols in the late 1840s. The case contains the standard accessories—powder flask, bullet mold, ramrods, cleaning rods, and boxes for percussion caps. The powder flask is decorated with Egyptian hieroglyphics—a reflection of the popularity of ancient Egyptian motifs in nineteenth-century France.

RARE PAIR
This set of Belgian-made, percussion .44 dueling pistols came with unusual accessories—hand guards that fitted over the lock and trigger guard. For training purposes, the pistols could be made to fire wax bullets (thus the hand guards for protection).

WOGDON PISTOL
This pistol by the celebrated English gunsmith Robert Wogdon could be fitted with a wooden shoulder stock for non-dueling use. Originally a flintlock, it was later converted to percussion action. Wogdon made the pistols used in the famous 1804 duel in which Vice President Aaron Burr mortally wounded his personal and political enemy Alexander Hamilton.

BELGIAN PISTOLS
Flintlock dueling pistols had all the disadvantages of the flintlock system—they misfired frequently, were unreliable in damp conditions, and the relative slowness of the firing mechanism hampered accuracy even with the use of set triggers (see main text). After 1815 (just as dueling was on the wane), makers of dueling pistols—like the Belgian gunsmith who produced the handsome pair above—increasingly switched to the more robust and reliable percussion-cap system.

THE BLUNDERBUSS

The blunderbuss was a short, usually flintlock, smoothbore musket with a barrel that ended in a flared muzzle. The weapon developed in Europe, probably in Germany at first, early in the seventeenth century, although it didn't come into widespread use until about a hundred years later. (The weapon got its name from the Anglicization of a Dutch term *donderbuse*, meaning "thunder-box" or "thunder-gun.") Firing lead shot, the blunderbuss was deadly at short range and was generally used as a defensive weapon—by coachmen against highwaymen, by merchants and homeowners against burglars, and by innkeepers against robbers. It was also used at sea, as it was an ideal weapon in a boarding attack.

THE "THUNDER-BOX"

There are a couple of popular misconceptions about the blunderbuss. The first is that its flared muzzle (often described as bell-shaped or trumpet-shaped) served to scatter its load of shot in the manner of a modern shotgun. In fact, the dispersal pattern for the shot was little different than that of a nonflared barrel. The muzzle's wide mouth, however, facilitated quick reloading. It also had a psychological effect. In the words of firearms historian Richard Akehurst, "[T]he great bell mouth was most intimidating: those at whom it was aimed were convinced that there was no escaping the dreadful blast." Akehurst also notes that some English blunderbuss owners upped the intimidation factor by having the inscription "Happy is he that escapeth me" engraved on the barrel.

The second misconception is that blunderbuss was often loaded not with conventional shot but with scrap metal, nails, stones, gravel, or even broken glass for a particularly devastating effect. This may have happened on occasion, but such loads would quickly ruin the weapon's barrel.

ON THE ROAD AND OFF

The Blunderbuss's heyday was in the eighteenth century, when more and more people were traveling the primitive roads of Europe, and the danger of being waylaid by pistol-wielding highwaymen was always present. The blunderbuss's barrel was usually made of nonrusting brass—a necessity as they were often carried by coach drivers and guards who sat exposed to the weather.

Besides its use at sea—by both the regular naval forces and by pirates and privateers—the blunderbuss saw some military service on land. The Austrian, British, and Prussian armies of the eighteenth century all fielded units armed with the weapon, and according to some sources, the American Continental Army considered adopting the blunderbuss in preference to the carbine for its mounted troops during the Revolutionary War. However, the blunderbuss's very short range limited its effectiveness in a conventional combat role.

The blunderbuss remained popular into the early decades of the nineteenth century, when the shotgun replaced it as the preferred short-range defensive firearm.

TRAP GUN

Made for hunting rather than for offense or defense against human targets, this nineteenth-century European percussion-cap trap gun utilizes a blunderbuss-style barrel. Trap guns were connected by string or wire to a baited trap; when the animal took the bait, the string or wire tripped the trigger and discharged the gun.

FRENCH

While most blunderbusses had musket type shoulder stocks, eighteenth- and nineteenth-century gunsmiths also produced blunderbuss pistols, like the French weapon shown here. They were often carried by French naval officers, and were also used widely in the street fighting that accompanied the French Revolution.

INDIAN

This eighteenth-century Indian blunderbuss differs from its European counterparts in that it has a steel rather than a brass barrel and uses matchlock ignition, a system long obsolete in Europe and the Americas. The 11in/28cm barrel is decorated with a fish-scale pattern. The needle-like object attached to the gun is a touch-hole pricker, used to clear gunpowder residue from the vent that communicated the match's flame to the powder charge.

AMERICAN

The U.S. government arsenal at Harper's Ferry, Virginia, produced this blunderbuss in 1814. Like other nations, the United States produced blunderbusses for use by sailors and marines and also as rampart guns for forts on land. Meriwether Lewis and William Clark also took a pair of blunderbusses with them on their famous exploring expedition in the American West (1804–1806).

TURKISH

This finely decorated blunderbuss was presented to French general Aimable-Jean-Jacques Pélissier, later the Duke de Malakoff, by his wife. He may have had it with him at the Siege of Sevastopol during the Crimean War (1854–55).

EUROPEAN

A particularly short-barreled example of the blunderbuss, probably made early in the ninteenth century. Some of the best gunsmiths of the era—like Henry Nock (1741–1804) of Birmingham and London, England—produced blunderbusses.

Naval Weapons

From ancient times until well into the sixteenth century, naval warfare in the Western World was, in a sense, an extension of land fighting. Sea battles were typically fought close to shore by fleets of oar-propelled galleys. The object was to ram the enemy with the galley's fortified bow or otherwise get close enough to grapple with the enemy vessel. Then soldiers armed with conventional infantry weapons—spears, swords, and bows—would board the opposing galley to fight on deck. By the mid-seventeenth century, however, the sailing ship had evolved into a stable platform for heavy cannon. In the resulting Age of Sail, which lasted until the introduction of steam power 200 years later, large-scale naval battles saw lines (columns) of warships battering each other with cannon at ranges of 300ft/122m or less, each side hoping to break the other's line and disable its ships. Many smaller actions between individual ships, however, were still decided by clashes between boarders and defenders, both armed with a variety of hand-held weapons.

THE BROADSIDE

Heavy guns had been mounted on European ships as early as the fourteenth century, but they were placed in "castles" on the main deck and they were limited in number and usefulness. During the reign of King Henry VIII (from 1509 to 1547), English warships began mounting cannon on lower decks, firing through gunports that could be closed when not in action. This began the evolution that ultimately led to the massive "ships of the line" of the Napoleonic Wars (see pp 110–13). These vessels carried as many as 136 guns on two to four decks.

The muzzle-loading, brass or iron-barreled ship's guns of the time were rated by the weight of the shot they fired, with 24- and 32-pounders the most common sizes. Round shot made of iron was the usual projectile, but specialized shot like chain shot (two small round shot joined by a length of chain, intended to tear the enemy's sails and rigging) were also used. In addition to these "long guns," warships of the era also carried carronades, or "smashers"—shorter guns that fired the same weight of shot, for use at close range.

The weight of a broadside (the combined weight of shot fired by all the guns on one side of a ship in a single volley) was devastating. The broadside weight of the Royal Navy's HMS *Victory* (flagship of Admiral Horatio Nelson at the Battle of Trafalgar in 1805) was 1150lb/522kg.

BOARDERS AWAY!

Warships in the Age of Sail usually also had a contingent of marines; in battle, these "sea soldiers" would take to the fighting tops (platforms on the masts) to fire at enemy sailors with muskets and—if the range was close enough—to throw grenades onto the enemy vessel's deck. If the ship came alongside its opponent, both marines and sailors would make up a boarding party, armed with weapons that could include pikes (see pp 40-43), cutlasses (short curved swords, also called hangers), blunderbusses (see pp 102–03), musketoons (short-barreled muskets), and pistols. Because it was virtually impossible to reload a muzzle-loading firearm in a pitched on-deck battle, guns were reversed and used as clubs after being fired.

GREEK FIRE

One devastating naval weapon has been lost to history—Greek Fire. Developed in the Byzantine Empire in the seventh century, this was an inflammable compound that burned anything (or anyone) it struck and was nearly impossible to extinguish. Needless to say, it was a terrifying weapon. Greek Fire was used in land battles, but it proved especially suited to naval warfare because it burned even in water. Discharging the flaming liquid from tubes mounted on ship's bows, the Byzantine Navy used it successfully to repel seaborne invasion attempts from several enemies between the eighth and eleventh centuries. The composition of this early "superweapon" was such a closely guarded secret that eventually the Byzantines discovered that no one remembered how to make it. Modern historians still debate just what made up Greek Fire, but it was likely a mixture of several chemicals in oil.

CUTLASS

A short, broad-bladed slashing sword, the cutlass was a mainstay of boarding parties during the Age of Sail. The weapon's name may derive from the Italian term coltelaccio ("large knife") or from the French cutteaux, a term applied to similar weapons. Its relatively compact size made it easily maneuverable in crowded and chaotic hand-to-hand fighting on a ship's deck. Most cutlasses—like the British model shown here—had a sturdy guard both to protect the user's hand and for use in clubbing an opponent.

GRENADE LAUNCHER

An interesting eighteenth-century British naval weapon, this "hand mortar" was used to fire a kind of incendiary grenade. A wooden projectile with one end soaked in pitch (an inflammable resin) and topped with a burning scrap of rag was inserted into the barrel. The weapon was then fired, lofting the flaming projectile onto the deck or into the rigging of an enemy ship in hopes of setting the vessel ablaze.

DIRK

Midshipmen (officers-in-training) traditionally carried a dirk (see pp 50–63) like the one shown here, which dates from the reign of King George III (r. 1760–1801). They typically had a blade of up to 24in/61cm in length and were worn on the belt.

BELGIAN PISTOL

A .74 Belgian naval pistol, manufactured around 1810, according to the proof marks on the barrel.

BRITISH NAVAL BOARDING AX

The crescent ax head and slightly curved rear spike is typical of the European naval form dating from the early nineteenth century. An ax such as this was ideal for cutting ropes and destroying masts to ensure a ship's immobility.

RAIL GUN

A rare ship's rail gun from an Austrian warship. The weapon consisted of a 66in/168cm section of ship's rail with ten pistol barrels mounted vertically. (Three barrels are missing.) Each barrel was loaded individually, with priming powder for all distributed in a channel inside the rail. The idea was to ignite the charge and fire all the barrels at the moment an enemy boarding party tried to board. Its actual effectiveness is not known.

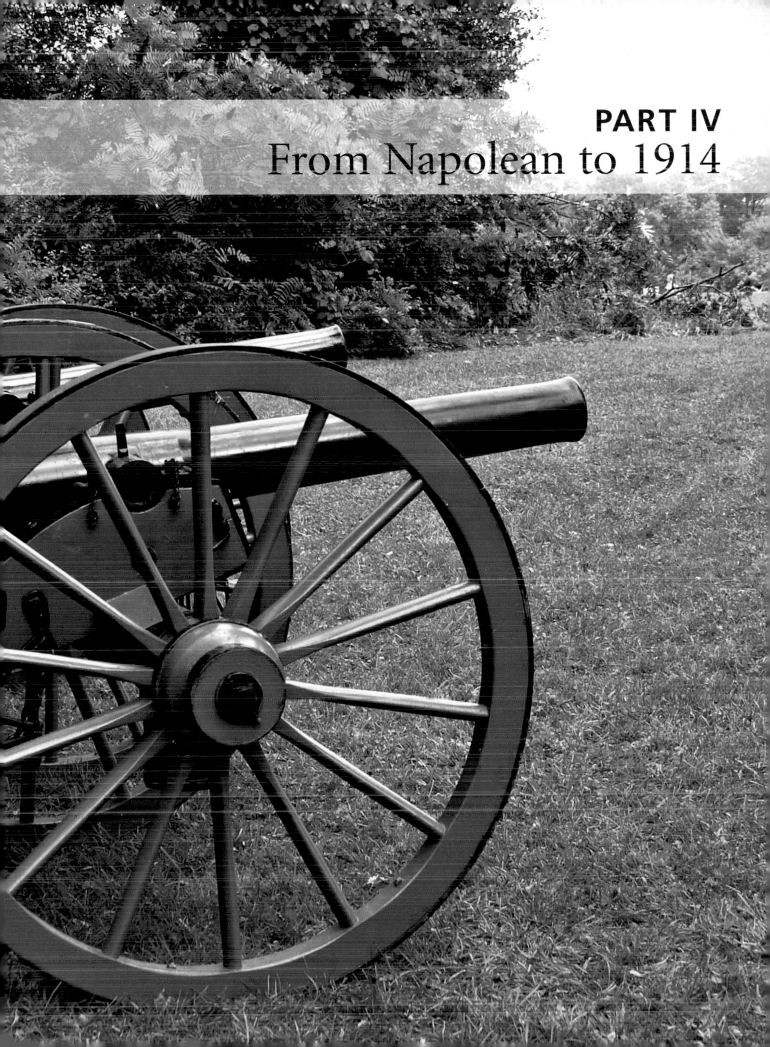

"On the right and left two seas enclose you, without even a single ship for escape; […] the Alps behind, scarcely passed by you when fresh and vigorous, hem you in. Here, soldiers, where you have first met the enemy, you must conquer or die."

—Hannibal, in an address to his troops, 218 BCE

The period from the Battle of Waterloo in 1815 to the outbreak of World War I ninety-nine years later saw weapons technology advance in leaps and bounds. By the mid-nineteenth century, the old smoothbore musket had given way to the rifle, a weapon of much greater range and accuracy. The flintlock firing mechanism was replaced, first by the percussion cap system, and later by weapons firing fully enclosed metallic cartridges.

The introduction of such cartridges made repeating weapons—which could fire multiple shots without reloading—a practical proposition, and by the end of the nineteenth century, most armies would be equipped with bolt-action, magazine-fed rifles. The revolver, popularized by Samuel Colt at mid-century, gave individuals a potent pistol, and inventors had developed automatic pistols by the end of the 1800s. The last years of the nineteenth century also saw the invention of the machine gun by Sir Hiram Maxim—a weapon that fired continuously as long as the trigger was pulled. With firearms now completely dominating the battlefield, edged weapons like swords were increasingly relegated to purely ceremonial roles, except in parts of the world that remained relatively untouched by Western technology.

WEAPONS OF THE NAPOLEONIC WARS

On July 14, 1789, a Parisian mob stormed the Bastille prison—an infamous symbol of royal power—sparking the French Revolution and setting off a series of events that plunged Europe, and eventually much of the world, into war. Out of France's revolutionary chaos emerged a leader, Napoleon Bonaparte, whose astonishing success as a military commander formed the foundation of his political power. The Napoleonic Wars—which lasted from 1799 until the Emperor's final defeat at Waterloo in 1815—did not see any extraordinary technological leaps in weaponry, but Napoleon masterfully exploited the existing weapons of the day to conquer much of Europe.

INFANTRY WEAPONS

The standard infantry weapon of the Napoleonic Wars was the smoothbore, muzzle-loading flintlock musket (see p 75). Napoleon's infantrymen typically carried the .69 Charleville musket, named for the armory at Ardennes where the weapon was first produced in 1777. Among Napoleon's enemies, the British used the venerable .75 Land Pattern musket, known popularly as the "Brown Bess," the Prussian Army was equipped after 1809 with a .75 musket based largely on the French Charleville, while the Russian Army made use of a variety of imported and domestically produced muskets of various calibers before standardizing, around 1809, on a 17.78mm weapon.

The smoothbore musket was inherently inaccurate, with an effective range of no more than 300ft/90m. Accuracy wasn't a factor in the tactics of the time, however, which relied on massed formations of infantry firing in volleys to send, in effect, a "wall of lead" at the opposing line. If the enemy broke ranks in the face of this intense fire, a bayonet charge usually followed, but the bayonet's effect was mostly psychological.

All armies of the time had units which carried the much more accurate rifle, but because rifles were even slower to load than muskets, their use was largely limited to these specialized and often elite troops. The best-known rifle of the time was the Baker rifle, designed by London gunsmith Ezekiel Baker and introduced in the British Army around 1800. In 1809, in Spain, a British rifleman using a Baker killed a French general from a distance that may have been as much as 1,800ft/550m.

CAVALRY WEAPONS

Mounted forces of Napoleonic-era armies were divided between light and heavy cavalry. Both carried swords, usually sabers designed for slashing, although the French retained a preference for "running through" their opponents with the point of their swords. Light cavalry often fought dismounted using carbines or pistols. Heavy cavalry, like the French Army's cuirassiers, usually fought from the saddle and were armed with heavy, straight-bladed swords.

The French Army also made use of mounted troops armed with lances, as did its opponents in the Russian, Prussian, and Austrian forces. Lancers were often pitted against infantry formations, because their lances could outdistance a bayonet thrust.

Edged weapons weren't limited to mounted troops. Officers of all military branches continued to carry swords, and noncommissioned officers in several armies carried pikes (see pp 40–45).

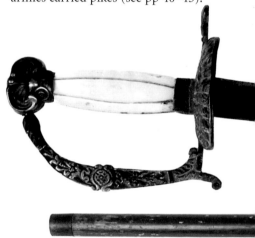

NAPOLEON'S SWORD CANE
A female admirer presented this sword cane to Napoleon in 1799, the year he became First Consul of France. The handle is inlaid with a mother-of-pearl shield bearing the letter "N". The wooden scabbard housing the 30in/76cm blade is framed in brass and copper.

NAPOLEONIC ARTILLERY

Napoleon began his military career as an artilleryman, and during his reign the French Army's artillery gained a reputation for excellence. This was particularly true of the horse artillery units, which were equipped with relatively light and mobile cannons (like the brass-barreled piece shown here) that could be rapidly moved into position and used in direct support of infantry. These weapons would fire round shot—solid iron balls—or, at closer ranges, canister shot, which consisted of scores of small metal balls that burst from the cannon's muzzle. Historians debate the effectiveness of Napoleonic artillery: Some contend it was the deadliest weapon, overall, in many battles; others argue that, like the bayonet, artillery fire served mainly to demoralize the enemy.

BRONZE ARTILLERY CANNON
With advances in construction and the use of bronze, the French were able to make a cannon such as this specimen that was half the weight of models of thirty years earlier. This greatly increased the mobility of the weapon, thus enabling more frequent usage.

YOUTH SABER
A scaled-down "youth" saber from the Revolutionary period, when the French government raised mass armies to fight off invasion from other European powers.

A NATION AT ARMS

Napoleon Bonaparte's success on the battlefield was due not to any great technological innovation in weaponry, but rather to his brilliance as a commander—and to his ruthless exploitation of available manpower. During the French Revolution, the relatively small professional army of the Bourbon regime was replaced by an army of conscripts—the famous Levée en Masse. Napoleon appropriated the innovation of conscription to his own dictatorial ends, drafting about 2.5 million Frenchmen into military service between 1804 and 1813. The Emperor's profligacy with the lives of his soldiers was legendary—as he told Count Metternich of Austria, "You can't stop me. I spend 30,000 men a month."

BRITISH PISTOLS

In 1796, the British Army introduced the New Land Pattern .65 holster pistol for cavalry use, although the pistol was not manufactured in large numbers until 1802. The weapon incorporated a swivel ramrod (visible on the upper pistol in this photo), which simplified loading while in the saddle. The lower pistol is a modified version.

DRUMMER BOY RIFLE

Picked up on the field after the Battle of Waterloo, this musket was carried by a French drummer boy; the weapon is 34.5in/88cm in length overall, in contrast to the 60in/152cm of the standard French Charleville musket, with a similarly downsized bayonet. It was later converted from a flintlock to percussion cap firing mechanism (see pp 118–19).

AIR RIFLE

One of the most unusual weapons used during the Napoleonic Wars were the air rifles fielded by the Austrian Army in 1808–09. Weapons using compressed air to fire a projectile (similar to the one pictured above) were introduced in the seventeenth century, and they had obvious advantages over gunpowder; the air weapon makes little sound and produces no smoke or muzzle flash to give away the firer's position. These qualities made them ideal for sniping. The Austrian weapon known as the windbüchse (German for "wind rifle") was first made by Bartolomeo Girandoni around 1780. Reports of the gun's specifications vary, but it could apparently discharge a .51 or .52 bullet at speeds of up to 1000ft/305m per second—and it could get off twenty rounds on a single charge of compressed air. At first windbüchse were parceled out to conventional infantry units, but eventually the Austrians formed a special unit armed solely with the weapon. While the use of the windbüchse wasn't enough to defeat French troops, the fear they inspired reportedly led Napoleon himself to authorize the summary execution of any Austrian soldier found carrying one. Despite its effectiveness, the air rifle never caught on as a military weapon—probably because of the time-consuming pumping process needed to produce the necessary air-pressure, plus their reputation as "terror weapons."

BRITISH CAVALRY SWORD

The British 1796 Pattern light cavalry saber was both a handsome and effective weapon—so effective that the Prussian Army, Britain's ally in the struggle against Napoleon, adopted it as well. Its design was likely inspired by the Indian tulwar (see p 92). Intended for use as a slashing weapon, the saber's 33in/84cm blade inflicted such terrible wounds that according to some sources, French officers protested its use.

GUARD'S SWORD

After Napoleon's abdication as emperor in April 1814, France was restored to royal rule under Louis VIII—a restoration temporarily interrupted by Napoleon's escape from exile on the Mediterranean island of Elba in 1815. A member of the King's Royal Bodyguard carried this Model 1814 saber, with its a brass half-basket guard decorated with the royal crest bearing three fleurs-de-lis—a flower that had symbolized the French monarchy since the fourteenth century. The blade also displays fleurs-de-lis around its engraved lettering identifying the blade as that of the King's Guard.

FROM FLINTLOCK TO PERCUSSION CAP

By the turn of the nineteenth century, the flintlock (see pp 78–79) had been the standard firing mechanism for guns for more than a century. The flintlock's deficiencies—its vulnerability to inclement weather, and the delay between the ignition of the powder in the priming pan and the main charge—led several inventors to develop firing systems that used the strike of a hammer on chemical compounds, like fulminate of mercury, as the means of ignition. First implemented mainly on sporting guns, the percussion system (sometimes called the caplock) came into widespread military use in the mid-nineteenth century.

EARLY PERCUSSION WEAPONS

The percussion system was inspired by a sportsman's frustration. A Scottish clergyman, the Rev. Alexander Forsyth, realized that the interval between the trigger pull and the actual firing of his fowling piece gave birds enough of a warning to fly away. Around 1805, Forsyth developed a new lock in which a hammer struck a firing pin inserted into a small bottle containing a special detonating charge, which in turn fired the powder charge in the barrel. Forsyth's "scent bottle" lock, as it was called from its shape, was a major advance, although weapons based on the system had their drawbacks, like the possibility of the entire "bottle" exploding. But it inspired several gunsmiths—including notables like Joseph Manton, to work on alternative systems, especially after Forsyth's British patent expired in 1821. In the words of firearms historian Richard Akehurst, a variety of percussion-fired "pills, tapes, tubes, and caps" containing several different types of detonating compounds came into use.

THE PERCUSSION CAP

The variety that ultimately won widespread adoption was a metallic cap—first made of steel, later of copper—filled with a compound based around fulminate of mercury. The cap was placed on a nipple in the lock and was struck by a hammer when the firer pulled the trigger.

There is some debate about how and when the metallic percussion cap was developed, but it's generally credited to a British-born American artist and inventor, Joshua Shaw (1776–1860), who developed it around 1814 but did not patent it until several years later. While some other percussion systems came into use—like the tape-primer system introduced in the 1840s by American inventor Edward Maynard (1813–1891), which operated much like a contemporary toy cap pistol—the stand-alone metallic cap became standard from the 1820s onward. The percussion system's popularity was helped by the relative ease with which flintlock weapons could be converted to the new mechanism.

The percussion system's advantages over the flintlock were considerable. It was reliable in all weathers and far less prone to misfire. The system also facilitated the introduction of reliable repeating weapons, especially the revolver (see pp 130–37). Still, it took several decades for the percussion system to win acceptance in military circles. (Napoleon Bonaparte was reportedly interested in developing weapons based on the Forsyth system, but the patriotic reverend rebuffed the French dictator's overtures.) It was not until the early 1840s, when the British Army began retrofitting its muskets with percussion locks, that percussion weapons became standard in the armies of the day.

The heyday of the percussion cap was relatively brief. Percussion firearms still had the drawbacks of muzzle-loading weapons, and after the introduction of self-contained metallic cartridges starting in the 1850s (see p 134), they rapidly gave way to cartridge-firing weapons.

HARPER'S FERRY

In 1841 the other major U.S. arsenal—at Harper's Ferry, Virginia—began producing a new smooth-bore percussion musket. The Springfield and Harper's Ferry arsenals together turned out about 175,000 Model 1842 muskets (like the one shown here) before 1855, when a rifled version was introduced. Many Model 1842's were returned to the arsenals to have their barrels rifled to take the new Minié ball ammunition (see p 139).

SPRINGFIELD

The .69 U.S. Army Model 1835 Musket, manufactured at the government armory at Springfield, Massachusetts, was among the last smoothbore long arms in official U.S. military service. Some 30,000 were made between 1835 and 1844. Originally flintlocks, these muskets were converted to percussion starting in the late 1840s. The detail shows the lock with the hammer down on the nipple on which the percussion cap was placed.

SPANISH

The incompatibility of percussion systems introduced in the early nineteenth century led to the development of "dual ignition" weapons. This rare brass-barreled pistol had a firing mechanism that could use both a Forsyth-type priming system and the later percussion cap.

SWISS
This heavy caliber (.70) pistol was made in a Swiss factory in 1855. However, it was assembled largely from French-manufactured parts

SINGLE-SHOT
A .17 French percussion pistol is a rare early example of the "salon" or "saloon" pistol—a handgun, small both in size and caliber, which could be fired indoors, for personal defense or for target practice.

TWIGG
One of a pair of percussion pistols made by British gunsmith John Twigg, this gun also has a spring dagger mounted below the barrel—a somewhat unusual configuration, as most combination weapons of this type place the blade above the barrel.

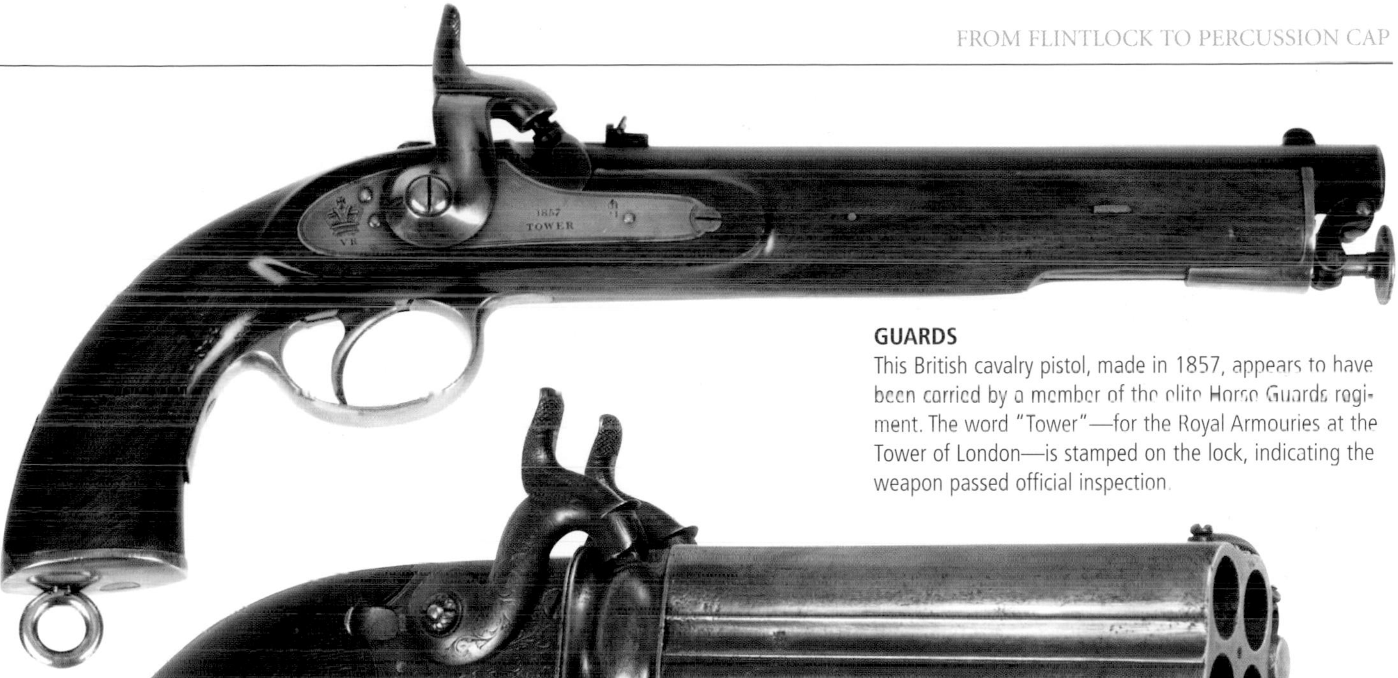

GUARDS

This British cavalry pistol, made in 1857, appears to have been carried by a member of the elite Horse Guards regiment. The word "Tower"—for the Royal Armouries at the Tower of London—is stamped on the lock, indicating the weapon passed official inspection.

TURNOVER

A rare four-barreled turnover (see pp 78 79) percussion pistol, made by London gunsmith Thomas Lloyd.

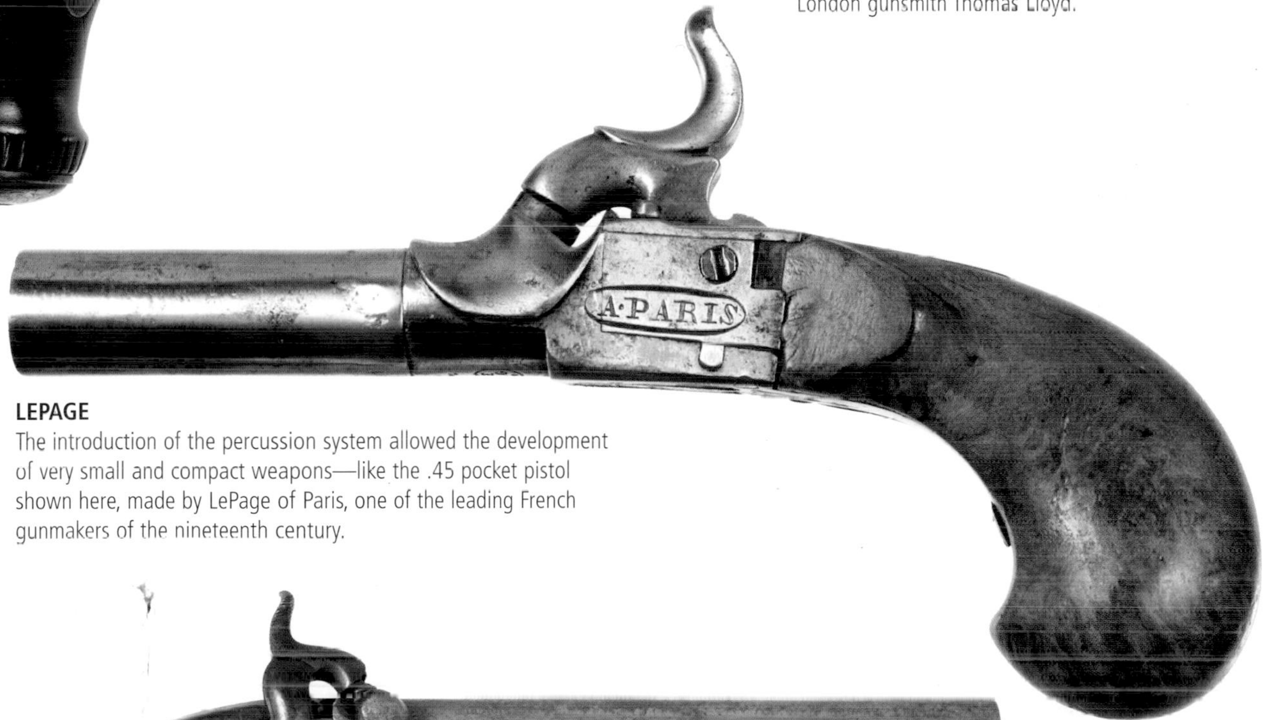

LEPAGE

The introduction of the percussion system allowed the development of very small and compact weapons—like the .45 pocket pistol shown here, made by LePage of Paris, one of the leading French gunmakers of the nineteenth century.

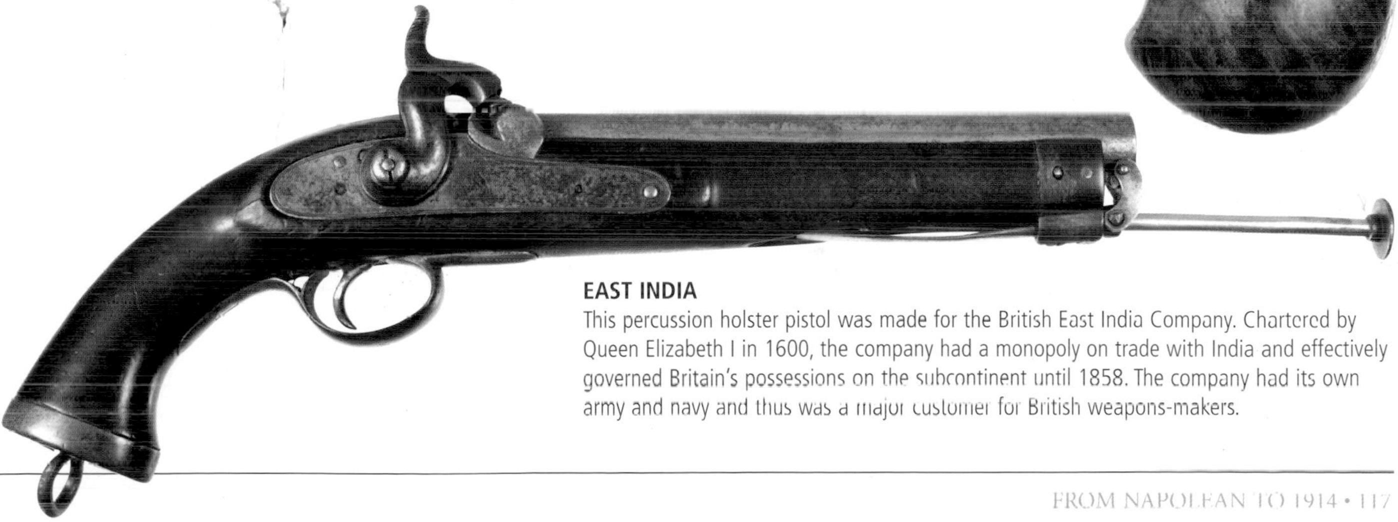

EAST INDIA

This percussion holster pistol was made for the British East India Company. Chartered by Queen Elizabeth I in 1600, the company had a monopoly on trade with India and effectively governed Britain's possessions on the subcontinent until 1858. The company had its own army and navy and thus was a major customer for British weapons-makers.

FLINTLOCK TO PERCUSSION CONVERSIONS

It was a fairly easy process to convert a flintlock weapon to the new percussion system; gunsmiths generally had only to replace the flintlock's priming pan with a nipple for the cap and to swap the flint cock with a hammer. As a result, countless flintlock muskets and other firearms were retrofitted as the percussion system grew in popularity. Some interesting and unusual conversions are show here.

SPANISH BLUNDERBUSS
This Spanish blunderbuss (see pp 102–03) was converted from flintlock to percussion; it also has a spring-out dagger mounted above the barrel.

INDIAN

A disadvantage of the percussion system was that the weapon could be fired only as long as the firer had caps. Some gunsmiths got around this by making weapons that used both percussion and flintlock mechanisms. The ingenious Indian rifle shown here has a revolving pan (for priming powder in flintlock mode) and nipple (for caps); the lower part of the flintlock cock doubles as a percussion hammer.

CHINESE

A Chinese gunsmith converted what was originally a matchlock gun (see pp 70–71), probably made in the eighteenth century, into a percussion gun. In this weapon, however, the original matchlock mechanism was modified instead of being totally replaced. The firer had to engage a hook around the back of the hammer, which fell forward to strike the percussion cap when the trigger was squeezed.

DUAL-FIRE PISTOL

Probably made in Switzerland around 1840, this pistol has both flintlock and percussion mechanisms.

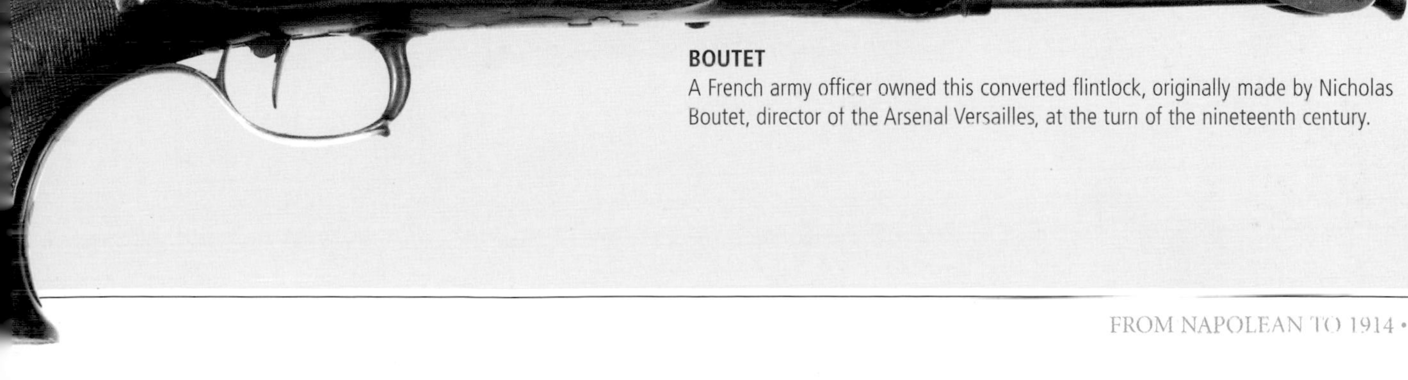

BOUTET

A French army officer owned this converted flintlock, originally made by Nicholas Boutet, director of the Arsenal Versailles, at the turn of the nineteenth century.

THE NINETEENTH-CENTURY SWORD

Even before the end of the Napoleonic Wars in 1815, the sword's role as a true fighting weapon was in decline in the Western world. Swords, especially sabers, continued to be used by mounted troops, but as the nineteenth century went on, the development of revolvers (see pp 130-37) and repeating carbines (see pp 140-41) largely replaced swords in actual cavalry combat. Still, in all military branches, the sword retained its longstanding role as a symbol of authority for officers—but with the pistol now the officer's battlefield weapon, swords were increasingly worn only with full-dress uniforms on ceremonial occasions. In the civilian world, dueling with swords continued in Europe into the nineteenth century, evolving into the modern sport of fencing, while the growth of fraternal organizations in Europe and America created a demand for purely decorative swords to be carried in parades or used in ceremonies.

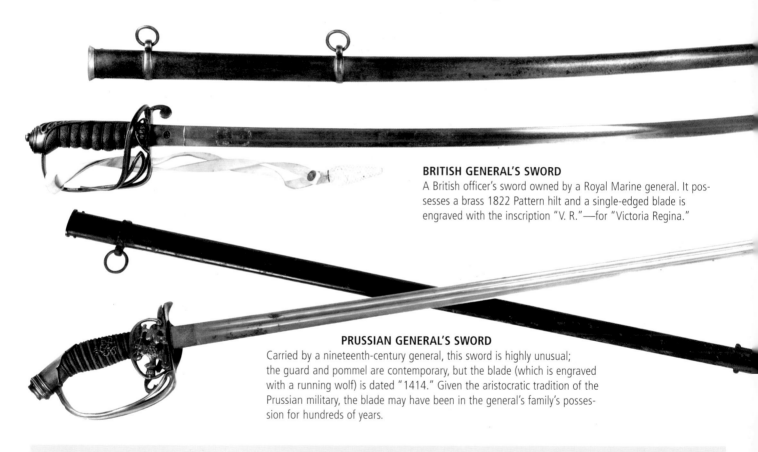

BRITISH GENERAL'S SWORD
A British officer's sword owned by a Royal Marine general. It possesses a brass 1822 Pattern hilt and a single-edged blade is engraved with the inscription "V. R."—for "Victoria Regina."

PRUSSIAN GENERAL'S SWORD
Carried by a nineteenth-century general, this sword is highly unusual; the guard and pommel are contemporary, but the blade (which is engraved with a running wolf) is dated "1414." Given the aristocratic tradition of the Prussian military, the blade may have been in the general's family's possession for hundreds of years.

THE WILKINSON SWORD COMPANY

Although the Wilkinson name has long been associated with sword-making, the company began when gunsmith Henry Nock set up shop in Ludgate Street, London, in 1772. Nock became one of the most celebrated gun-makers of the time, later (1804) receiving a Royal Appointment as gun-maker to King George III. The company also made bayonets for its long arms, and following Nock's death in 1805, his son-in-law, Henry Wilkinson, diversified the product line to include swords. Wilkinson moved the company's production facilities to Pall Mall, and the Wilkinson Sword Company soon gained an international reputation for its high-quality swords and other edged weapons. Later in the nineteenth century, the company began making other metal products, from typewriters to garden tools. Wilkinson Sword also became a leading manufacturer of razors after introducing one of the first "safety" razors in 1898—a position it retains today.

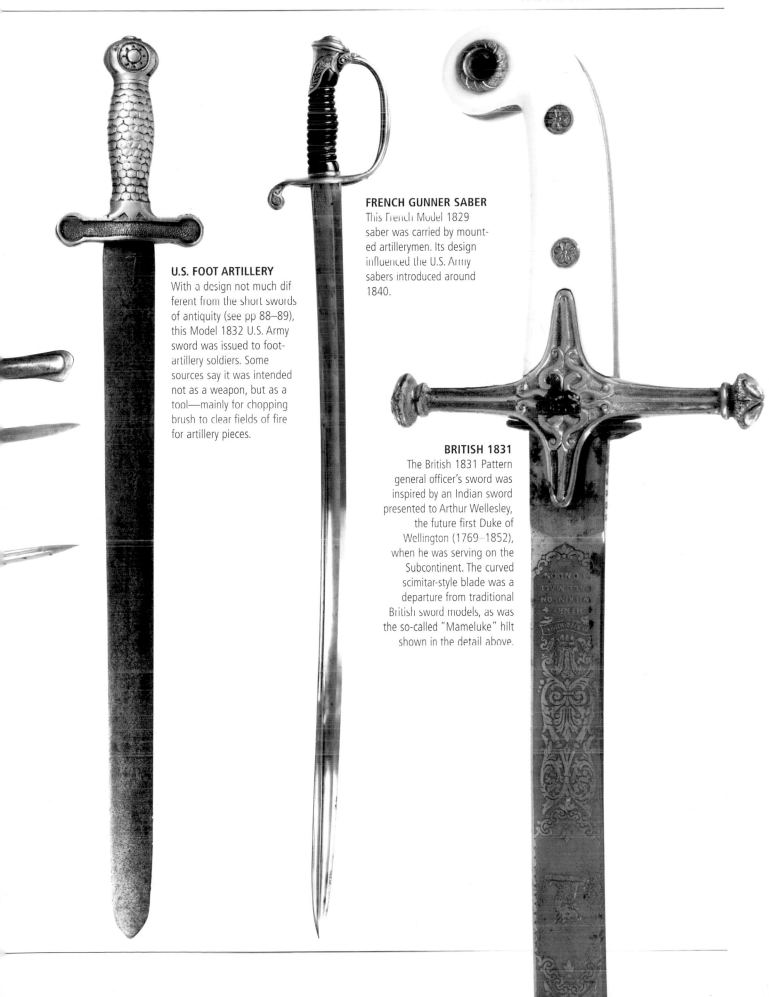

U.S. FOOT ARTILLERY

With a design not much different from the short swords of antiquity (see pp 88–89), this Model 1832 U.S. Army sword was issued to foot-artillery soldiers. Some sources say it was intended not as a weapon, but as a tool—mainly for chopping brush to clear fields of fire for artillery pieces.

FRENCH GUNNER SABER

This French Model 1829 saber was carried by mounted artillerymen. Its design influenced the U.S. Army sabers introduced around 1840.

BRITISH 1831

The British 1831 Pattern general officer's sword was inspired by an Indian sword presented to Arthur Wellesley, the future first Duke of Wellington (1769–1852), when he was serving on the Subcontinent. The curved scimitar-style blade was a departure from traditional British sword models, as was the so-called "Mameluke" hilt shown in the detail above.

FRENCH 1845/55
The French Model 1855 sword featured a brass hilt and a grip made of wire-wrapped sha-green—a sort of untanned leather often made from the skin of sharks or other fish. Like the French Model 1829 saber shown on these pages (see pp 121), the sword's design influenced the development of the U.S. army and navy swords of the same era.

DRAGOON
A British dragoon officer's sword with a black fishskin grip and a straight-single-edged, spear-pointed blade. The barrel is engraved with battle honors commemorating Sevastopol (the Crimean War, 1854–55) and Delhi (the Indian "Mutiny" of 1857).

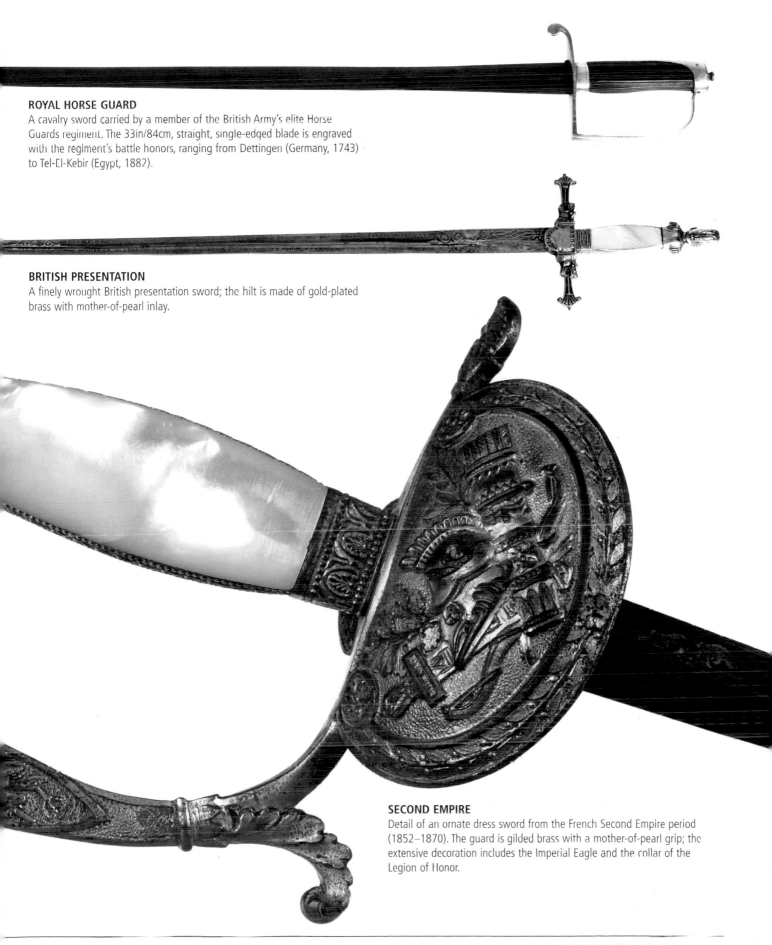

ROYAL HORSE GUARD

A cavalry sword carried by a member of the British Army's elite Horse Guards regiment. The 33in/84cm, straight, single-edged blade is engraved with the regiment's battle honors, ranging from Dettingen (Germany, 1743) to Tel-El-Kebir (Egypt, 1882).

BRITISH PRESENTATION

A finely wrought British presentation sword; the hilt is made of gold-plated brass with mother-of-pearl inlay.

SECOND EMPIRE

Detail of an ornate dress sword from the French Second Empire period (1852–1870). The guard is gilded brass with a mother-of-pearl grip; the extensive decoration includes the Imperial Eagle and the collar of the Legion of Honor.

PRUSSIA'S DOWNFALL

To paraphrase a historian's words, the German state of Prussia was an army with a nation attached. Prussia's reputation for military prowess began during the reign of King Frederick II (r. 1740–86), often called "Frederick the Great," who used the army his father had built with great success in several wars with Prussia's neighbors. After wars with Denmark (1864), Austria (1866), and France (1870), Germany became a unified nation with the kaiser (emperor) of the Prussian Hohenzollern dynasty as head of state. In 1888, Wilhelm II (shown above at right), a grandson of Britain's Queen Victoria, became kaiser after his father's brief reign. Wilhelm was a staunch militarist, maintaining a large standing army—raised by conscription—and greatly expanding Germany's navy. In 1914, Wilhelm went to war against France, Britain, and other allied nations; despite the excellence of the German army—equipped, for example, with state-of-the-art cannon from the legendary arms-makers Krupp—Germany sued for peace in November 1918. Wilhelm abdicated his throne and went into exile in Holland, where he died in 1941.

HUNTING SWORD

European hunters have long used swords to kill wild boar, but by the nineteenth century many hunting swords were produced mainly for ceremonial use or for presentation. This German sword, made by the well-known Solingen firm of WKC (Weyersberg, Kirschbaum, & Co.), belonged to Kaiser Wilhelm II (1859–1941) and bears his coat of arms.

KING OF SIAM

In 1898, the Wilkinson company (see p 120) made this handsome presentation sword for King Chulalongkorn (1853–1910) of Siam (now Thailand). The hilt is sterling silver with an ivory grip; the slightly curved blade is 32in/81cm in length. Its decoration includes a silver elephant head pommel and the coat of arms of the Siamese royal family on the guard.

BRITISH 1897

This unusual infantry officer's sword of the late 1890s was patterned after the sickle-shaped shotel, the traditional sword of Ethiopia.

PARADE SWORD

Dress swords, like the nineteenth-century American model shown here, were carried by members of organizations such as the Freemasons, the Knights of Columbus, and the Grand Army of the Republic (an association of Union army veterans).

1886 CHASSEPOT BAYONET SWORD

The chassepot bayonet sword was crafted in the Manufactory of Châtellerault, and the initial model of the bayonet was created for the bolt-action rifle of the same name. The blade of this sword is hand-forged, as chassepot blades continued to be until 1916. The ribbed brass hilt has a curved quillion.

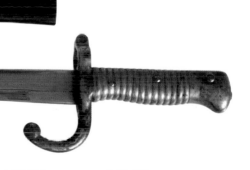

PEPPERBOXES AND DERRINGERS

Before Samuel Colt's revolvers (see pp 130–33) gained a widespread following in the 1850s, the most popular multiple-shot handgun was the pepperbox pistol. Unlike the revolver, which loads from a cylinder rotating around a single barrel, the pepperbox had multiple rotating barrels—usually four to six. Around the same time, the compact but powerful handguns known as derringers also became popular while gunsmiths around the world developed handguns suited to local requirements, like the "howdah" pistols used in British-ruled India, and the weapons made by indigenous gunsmiths in Darra on what was, in the nineteenth century, the frontier between India and Afghanistan.

THE PEPPERBOX

The pepperbox was the brainchild of Massachusetts gunsmith Ethan Allen (1806–71; apparently no relation to the Revolutionary War hero of the same name), who patented the weapon in 1837 (some sources say 1834) and manufactured it first in Grafton, Massachusetts, then in Norwich, Connecticut, and finally in Worcester, Massachusetts, most of that time in partnership with his brother-in-law under the company name of Allen & Thurber. The weapon is said to have got its name from the fact that the percussion-cap firing system sometimes accidentally discharged all the barrels at once, "peppering" anything (or anyone) in front of it.

The pepperbox was capable of rapid fire, thanks to its double-action firing system (see pp 134–37)—one long pull of the trigger rotated the barrel into position and fired the weapon, and it was immediately ready to fire again with the next trigger pull. Pepperboxes, however, were never renowned for their accuracy. In *Roughing It*, Mark Twain's best-selling account of his Western adventures, the author quotes a stagecoach driver's experience with the weapon: "'If she [the gun] didn't get what she went after, she would fetch something else.' And so she did. She went after a deuce of spades nailed against a tree, once, and fetched a mule standing about thirty yards to the left of it."

The pepperbox fell victim to the growing popularity of the revolver, and Allen & Thurber ceased production of the weapon in the mid-1860s.

THE DERRINGER

"Derringer" is a catch-all term for the small, short-barreled, easily concealable pistols introduced in the 1830s. The name derives from a Philadelphia gunsmith, Henry Deringer (1786–1878).

(Generally, firearms historians refer to the weapons made by Deringer himself as "deringers" and those made by his imitators as "derringers.") The original deringers were single-shot, muzzle-loading, percussion-cap weapons, usually .41, and with barrel lengths as short as 1.5in/38mm. Actor John Wilkes Booth used such a weapon to assassinate President Abraham Lincoln at Ford's Theater in Washington, D.C., on the Saturday evening of April 15, 1865.

Later weapons of the type were made by a number of manufacturers, including Colt and Remington; they typically fired cartridges and often had two barrels in an over-and-under configuration. Derringers had widespread appeal as personal-defense weapons because they provided considerable "stopping power"—at least at close range—in a weapon that could be stowed inconspicuously in a coat pocket, or a boot, or tucked into a "lady's" garter belt.

ALLEN & THURBER
A classic Allen & Thurber pepperbox. This six-shot, .36 model was made sometime after 1857. Allen & Thurber guns were famed for their excellent construction; for example, the barrel assembly was machined from a single piece of steel.

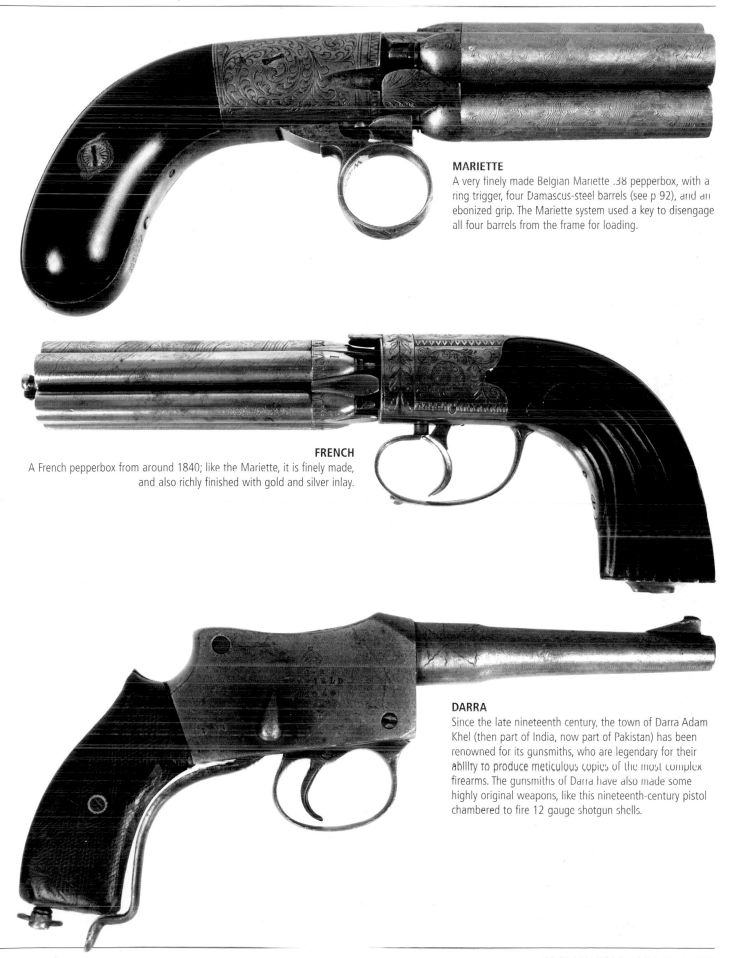

MARIETTE

A very finely made Belgian Mariette .38 pepperbox, with a ring trigger, four Damascus-steel barrels (see p 92), and an ebonized grip. The Mariette system used a key to disengage all four barrels from the frame for loading.

FRENCH

A French pepperbox from around 1840; like the Mariette, it is finely made, and also richly finished with gold and silver inlay.

DARRA

Since the late nineteenth century, the town of Darra Adam Khel (then part of India, now part of Pakistan) has been renowned for its gunsmiths, who are legendary for their ability to produce meticulous copies of the most complex firearms. The gunsmiths of Darra have also made some highly original weapons, like this nineteenth-century pistol chambered to fire 12 gauge shotgun shells.

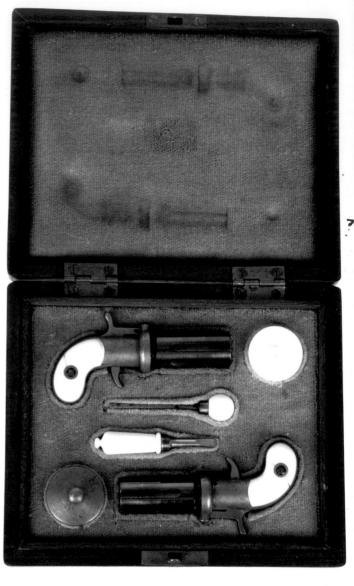

LADIES CASE WITH PISTOL COMPARTMENT

The derringer's compact size made it a popular personal-defense gun for women—whether "respectable," by nineteenth-century standards, or otherwise. This traveling case, made by Halstaffe of Regent Street, London, has a tray for cosmetics, a hidden compartment for money—and a concealed drawer fitted for two .44, single-shot Colt Model No. 3 derringers. The Model No. 3 was manufactured between 1875 and 1912.

ENGLISH MINIATURES

British gunsmith John Maycock produced this cased set of miniature pepperboxes. The six-shot, 2mm pistols feature 1in/2.5cm blued steel barrels, ivory butts, and brass frames; the mahogany case also holds an ivory cartridge box, ivory-handled screwdriver and cleaning rod, and a brass flask for lubricating oil. These tiny pistols are single-action—i.e., each barrel had to be manually rotated into place—as a double-action mechanism would have been impossible to incorporate into weapons of this diminutive size.

REMINGTON

While perhaps not strictly a derringer, the Remington-Rider magazine pistol, manufactured between 1871 and 1888, meets the derringer criteria of compact size (it had a barrel of 3in/7.6cm), but it fired a special short .32 cartridge. Also, it used an unusual repeating mechanism, with five rounds in a tubular magazine below the barrel. The firer pressed downward on a projection to depress the breechblock, ejecting the spent cartridge and chambering a new one.

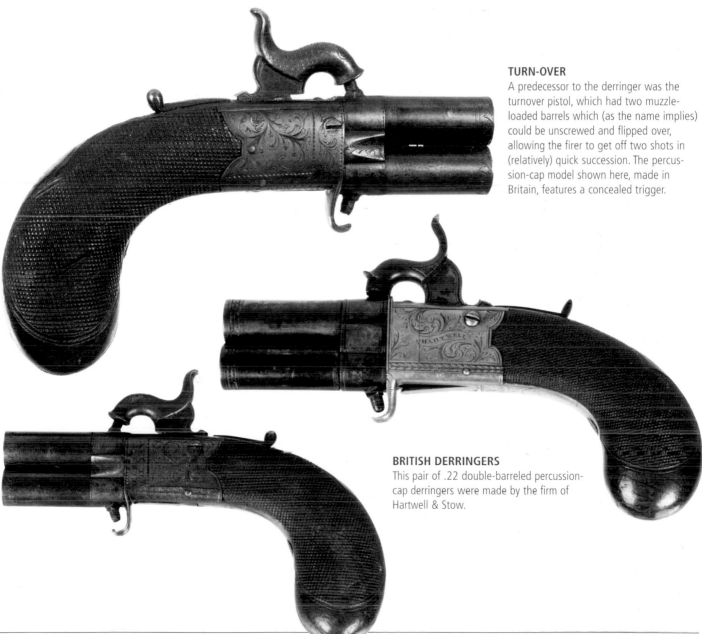

HOWDAH

One unusual category of nineteenth-century handguns are the "howdah" pistols used by British officers and colonial officials in India. Howdahs are the passenger-carrying platforms mounted on the backs of elephants, which were a common form of transportation on hunting trips or administrative rounds in rural areas of the Subcontinent. Riders needed a hard-hitting weapon to fend off attacks by tigers, so British gunsmiths produced heavy-caliber pistols (usually .50—like the one shown here—or .60), which were often double-barreled, to give the firer a second shot if the first one missed.

TURN-OVER

A predecessor to the derringer was the turnover pistol, which had two muzzle-loaded barrels which (as the name implies) could be unscrewed and flipped over, allowing the firer to get off two shots in (relatively) quick succession. The percussion-cap model shown here, made in Britain, features a concealed trigger.

BRITISH DERRINGERS

This pair of .22 double-barreled percussion-cap derringers were made by the firm of Hartwell & Stow.

COLT'S REVOLVERS

While Samuel Colt didn't invent the revolver, his name is now synonymous with the weapon—and for good reasons. First, while the mechanical advances that Colt patented in 1835–36 weren't a huge leap forward in innovation, they collectively made the revolver a practical weapon for both military and civilian use. Second, although it took years for Colt to win widespread acceptance for his revolvers, his skill in marketing the weapon ultimately established the Colt revolver as the standard by which all similar pistols were judged. Finally, Colt's significance to weapon history extends beyond his designs: His factory situated in Hartford, Connecticut, was the first to harness the technical advances of the Industrial Revolution—mass-production using interchangeable parts—and bring them to gunmaking on a large scale.

THE EVOLUTION OF THE REVOLVER

The idea of a repeating firearm that fired successive shots from a cylinder rotating around a single barrel (the opposite of the pepperbox system—see pp 126–27) was not new in the early nineteenth century. Flintlock revolvers were made in England as early as the mid-1600s. The problem with these early revolvers was that each chamber of the cylinder needed its own pan of priming powder, and firing one round sometimes ignited the powder in the rest of the pans, discharging all the cylinders at once.

Around the turn of the nineteenth century an American inventor, Elisha Collier, designed a much improved flintlock revolver that used a single priming pan. A number were manufactured in Britain after around 1810. Despite Collier's advances, it would take the introduction of the percussion cap—and Samuel Colt's basic design, which linked the cylinder to the firing mechanism, eliminating the need to manually rotate the cylinder—to make a truly safe and practical revolver.

Colt's revolvers earned their high reputation because they were powerful, well made, and reliable. That reliability stemmed in large part from their relative mechanical simplicity. Until the mid-1870s, all Colt models were single-action. To fire, the user pulled back the hammer, which rotated the cylinder and lined up the chamber with the barrel. Then the user had only to pull the trigger to discharge the weapon. This required a mechanism with fewer moving parts than the double-action revolvers (see pp 134–37) developed in the early 1850s. For the same reason, Colts were also more accurate than their double-action counterparts, if slower to fire. (An experienced user could, however, discharge his Colt quickly by "fanning" the hammer with the palm of his non-shooting hand—a technique familiar from countless Western movies and TV shows.)

PATERSON AND CHARGER

The largest of the first three Colt revolvers—the five-shot .36 "Texas Paterson"—is shown here. Like all revolvers before the introduction of the metallic cartridge, it was a "cap and ball" weapon. Each chamber had to be individually loaded with gunpowder and a bullet (usually known as a ball at the time); a percussion cap was then fitted to a nipple at the rear of the chamber. The Texas Paterson was probably the first revolver to be in used in combat, during one the U.S. Army's several wars against the Seminole Native Americans in Florida in 1835–42.

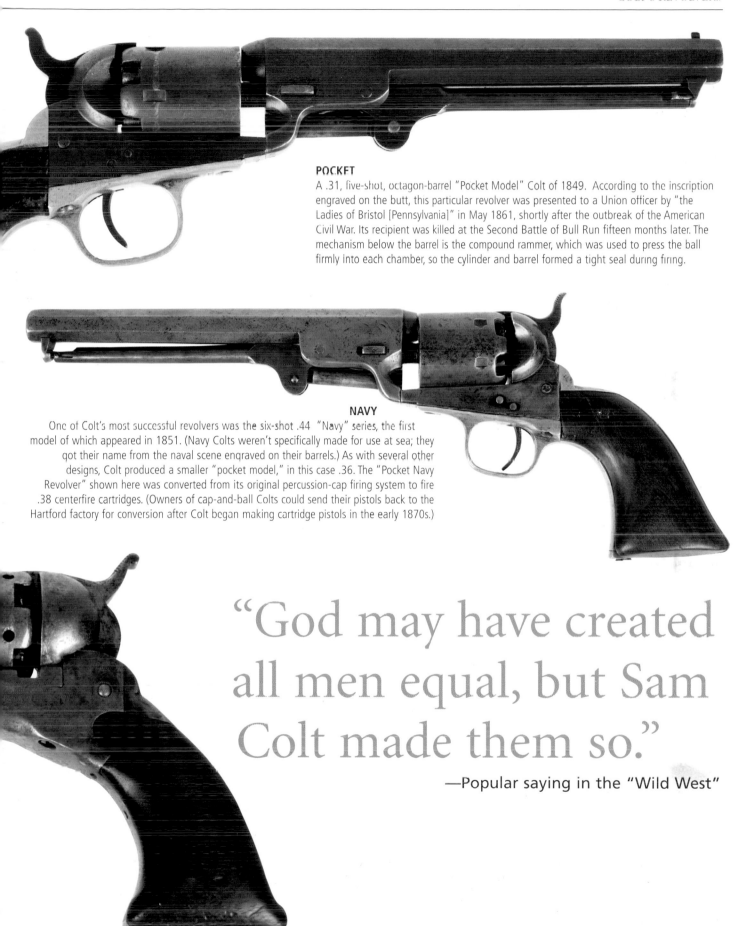

POCKET

A .31, five-shot, octagon-barrel "Pocket Model" Colt of 1849. According to the inscription engraved on the butt, this particular revolver was presented to a Union officer by "the Ladies of Bristol [Pennsylvania]" in May 1861, shortly after the outbreak of the American Civil War. Its recipient was killed at the Second Battle of Bull Run fifteen months later. The mechanism below the barrel is the compound rammer, which was used to press the ball firmly into each chamber, so the cylinder and barrel formed a tight seal during firing.

NAVY

One of Colt's most successful revolvers was the six-shot .44 "Navy" series, the first model of which appeared in 1851. (Navy Colts weren't specifically made for use at sea; they got their name from the naval scene engraved on their barrels.) As with several other designs, Colt produced a smaller "pocket model," in this case .36. The "Pocket Navy Revolver" shown here was converted from its original percussion-cap firing system to fire .38 centerfire cartridges. (Owners of cap-and-ball Colts could send their pistols back to the Hartford factory for conversion after Colt began making cartridge pistols in the early 1870s.)

"God may have created all men equal, but Sam Colt made them so."

—Popular saying in the "Wild West"

SAMUEL COLT

Born in Hartford, Connecticut, in 1814, Samuel L. Colt was—like most of the great gunmakers—something of a mechanical prodigy: As a boy, he liked to disassemble and reassemble clocks, firearms, and other devices. Bored with working in his father's textile mill, he went to sea at age fifteen as an apprentice seaman. It was on this voyage that he conceived his initial design. The origin of Colt's inspiration is shrouded in legend, variously attributed to his observation of the ship's wheel; or the capstan used to raise the anchor; or a steamboat's paddlewheel—or, more prosaically, he may have seen Collier flintlock revolvers in India, where they were used by British troops. In any event, by the time he returned to the U.S., he had carved a working model out of wood.

To get his gun built, Colt needed money. Billing himself as "Dr. S. Coult," he became a traveling "lecturer" whose specialty was demonstrating the effects of nitrous oxide—laughing gas—on curious locals. With the proceeds he had two gunsmiths, Anton Chase and John Pearson, make experimental models. After receiving his U.S. Patent in 1836, Colt set up the Patent Arms Manufacturing Company in Paterson, New Jersey, to make the new weapon. The three "Paterson" revolver models that appeared that year, however, found few takers. In 1842, Colt went bankrupt. That experience—and the years of litigation that followed—might have driven a lesser personality into despairing retirement. As determined as he was ambitious, Colt made an astonishing comeback a few years later.

Some early Colts had found their way into the hands of soldiers and frontiersmen, including Captain Samuel Walker of the Texas Rangers. In 1844, Walker and fifteen rangers, armed with Colts, fought off a war party of about eighty Comanche Native Americans. When the Mexican-American War broke out in 1846, Walker (now an army officer) and Colt collaborated on a design for a new revolver. The result was the huge (4.9lb/2.2kg), powerful (.41), "Walker Colt." A government order for a thousand put Colt back in business; because he no longer had his own plant, Colt contracted with Eli Whitney Jr. (son of the famous inventor) to make them in Whitneyville, Connecticut.

The success of Colt revolvers in the Mexican-American War greatly raised the weapons' profile, and they began to attract international orders when Colt exhibited his guns at the Great Exhibition in London in 1851 and also when they proved their worth in the Crimean War (1854–55). By 1855, Colt was so successful that he was able to build a huge and highly advanced factory in Hartford, Connecticut—soon to become the world's largest non-government armory.

Colt died in 1862, eleven years before his company's single most successful revolver—the single-action Army Model, and its civilian variants—came into being. Made in several calibers (including 44. and .45), this was the legendary "Peacemaker" and "Six-Shooter" of the American West.

RIFLE
From its beginnings in Paterson, New Jersey, Colt manufactured carbines, rifles, and even shotguns as well as pistols. Most early Colt long arms (such as the Model 1855 .56 carbine shown here) used a revolving cylinder, but later the company made lever- and slide-action (see pp 146–47) guns as well. While Colt's nineteenth-century long arms enjoyed some success in both military and civilian hands, their popularity never reached the level that the company's pistols achieved. At some point in this rifle's history, the barrel was shortened.

NEW NAVY

Introduced in 1892 and produced through 1908, the double-action Colt "New Navy" revolver was typical of the revolvers made by Colt from the late 1880s through the 1910s. (These guns, unlike the earlier "Navy Colts," were actually bought by the U.S. Navy and were the standard sidearm during the Spanish-American War.) Colt revolvers of this era were available in several different barrel lengths and chambered for a range of calibers. The New Navy series was made in .38 and .41—the latter version is shown here.

NEW DOUBLE-ACTION REVOLVER

In the mid-1870s Colt finally began to make double-action pistols, starting with the "Lightning" model. The pistol shown here—which makes use of a slide-rod ejector to push spent cartridges from the cylinder chambers—is a model .38 made for export to Britain.

COLT'S COMPETITORS

While Colt's revolvers (see pp 130–33) dominated the field thanks to a combination of patents, marketing, and general excellence, gunmakers on both sides of the Atlantic introduced a number of competing revolver designs, many of which would be combat-tested in battlefields ranging from the Crimea (1854–55) to India (the "mutiny" of 1857), and the United States itself, in the Civil War of 1861–1865 (see pp 138–43), in which an amazing variety of revolvers were used on both sides. The 1850s and 1860s also saw a sort of civil war among gunmakers themselves over real and perceived patent infringement. However, by the 1870s, it was clear that the overall victor (whether double- or single-action) was the cartridge-firing revolver.

DOUBLE VERSUS SINGLE ACTION

At the 1851 Great Exhibition in London—the same "world's fair" at which Samuel Colt proudly displayed his revolvers—British gunsmith Robert Adams (1809–70) exhibited a new type of revolver. Instead of requiring the separate step of cocking the hammer before pulling the trigger, Adams's "double-action" revolver could be cocked and fired with one pull of the trigger. This made it faster to fire than Colt's single-action revolvers, but also less accurate because of the heavy pressure the firer had to exert on the trigger. Early Adams revolvers suffered from various technical problems, but based on combat experience in the Crimean War, an improved version, the Beaumont-Adams, was introduced in 1855.

Revolvers of this type—which could be fired using either single- or double-action—soon became the standard sidearm in the British Army, more or less shutting Colt out of the British market. Although Adams revolvers were purchased for use by both the Union and Confederate armies during the Civil War, Colt retained its dominance in both camps during this era; unlike Colt, which mass-produced its pistols, Adams revolvers were hand-crafted and thus more expensive. The simpler Colt

revolvers were also more suited to rugged American conditions, whether on Civil War battlefields or on the plains and deserts of the postwar Western frontier.

THE CARTRIDGE PISTOL

Another potential challenge to Colt came from the introduction of fully enclosed metallic cartridges. In the mid-1850s, Americans Horace Smith and Daniel Wesson (see p 136), who had pioneered both the metallic cartridge and the repeating rifle, developed a revolver firing rimfire cartridges based on a cylinder design purchased from a former Colt employee, Rollin White. (According to some sources, White first offered his design to Samuel Colt, but with an uncharacteristic failure of foresight, Colt didn't think metallic cartridges had any potential.) Smith & Wesson put their pistol, in a .22 model, on the market in 1857, after Colt's patents expired.

The combat advantages of a revolver that could load cartridges quickly—as opposed to the slow-loading cap-and-ball system (see pp 130–33) used by Colt and others—were obvious, and a .32 version proved popular with Union forces during the Civil

War. But again, Colt's dominance was not seriously challenged, because S&W's production couldn't keep up with demand, both in pistols and in ammunition. In the last years of the conflict, Colt revolvers did face a serious competitor in the form of the Remington Model 1863 Army revolver. While a cap-and-ball weapon, many soldiers found it to be easier to load and fire than its Colt counterparts. When S&W's patent expired in 1872, Colt and a host of other gunmakers rushed to get cartridge revolvers on the market.

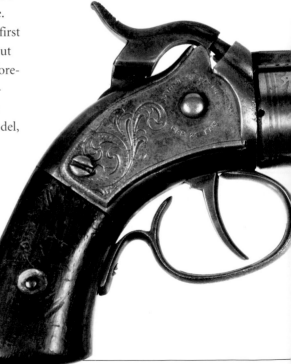

TURRET PISTOL
This very rare and interesting American revolver design appeared around the same time as Samuel Colt's first pistol. Patented by J. W. Cochran of New York City and made by C. B. Allen of Springfield, Massachusetts, the "turret" or "monitor" pistol had a .40, seven-shot, horizontally oriented cylinder. The percussion-cap weapon was fired by a sideways-mounted hammer. Only five or so were made.

COGSWELL TRANSITION GUN
A major maker of pepperbox pistols (see pp 126–27), the London gunmakers Cogswell & Harrison also produced this revolver—known to firearms historians as a "transition gun"—in the early 1850s. The single-action weapon had a six-shot cylinder firing .44 rounds.

MASSACHUSETTS ARMS CASED SET
Between about 1849 and 1851, Massachusetts Arms also made Wesson & Leavitt revolvers, like the .31, six-shot model one shown here cased with its accessories.

MASSACHUSETTS ARMS COMPANY .28
In 1851, Colt sued the Massachusetts Arms Company of Chicopee Falls, Massachusetts, for patent infringement. The Massachusetts Company claimed that its revolvers—which used a bevel-gear system to rotate the cylinder, rather than the pawl-and-ratchet system used by Colt—were significantly different than Colt's, but the court eventually ruled in favor of Colt. The Massachusetts Arms Company, however, stayed in business and produced some popular pistols, like the .28 six-shot revolver shown here, which was unusual in that it could use either single percussion caps or the Maynard tape-primer system.

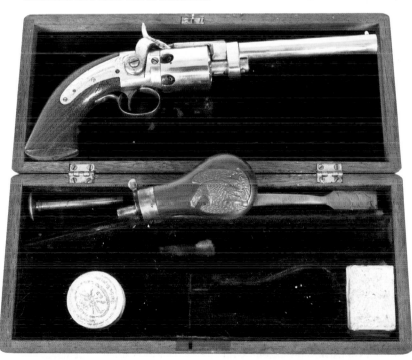

SMITH & WESSON

Horace Smith (b. Cheshire, Massachusetts; 1808–93) and Daniel Wesson (b. Worcester, Massachusetts; 1825–96) both entered the gunmaking trade in their youth: Smith as an employee of the federal armory at Springfield, Massachusetts, and Wesson as an apprentice to his elder brother Edwin, a leading New England gunsmith. The two first joined forces in Norwich, Connecticut, in the early 1850s, when they collaborated to produce a repeating rifle that could fire metallic cartridges. As with Samuel Colt, their techno-logical innovation didn't meet with commer-cial success at first, and they had to sell out to Oliver Winchester (see p 147). But also like Colt, they persevered, patenting a revolver firing a rimfire cartridge (1854) and reconstituting their company (1856). The suc-cess of their designs during the Civil War and in the years that followed—especially the Model 3 revolver, introduced in 1870—laid the foundations of a company that remains one of the foremost gunmakers in the twen-ty-first century. While Smith & Wesson today manufacture automatics, revolvers continue to be the firm's signature product, and long after the death of its founders, their tradition of innovation continued in such weapons as the .38 Model 1910 "Military & Police" revolver (introduced in 1899 and still in pro-duction through numerous variations, and probably the most popular pistol ever made for law-enforcement use); the .357 (1935) and .44 (1956) magnums (beloved by Hollywood—Clint Eastwood's character "Dirty Harry" wielded the latter); and the Model 60 (1965), which ushered in the era of the stainless steel pistol.

SLOCUM

In 1863, the Brooklyn Arms Company of New York introduced a .32 five-shot revolver, the "Slocum," named apparently for a New York–born Civil War gen-eral. The pistol loaded from the front; the chambers were actually sliding tubes that moved forward over a fixed ejecting mechanism.

REMINGTON NEW ARMY

The .44 six-shot "New Army" revolver was (after the Colt Model 1860) perhaps the second most widely issued revolver for Union troops during the American Civil War (1861–65; see pp 138–39). At least 130,000 were manufactured at Remington's Ilion, New York, factory.

SMITH & WESSON

The six shot, .32 Smith & Wesson No. 2 revolver, which saw much use in the Civil War and on the Western frontier, was—like other early Smith & Wessons—known as a "tip-up" revolver from the system it used for loading and extracting cartridges: Manipulating a catch released the barrel to swing upward, allowing the cylinder to be removed completely from the frame; the firer used the spike below the barrel to push out the spent cartridges; the cylinder was then reloaded, replaced, and the barrel swung downward into firing position. Later Smith & Wesson revolvers pioneered the "break-open" system, in which the barrel swung downward and an extractor mechanism in the cylinder (which remained attached to the frame) ejected all the spent cartridges at once.

TRANTER

Based in Birmingham, England, British gunsmith William Tranter (1816–1890) produced a variety of revolver designs in his long career; his pistols had a high reputation for quality, and large numbers were purchased by the Confederate government for issue to its forces in the American Civil War (1861–65), while others (like the five-shot .54 pistol shown here) were bought privately by British officers. This model used a double-trigger firing system; the lower trigger cocked the weapon, the upper one fired it. It's a cap-and-ball pistol, but after the Civil War, Tranter produced many cartridge-firing designs.

ALLEN & WHEELOCK

Another interesting early cartridge pistol was the .32 "lipfire" revolver made by the Allen & Wheelock Company of Worcester, Massachusetts. First made in 1858, these pistols not only fired a unique cartridge, but also utilized a lever-operated, rack-and-pinion ejection system.

MOORE

In an effort to get around Smith & Wesson's patent on cartridge revolvers, Moore's Patent Firearms Company of Brooklyn made a number of revolvers based on a design by Daniel Moore and Daniel Wilson in the 1860s. Instead of loading from the rear of the cylinder, these revolvers loaded from the front; the cartridge's priming charge was contained in a "teat" in its base, and so these revolvers became known as "teat," or "tit," guns. The courts eventually found for Smith & Wesson.

The American Civil War

The American Civil War (1861–65) is often described, with much justification, as the first modern war. The conflict saw the introduction (or at least the first widespread use) of innovations like photography, the telegraph, aircraft (balloons, used for observation of enemy forces), submarines, armored ships, breech-loading artillery, and infantry weapons, repeating rifles, and rapid-fire guns. Almost a century and a half later, the Civil War remains both the greatest war fought in the Western Hemisphere and America's deadliest conflict, with a combined death toll estimated at 700,000—more than in all other American wars combined. While disease claimed twice as many men as combat, the high casualty rate owed much to technical advances in weaponry.

TACTICS AND TECHNOLOGY

The Civil War was a classic example of technology outstripping tactics. At the beginning, commanders on both sides envisioned that the war would be fought in the traditional style—by masses of men maneuvering in the open in stand-up combat, with infantry exchanging volleys and charging the opposing line with the bayonet, with artillery in support and cavalry waiting to exploit any breakthrough.

These tactics worked in the eighteenth century and the Napoleonic Wars (see pp 110–13), when armies fought with smoothbore muskets that were inaccurate at all but the closest ranges. The years before the Civil War, however, saw a revolution in infantry weapons. The old smoothbore musket had given way to the rifle (or rifled musket, as it was also known), which was the standard infantryman's weapon on both sides. These fired a heavy lead bullet (usually .58 caliber) to an effective range of up to 500yd/0.45 kilometer. While still muzzle-loaders, these rifles used a new type of bullet, the Minié ball (named for French army officer, Claude Minié, who invented it in 1847). The Minié ball expanded upon firing to snugly fit the grooves of a rifled barrel, greatly increasing accuracy.

The result of these innovations, when translated into impact on human flesh, was horrifying. If not killed outright, a Civil War soldier hit in the abdomen would likely die of infection, given the crude medical treatment of the era. If hit in a limb, amputation was the usual outcome. Head shots were generally immediately fatal.

The introduction of the rifle shifted the advantage from the offensive to the defensive on the battlefield. Riflemen "dug in" to the ground or otherwise behind cover, firing several shots a minute, could easily mow down several times their number attacking in the open.

Confederate commanders, especially Robert E. Lee, were quicker to grasp that the rules of warfare had changed than their Union counterparts. However, even Lee made the mistake of sending infantry across open ground against fixed positions in the Battle of Malvern Hill (July 1, 1862) during the Peninsular Campaign and again a year later in "Pickett's Charge" during the Battle of Gettysburg—the latter a miscalculation that probably doomed the Confederacy to ultimate defeat.

EXPERIMENTATION AND INNOVATION

The Civil War also saw the introduction of weapons that were "high-tech" for their time. Because it was virtually impossible to use a muzzle-loading weapon in the saddle,

Union cavalry rode into battle armed with breech-loading weapons like the Burnside and Sharps (see p 148) carbines. Especially effective was the repeating Spencer carbine, which had a seven-shot magazine—Confederate soldiers called it "That damned Yankee gun that can be loaded on Sunday and fired all week." Because the Confederacy was largely unable to manufacture similar weapons, captured breech-loaders and repeaters were prized by Southern soldiers.

Both sides also raised units of marksmen to engage in what would later become known as sniping. The best-known of these units was the Union army's Berdan's Sharpshooters, commanded by Hiram Berdan (1823–1893), who was already famous as a civilian target-shooting champion. (The term "sharpshooters" may derive from their use of Sharps breech-loading rifles. Confederate snipers tended to use the British-designed Whitworth rifle.)

While the technology of the time was not sufficient to permit the development of machine guns in the modern sense, both sides experimented with manually operated rapid-fire weapons. The Confederacy apparently used a crank-operated light cannon during the Peninsular Campaign, and the Union deployed a multiple-barreled bullet-firing weapon, the Requa-Billnghurst battery gun, mainly to defend bridges and other positions. The best-known of these weapons is the Gatling gun (see p 141), although it only saw limited service very late in the war.

UNION WEAPONS OF THE AMERICAN CIVIL WAR

In terms of weapons production, the Union was much more fortunate than the Confederacy (see pp 142–43); the northern states contained not only most government arsenals, but the region was also much more heavily industrialized than the South. Although the Union, like the Confederacy, had to scramble for weapons to equip its troops early in the war, by 1862 the Union had largely settled on a few standardized firearms whose manufacture could be contracted out to private firms. By 1864, the Union was self-sufficient in weapons production, while the Confederacy still relied on imports for many of its firearms.

THE SPRINGFIELD RIFLED MUSKET

The closest thing to a standard Union infantry long arm was the Springfield rifled musket. The weapon got its name from the federal government's arsenal at Springfield, Massachusetts, which had been founded in 1794, and where many were manufactured—although during the war, more than thirty companies produced Springfields under contract, for a total of about 1.5 million pieces. The most common version of the weapon was the Model 1861, but the first of the .58 Springfield series appeared in the 1840s, when the U.S. Army began to replace .69 flintlock muskets with percussion-cap weapons, which after 1855 incorporated a rifled barrel as well. The greater accuracy of the rifle over its smoothbore predecessors also led to the introduction of a ladder-style rear sight, and it came with a spike bayonet. It was a heavy piece, weighing in at 9.25lb/4.2kg, with an overall length of about 58in/147cm—which meant that with bayonet fixed, the Springfield was about as tall as the average Civil War soldier.

Springfields were also widely used by the Confederacy—some were seized when the federal arsenal at Harper's Ferry, Virginia, fell to Stonewall Jackson's troops during the campaign that culminated in the Battle of Antietam (September 1862), and many others were obtained by battlefield scavenging.

CARBINES AND PISTOLS

The Union was also fortunate in being able to take advantage of the designs of gunmakers like Christian Sharps, Christopher Spencer, and Benjamin Tyler Henry, who produced innovative breech-loading (and, in the case of Spencer and Henry, repeating) rifles and carbines. However, these weapons were never issued in large numbers by the Union's Ordnance Department; many of them were purchased by state governments for issue to their regiments, or were personally bought by individual soldiers. In the opinion of some historians, the Union might have defeated the Confederacy more quickly had it been less conservative in adopting these kinds of weapons.

As for the Union Army's pistols, these, too were a mix of government-issue and privately purchased weapons. The .44 Colt Model 1860 was probably the most popular single revolver among Union officers, but a wide variety of revolvers were used, including the Starr (also .44), British-made Adams revolvers, and the .36 Savage-North "Navy" model shown below.

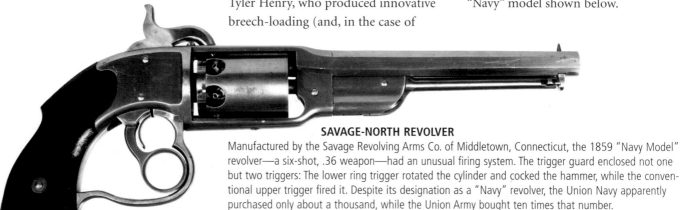

SAVAGE-NORTH REVOLVER
Manufactured by the Savage Revolving Arms Co. of Middletown, Connecticut, the 1859 "Navy Model" revolver—a six-shot, .36 weapon—had an unusual firing system. The trigger guard enclosed not one but two triggers: The lower ring trigger rotated the cylinder and cocked the hammer, while the conventional upper trigger fired it. Despite its designation as a "Navy" revolver, the Union Navy apparently purchased only about a thousand, while the Union Army bought ten times that number.

SPRINGFIELD MUSKET

In the first year or so of the war, many Union troops were issued with a version of the old .69 flintlock musket converted to the percussion cap firing system, like the gun shown here. The Springfield rifled musket would largely replace these obsolete weapons during the course of the conflict, although many of the conversions remained in service with state militias.

SPENCER CARBINE

The Spencer rifle, model 1860, has the distinction of being the first magazine-fed repeating rifle officially adopted by a major army. The gun, designed by Christopher Spencer (1833–1922), utilized a falling-block breech, operated by a lever that doubled as a trigger, fed by a tubular magazine of seven .56 copper-jacketed cartridges located in the stock. After the war started, both the Union army and navy placed orders for the weapon, but Spencer's company had an impossible delivery deadline, and unfortunate accidents in testing led the government to have second thoughts. Spencer personally called on President Abraham Lincoln in August 1863, and the president test-fired the weapon to his satisfaction. The Union ultimately bought more than 100,000 Spencers, including the carbine model shown here.

GATLING GUN

The original Gatling gun of 1861 had six barrels and fed from a hopper containing paper cartridges; a later model took metallic cartridges, greatly increasing the rate of fire, and post–Civil War models—like the one shown here—had ten barrels and utilized a drum magazine. The Gatling is often cited as the world's first machine gun, but this is an inaccurate description, as the weapon was manually operated, rather than functioning by means of recoil or gas energy. Still, Gatlings could achieve a rate of fire in excess of 1,000 rounds per minute.

RICHARD GATLING

Ironically, Richard Jordan Gatling (1818–1903), the inventor of the Gatling gun—which first saw action with the Union Army in the siege of Petersburg, Virginia, in 1864—was a North Carolinian by birth and (according to some historians) a Confederate sympathizer. In another irony, Gatling (a doctor by training) claimed that his inspiration in developing the weapon—considered to be the first successful rapid-fire gun—was the desire to lower the number of men needed to fight battles in order to reduce the spread of disease: "It occurred to me that if I could invent a machine—a gun—which could by its rapidity of fire, enable one man to do as much battle duty as a hundred, that it would, to a large extent supersede the necessity of large armies, and consequently, exposure to battle and disease [would] be greatly diminished." In 1861, Gatling designed a multiple-barreled, hand-cranked weapon, which he demonstrated to the U.S. Ordnance Bureau a year later. The weapon was rejected in 1862 as too complicated and heavy, and it was not officially adopted until 1866, after the war's end—but, as per above, some commanders purchased Gatlings on their own initiative and these saw service toward the end of the conflict. In later decades, Britain's Royal Navy adopted guns based on the Gatling design, and Gatlings were used to good effect by the U.S. Army in Cuba during the Spanish-American War (1898). After World War II, the multiple-barrel Gatling concept was revived by the U.S. military—in an electrically operated form—in aircraft weapons like the M1961 Vulcan 20mm cannon and the 7.62mm "minigun" machine gun.

CONFEDERATE WEAPONS OF THE AMERICAN CIVIL WAR

Both "Johnny Reb" and "Billy Yank," the ordinary infantrymen of the American Civil War (1861–65), carried essentially the same weapon—a muzzle-loading rifled musket, usually .58 or .577 caliber. While the workshops and factories of the North kept the Union armies relatively well supplied with weapons (despite shortages early in the war), the South lacked industry and had to import most of its arms from Europe, something that became increasingly difficult as the war went on and the Union Navy's blockade of Southern ports cut the Confederacy off from its sources of supply.

STARTING FROM SCRATCH

Early in the war, the severe Southern arms shortage forced many Confederate soldiers to arm themselves with shotguns and hunting rifles from home.

Contemporary historian Andrew Leckie writes that "When the 27th Alabama [Regiment] marched off to war it was said the men carried a thousand double-barreled shotguns and a thousand homemade Bowie knives." The situation improved somewhat when arms began arriving from overseas, and when Confederate forces captured the federal arsenal at Harper's Ferry, Virginia, in 1861. Some of the machinery from Harper's Ferry was used to set up arms factories throughout the South, but these small manufacturers could produce only a fraction of the rifles, artillery pieces, and other weapons needed by the Confederacy.

IMPORTS AND IMITATIONS

The closest thing to a standard infantry weapon in the Confederate armies was the British-made .577 Enfield rifled musket. Despite the name, the Enfields used in the Civil War were not in fact made at the Royal Arsenal at Enfield, England, because Great Britain was officially neutral in the conflict; instead, private manufacturers produced rifles to the Enfield

JEFFERSON DAVIS

Unlike Abraham Lincoln—whose only military experience was a brief stint in the Illinois militia—Jefferson Davis spent many years as a professional soldier before assuming the presidency of the Confederate States of America in February 1861. Born in Kentucky in 1808, Davis graduated from West Point and saw service on the frontier before resigning his commission in 1835. He later fought with distinction—and was wounded—in the Mexican-American War (1846–48). Entering politics as Secretary of War in President Franklin Pierce's cabinet, he pushed through significant reforms like the adoption of the rifled musket. Davis was a U.S. Senator from Mississippi when the war broke out. Imprisoned for two years after the Confederacy defeat in the spring of 1865, he died in Louisiana in 1889.

CONFEDERATE CARBINE

Early in the war the Confederacy managed to obtain a small quantity of breech-loading carbines made by the Massachusetts Arms Company, like the one shown here. The carbine used the Maynard Percussion Tape Primer system, rather than the more common percussion cap.

pattern for export. The Confederate government purchased about 400,000 Enfields over the course of the war, and the rifle was also widely used by Union forces. Besides the Enfield, the Confederacy bought around 50,000 Model 1854 Infanteriegewehr (infantry rifles) from Austria.

Throughout the war, the Confederate cavalry lacked an effective breech-loading saddle weapon like the Sharps carbine (see p 148) used by Union horsemen. Confederate gunsmiths tried to copy the Sharps, but the result—the so-called "Richmond Sharps," named for the Confederate capital, where it was manufactured—performed so poorly that Confederate General Robert E. Lee described the gun as "so defective as to be demoralizing to our men." Only about 5,000 were made.

HOMEMADE BLADES

Confederate privates carried these crude knives, which may well have made himself from a saw or farm-implement blade. The design of this and similar Southern knives was inspired by the famous Bowie knife, the long-bladed weapon popularized by the frontiersmen Jim and Rezin Bowie in the 1830s.

LEMAT PISTOL

A favorite sidearm of Confederate officers, the LeMat pistol had two barrels: The upper discharged .40 bullets via a nine-shot cylinder, the lower a single charge of buckshot. This powerful hybrid of revolver and shotgun was first made in New Orleans in 1856 by a French-born doctor, Jean Alexander Francois LeMat, who later moved production to Europe when the war broke out.

JEFFERSON DAVIS' PISTOLS

This magnificent set of cased pistols was made in Belgium in 1861 for presentation to the newly appointed president of the Confederate States of America. They feature Damascus steel barrels (see p. 92), grips of fluted, carved ivory, and gold inlay on the frames and other parts. Davis never got to enjoy this gift, however; the ship carrying them to the Confederacy was captured as it tried to run the Union blockade.

AUSTRIAN STEEL

This socket bayonet fit the Model 1854 Austrian Infanteriegewehr, also known as the Lorenz rifled musket. Despite being purchased in large numbers by both sides, the Lorenz, according to one historian, was "universally loathed by many of the soldiers who used them." In fact, the Union government bought thousands of these guns simply to keep them from being bought by the Confederacy.

WEAPONS OF THE AMERICAN WEST

Few eras in history are more identified with the widespread use of firearms than the settling of western United States in the nineteenth century: The phrase "Wild West" instantly conjures up images of cowboys, outlaws, and lawmen wielding "six-shooters"; scouts and buffalo-hunters with their lever-action "repeaters" and high-powered single-shot rifles; Cavalrymen and Native Americans skirmishing with carbines and revolvers pitted against arrows and lances. Countless books and movies have established this romantic period in the popular imagination—not always accurately—but the fact is that on the frontier, having a reliable gun (or two, or three) to hand often meant the difference between life and death.

ACROSS THE MOUNTAINS

At the start of the nineteenth century, the frontier was just over the Appalachian Mountains; westward-moving pioneers from the states of the Eastern Seaboard brought with them their long Kentucky rifles both to bag game for the pot and to fight the Native Americans who resisted the tide of settlement. When the Louisiana Purchase (1803) pushed the frontier to the Rocky Mountains and beyond, the legendary "Mountain Men" went into the wilderness in search of furs, often armed with the heavy caliber rifles manufactured by the brothers Samuel and Jacob Hawken of St. Louis.

In the 1850s, during the run-up to the American Civil War the western territory of Kansas became a battleground as antislavery settlers from the North clashed with proslavery settlers from the South, each side hoping to gain a majority when the time came for the territory to apply for statehood. Many of the Northern settlers were armed with a new and technically advanced weapon—the carbine designed by Christian Sharps (1811-74) in 1848. The breech-loading Sharps had a falling-block action; a lever (which doubled as the trigger guard) dropped the breech-block for loading. Rifles and carbines based on the Sharps design remained popular in the West for decades.

ON THE FRONTIER

The original Sharps was a single-shot weapon, but in 1860 Christopher Spencer (1833-1922) introduced a falling-block rifle with a tubular seven-round magazine under the barrel—a true "repeater"—which also saw widespread use in the West. Around the same time, the Winchester Repeating Arms Co. was developing a lever-action magazine rifle, which it introduced in 1866; its successor, the Model 1873, proved immensely popular and has often been called "the gun that won the West."

The U.S. Army's main task from the end of the Civil War until the "end of the frontier" in 1890 was fighting the Native Americans. Although repeaters had proved their worth in the Civil War, the army had so many Springfield muzzle-loaders left over from that conflict that they fought the Indian Wars largely with "trap-door" Springfields—so-called because they'd been converted to single-shot breech-loaders,

Another category of Western weapon was the high-powered (usually .50 caliber) rifles used by professional buffalo hunters. Killed for their hides, to keep them from blocking railroad construction, or just for sport, the buffalo—whose herds had once ranged across the Western plains in hundreds of thousands—were nearly extinct by the mid-1880s.

As for pistols, those on either side of the law used a wide variety, but Colts—especially the 1873 single-action Army model—were favorites.

WINCHESTER 66
The Winchester Model 1866 was nicknamed "the Yellow Boy," because of the color of its receiver. A direct descendant of the Henry rifle, the gun fired the same .44 rimfire cartridge, but its tubular magazine more than doubled the Henry's capacity, from seven to fifteen rounds. This particular model (converted to centerfire) was owned by Czar Alexander II of Russia (1818–81) and is engraved with the czar's royal cipher and other symbols of the Russian monarchy.

OLIVER WINCHESTER

Born in Boston in 1810, Oliver Fisher Winchester made his first fortune as a manufacturer of men's shirts in Baltimore, New York City, and New Haven. As his clothing business prospered, he invested in the Volcanic Repeating Arms Company, taking control of that firm in 1856 and renaming it the New Haven Arms Co., and, later, the Winchester Repeating Arms Co. The Volcanic Company had produced a briefly popular repeating rifle, and Winchester hired gunsmith Benjamin Tyler Henry (1821-98) to refine the design. The result, in 1860, was the so-called Henry rifle, a lever-action repeater, which saw service in the American Civil War (1861-65; see pp 150 155), even though the Union Army never officially adopted it. After the war Winchester introduced the Model 1866, the Model 1873, and their successors. Winchester was also a politician, serving as lieutenant governor of Connecticut (1866-67). Oliver Winchester died in 1881 and control of the company passed to his son, William Winchester. William died the following year, but the company went on, and it remains one of the great American armsmakers, producing a wide range of rifles and shotguns for the sporting market. In a curious footnote to the Winchester story, William's widow, Sarah Pardee Winchester, was supposedly told by a Spiritualist medium that she had to build a home for the souls of those killed by Winchester weapons, or else the family would be forever cursed. Whether this is true or not is still debated, but in 1884 Sarah moved to San Jose, California, where she bought a modest house, which she proceeded to expand, at enormous cost, until her death in 1922. By that time the dwelling had 160 rooms and a host of bizarre features like staircases that went nowhere and doors that opened onto walls. The Winchester "mystery house" is now a major tourist attraction.

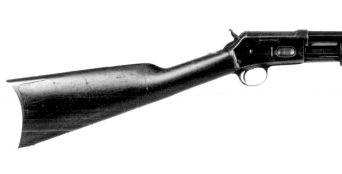

COLT LIGHTNING RIFLE
In the early 1880s Colt introduced its "Lightning" series of rifles, based on a patent by William Elliott. Unusual for the time, the rifles used a pump, or slide, action, and they were never as popular as the lever-action guns of competitors like Winchester. The several models of the series were chambered for .32, .38, and .44.

MASSACHUSETTS ARMS COMPANY CARBINE
A breech-loading percussion .50 caliber carbine made by the Massachusetts Arms Company; this type of rifle, accurate up to 600, was known as a Maynard Carbine because it used Maynard primer tape for igniting the powder. The carbine was popular with the military as well as sportsmen. It was patented in 1851 and later saw wide use in the Confederate Army during the Civil War. However, this particular rifle, with its silver cartouche and the Napoleonic emblem, was actually owned by Napoleon III (1808–73; r. 1852–70), Napoleon Bonaparte's nephew.

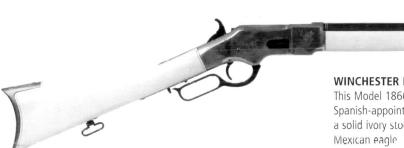

WINCHESTER M1866 MAXIMILIAN RIFLE
This Model 1866 rifle was created by the Winchester Arms Company as a gift to Spanish-appointed Mexican ruler Emperor Maximilian. Maximilian's weapon has a solid ivory stock, gold-plated lock mechanism, and is engraved with the Mexican eagle

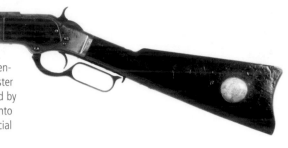

WINCHESTER 73

In 1873 Winchester produced an improved version of the Model 1866 chambered for a new, centerfire version of the .44 round. The "Winchester '73" became the most famous of the Winchester rifles and one of the most celebrated guns of the West, period. The gun shown here was owned by Albert Edward, Prince of Wales, later King Edward VII (1841–1910); the silver medallion inset into the stock is engraved with imperial symbols including the Star of India. The rifle received a special blued vision by the gunsmith James Kerr at the London Armoury Co.

SHARPS 1859

The rolling-block carbines and rifles designed by Christian Sharps (1811–74) were popular with hunters, scouts, and other Western denizens. Shown here is the 1859 Sharps New Model carbine, with a pair of colored "sharpshooter's glasses" used to cut down on glare. Perhaps the most famous Sharps model was the .50 rifle—known as the "Big Fifty"—which was widely used by buffalo hunters. The weapon could reportedly drop a buffalo at 200yd/183m with a single shot.

PUSH DAGGER

Described as a "gambler's push dagger," this nasty little weapon, made in San Francisco around 1870, was presumably useful in settling disputes about where that fifth ace came from. It has a bone grip and a 5in/12.5cm blade.

ADAMS REVOLVER

The revolvers made by the British gunsmith Robert Adams (1809–70) were a serious competitor to Colt's products both during the Civil War and on the Western frontier. As double-action revolvers, they were faster firing, but Colts were generally more accurate and powerful. The finely crafted Adams pistols were also more expensive. Colonel George Armstrong Custer of the U.S. Seventh Cavalry, which was famously wiped out by Sioux and Cheyenne warriors at the Battle of the Little Bighorn in 1876, is said to have carried an Adams pistol similar to the one shown here—although in that fateful battle Custer apparently went to his death firing a pair of Schofield revolvers.

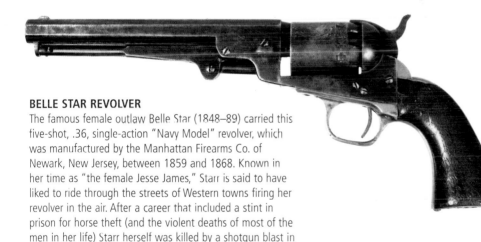

BELLE STAR REVOLVER

The famous female outlaw Belle Star (1848–89) carried this five-shot, .36, single-action "Navy Model" revolver, which was manufactured by the Manhattan Firearms Co. of Newark, New Jersey, between 1859 and 1868. Known in her time as "the female Jesse James," Starr is said to have liked to ride through the streets of Western towns firing her revolver in the air. After a career that included a stint in prison for horse theft (and the violent deaths of most of the men in her life) Starr herself was killed by a shotgun blast in Eufaula, Oklahoma.

ELIPHALET REMINGTON

Born in Connecticut in 1793, Eliphalet Remington moved—like many New Englanders of the time—to upstate New York, where he worked as a blacksmith alongside his father. In his early twenties, he decided that he could make a better gun than those available for commercial purchase. The resulting weapon impressed local users so much that he entered into gunmaking full-time, establishing what would become E. Remington & Sons (later the Remington Arms Co.) in Ilion, New York. By the time Remington died in 1861, the small firm was on its way to becoming one of the nation's leading gunmakers—a status that, like Winchester, it retains today. Although Remington diversified to produce products ranging from typewriters to bicycles, it's said that the Remington Arms Co. is the oldest American company still making its original product.

REMINGTON RIFLE

The single-shot, rolling-block Remington rifles of the 1860s and 1870s were of extremely rugged construction. In America they remained mainly a civilian weapon, although the U.S. Army and Navy purchased some rifles and carbines in small numbers. Remington, however, sold hundreds of thousands of the weapons to foreign governments—some of which remained in service well into the twentieth century.

BOLT-ACTION MAGAZINE RIFLES

The bolt-action, magazine-fed rifle, firing a completely enclosed metallic cartridge of substantial caliber and firepower, was the principal infantry weapon of modern armies for about seventy-five years, from the 1860s until the World War II era, when it was replaced by self-loading rifles (see pp 180–83) and later by selective-fire assault rifles (see pp 216–19). Simple, robust, and reliable, this type of rifle continues in use into the twenty-first century among civilians for hunting and target shooting.

NEEDLE-GUN AND CHASSEPOT
While the American Civil War (1861–65; see pp 138–43) demonstrated the effectiveness of rapid-fire, breech-loading rifles and carbines, the powerful German state of Prussia had already adopted such a weapon for its army in 1848. This was the so-called "needle gun" developed by Nikolaus von Dreyse (1787–1867). The 15.4mm gun got its name because it used a needle-shaped firing pin to explode a primer cap embedded in a paper cartridge that also comprised the main powder charge and bullet.

The needle gun's great innovation, besides the incorporation of a self-contained cartridge, was the introduction of a bolt-handle firing mechanism. Together, these advances made for faster loading and firing than was possible with the muzzle-loading, percussion-cap muskets and rifles in use at the time. The weapon's chief disadvantages were that the explosion of the primer cap tended to weaken and eventually corrode the needle firing pin, and the design of the breech, which allowed much propellant gas to escape in firing.

The needle gun first saw action against revolutionary mobs in 1848–49 and then in Prussia's wars against Denmark (1864), Austria (1866), and France (1870–71). In the Franco-Prussian War, Prussian troops with needle guns faced French infantry armed with a similar weapon, the chassepot, named for its inventor, Antoine Chassepot (1833–1905), which the French Army had adopted in 1866. The 11mm chassepot was technically superior to the needle gun in several respects and had a longer range, but Prussian superiority in artillery and tactics countered its advantages.

ENTER THE MAGAZINE
The success of the needle gun and the chassepot led to the adoption of the bolt-action rifles by other Western armies. The needle gun and chassepot, however, were single-shot weapons; the next step forward was the development of multiple-shot magazine weapons utilizing the new firing system. In 1868, for example, the Swiss Army adopted a rifle developed by Freidrich Vetterli (1822–82), which fed from a tubular magazine under the barrel.

Most of this new generation of rifles, though, used a fixed or detachable box magazine holding five or more cartridges, charged either with individual rounds or by means of a stripper clip, which held several cartridges in a metal frame and which was inserted into the magazine from either the top or bottom.

The British Army adopted its first magazine bolt-action rifle, the Lee-Metford, in 1877. In 1889, Denmark adopted the Krag-Jorgensen, which was later adopted by Norway and the United States. The most successful of the new-style rifles, however, were the designs produced by the German brothers Wilhelm and Paul Mauser (see feature).

BELGIAN POLICE CARBINE
This Belgian police carbine is a percussion-cap weapon manufactured in 1858.

THE MAUSERS

Wilhelm (1834–1882) and Paul Mauser (1838–1914) followed in their father's footsteps as gunsmiths at the royal armory in the German kingdom of Wurttemberg. When the government of the newly unified Germany sought an improved rifle in response to the performance of the French chassepot in the Franco-Prussian War, the brothers developed a single-shot bolt-action weapon, the Gewehr (rifle) Model 1871, which Germany adopted that same year. After Wilhelm's

death, Paul came up with a new 7mm design based on the newly developed box magazine. In Models 1893, 1894, and 1895, the rifle proved hugely successful and orders poured in from around the world. While the Mauser's straight-pull bolt didn't allow for as rapid a rate of fire as, say, the British SMLE, it was strong, safe, and effective. In 1898 Mauser introduced the 7.92mm Gewehr 98—the finest bolt-action rifle ever made, in the opinion of many weapons historians. The G98 remained in service with the Germany

Army until the mid-1930s, when it was replaced by a shorter version, the Karabiner (KAR) 98. The three principal Mauser factories were destroyed during World War II; today, the company—now owned by Rheinmetall—makes mostly hunting rifles. Several former Mauser engineers, however, were instrumental in founding Heckler & Koch, Germany's greatest weapons-maker of the post–World War II era.

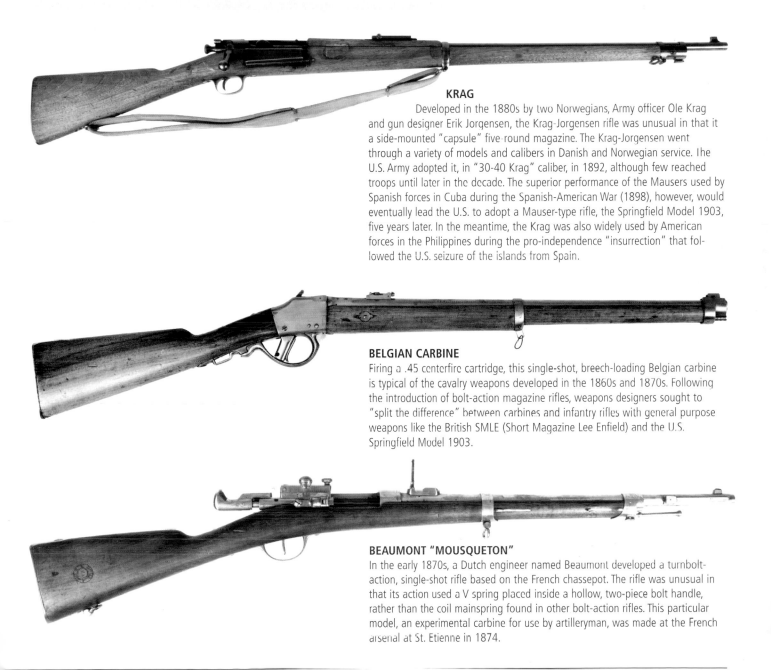

KRAG

Developed in the 1880s by two Norwegians, Army officer Ole Krag and gun designer Erik Jorgensen, the Krag-Jorgensen rifle was unusual in that it a side-mounted "capsule" five-round magazine. The Krag-Jorgensen went through a variety of models and calibers in Danish and Norwegian service. The U.S. Army adopted it, in "30-40 Krag" caliber, in 1892, although few reached troops until later in the decade. The superior performance of the Mausers used by Spanish forces in Cuba during the Spanish-American War (1898), however, would eventually lead the U.S. to adopt a Mauser-type rifle, the Springfield Model 1903, five years later. In the meantime, the Krag was also widely used by American forces in the Philippines during the pro-independence "insurrection" that followed the U.S. seizure of the islands from Spain.

BELGIAN CARBINE

Firing a .45 centerfire cartridge, this single-shot, breech-loading Belgian carbine is typical of the cavalry weapons developed in the 1860s and 1870s. Following the introduction of bolt-action magazine rifles, weapons designers sought to "split the difference" between carbines and infantry rifles with general purpose weapons like the British SMLE (Short Magazine Lee Enfield) and the U.S. Springfield Model 1903.

BEAUMONT "MOUSQUETON"

In the early 1870s, a Dutch engineer named Beaumont developed a turnbolt-action, single-shot rifle based on the French chassepot. The rifle was unusual in that its action used a V spring placed inside a hollow, two-piece bolt handle, rather than the coil mainspring found in other bolt-action rifles. This particular model, an experimental carbine for use by artilleryman, was made at the French arsenal at St. Etienne in 1874.

"TORINO"

In 1887, the Italian Army began retrofitting an 1870 Vetterli single-shot bolt-action rifle design with a box magazine designed by artillery officer G. Vitali. The result, a 10.4mm Vetterli-Vitali, saw much service in Italy's colonial wars in Africa during the late nineteenth and early twentieth centuries.

GEWEHR 1888

Afraid of falling behind the French in rifle development, the German Army set up a commission in 1888 to spur innovation. One result was the Gewehr Model 1888, aka the 7.92mm "commission rifle," which incorporated elements from both Mauser and Austrian Mannlicher designs. One unusual feature was that a metal sleeve, rather than the usual wooden forestock, surrounded the barrel: It was thought that this would be a more effective means of keeping the barrel from overheating during rapid fire.

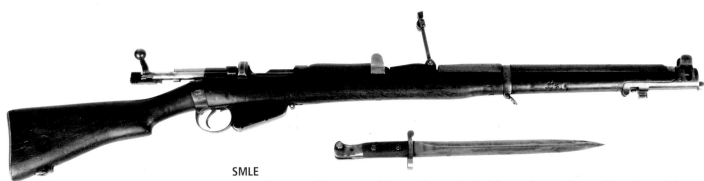

SMLE

During the Boer War (1899–1902) the British Army decided that modern combat conditions demanded a shorter infantry rifle that could double as a carbine, greatly reducing the logistical hassles of supplying two types of parts and ammunition. The result, introduced in 1907, was the .303 SMLE (Short Magazine Lee Enfield), which would remain in service, in various models, for more almost a half-century. Shown here is the Mark III model, with its 18in/46cm sword-type bayonet. The SMLE had a magazine capacity of ten rounds, at a time when most other magazine rifles held five rounds.

MOSIN

Few service rifles have had a longer active life than the Russian 7.62mm Model 1891 Mosin-Nagant; with variations, it served with Russian and Soviet forces through the late 1940s. Prior to the Russian Revolution, many Mosin-Nagants were manufactured in the U.S., including this one, shown with its spike bayonet, which was made by the Westinghouse Corporation in the 1890s.

VETTERLI

Preceding the more famous Mauser by several years, Switzerland's .41 Model 1869 Vetterli infantry rifle was the first multiple-shot, bolt-action rifle adopted by a major army—though it fed from a twelve-round tubular magazine, in a manner similar to the Winchester and Henry rifles, rather than from a box magazine. The model shown here is an Italian version from 1878.

A MULTITUDE OF MAUSERS

Scores of nations adopted Mauser designs for their armed forces; according to the company, some 100 million Mauser rifles were manufactured worldwide from the late nineteenth-century through World War II. Shown here are just a few of the many Mauser variants from across the globe.

TURKISH MAUSER
A Turkish model from 1890, chambered for a slightly different version of the standard 7.65 round.

PERSIAN MAUSER
An 8mm Persian (later Iranian) Army Mauser with bayonet. Many of these were manufactured at the Brno Arms Works in Czechoslovakia.

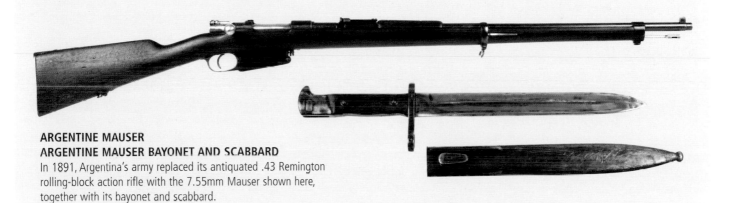

ARGENTINE MAUSER
ARGENTINE MAUSER BAYONET AND SCABBARD
In 1891, Argentina's army replaced its antiquated .43 Remington rolling-block action rifle with the 7.55mm Mauser shown here, together with its bayonet and scabbard.

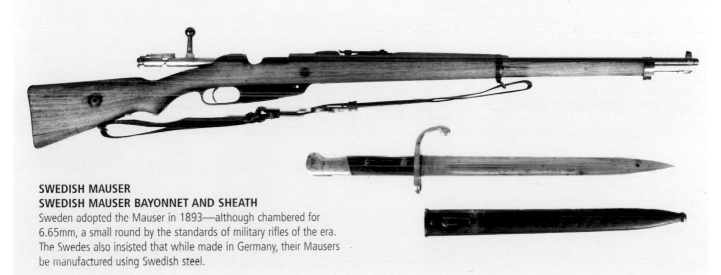

SWEDISH MAUSER
SWEDISH MAUSER BAYONNET AND SHEATH
Sweden adopted the Mauser in 1893—although chambered for 6.65mm, a small round by the standards of military rifles of the era. The Swedes also insisted that while made in Germany, their Mausers be manufactured using Swedish steel.

THE AUTOMATIC PISTOL

The automatic pistol can be considered a stepchild of the machine gun. After Hiram Maxim (see p 185) figured out how to use a weapon's recoil to load, fire, eject, and reload a cartridge in the 1880s, weapons designers in several countries worked to scale down the system to the handgun level. (Strictly speaking, automatic pistols are really semiautomatic weapons, because they fire once with every trigger pull, and not continuously, like a machine gun—though fully automatic pistols have been developed.) Early automatics had some teething pains, particularly concerning cartridge size, but designers like John Browning (see sidebar) made the weapon viable.

BORCHARDT, BERGMANN, AND LUGER

The first successful automatic pistol was the brainchild of a German-born American inventor, Hugo Borchardt (1844–1924), who worked for several U.S. arms manufacturers, including Colt and Winchester. In 1893 Borchardt designed a pistol that used the Maxim recoil principle to send a toggle backward and upward to eject the spent cartridge and chamber a new one, fed from a magazine in the grip. (Reportedly, Borchardt's design was inspired by the movement of the human knee.) Borchardt found no takers for his pistol in America, so he moved to Germany, where the firm of Ludwig Loewe & Company brought the pioneering pistol on the market.

Also in Germany, around the same time, Austrian-born entrepreneur Theodor Bergmann (1850–1931) and the German designer Louis Schmeisser

(1848–1917—father of Hugo Schmeisser) began developing a series of blowback-operated automatics, although these fed from a magazine in front of a trigger guard instead of in the grip—as did the "Broomhandle" Mauser developed around the same time.

Deutsch Waffen & Munitions Fabriken (DWM), the successor to Ludwig Loewe & Co., failed to sell the Borchardt pistol to the U.S. Army in the 1890s, but one of its employees, Georg Luger, improved on its design and eventually developed the first version of the famous pistol that would bear his name. The Swiss Army's adoption of the Luger in 1900 marked a major step forward in military acceptance of the automatic pistol. The German Army, however, considered the original Luger's 7.65mm round too weak. Luger then developed a new 9mm round (the parabellum, from the Latin "for war"). Germany adopted the 9mm version in 1908.

ENTER JOHN BROWNING

The main objection military customers had to the early automatics was the perceived lack of "stopping power" of their cartridges. (Automatic mechanisms couldn't function using the heavy revolver cartridges of the era.) In the early 1900s, the U.S. Army, however, found that even its .38 revolver was insufficient when used against determined Muslim insurgents in the Philippines (then an American colony). John Browning met the challenge with a pistol that, while automatic, fired an extremely powerful .45 round; the cartridge was called .45 ACP (Automatic Colt Pistol). Officially adopted by the U.S. Army in 1911, the Colt M1911 automatic went on to become one of the world's most successful and long-serving handguns.

BORCHARDT
Hugo Borchardt essentially designed his pistol, the first successful autoloader, around a new 7.65mm cartridge, which eventually became known as the 7.65 Mauser. The firing system was based around a locked breech; when fired, the barrel recoiled, unlocking the breechblock and activating a toggle that moved the barrel away from the breechblock, ejected the spent cartridge, and loaded a new one from the eight-round magazine in the grip. The awkward layout of the Borchardt, however, made it difficult to fire with one hand, so (like several other early automatics) it was supplied with a detachable stock.

BERGMANN

The blowback-operated Bergmann automatics developed in the mid-1890s (the Model 1894 is shown here) were unusual in that they didn't incorporate an extraction mechanism to eject spent cartridges; instead, the spent rounds were blown out of the gun by gas pressure from the cartridge's firing. The so-called "gas-extraction" mechanism made these pistols somewhat prone to jamming. The Bergmann series were chambered for various calibers and had a revolver-style grip, with rounds feeding from a magazine forward of the trigger guard. Later Bergmann models included the "Mars" and "Simplex" automatics, which saw widespread military service before and during World War I.

LUGER

The Luger model adopted by the Swiss Army (like the one shown here, with the Swiss Cross stamped on the receiver) were in 7.65mm; the German P08 model, adopted in 1908, fired the 9mm parabellum round which remains, almost a century later, the most popular caliber for automatic pistols and submachine guns. While the Luger was undoubtedly an excellent weapon, its legendary status—it was a coveted souvenir among Allied troops in both world wars—exaggerates its overall performance.

JOHN M. BROWNING

Browning was certainly the most influential and versatile gunmaker of all time. His work encompassed both civilian and military weapons and includes shotguns, machine guns, automatic rifles, and automatic pistols. Indeed, many of his designs are still in production today. John Moses Browning was born in Ogden, Utah, in 1855. Browning's father, a gunsmith, was among the Mormon pioneers who had trekked westward to Utah, and it was in his father's shop that he built his first gun at the age of thirteen. In 1883, Browning went to work for Winchester, where he designed several legendary shotguns and rifles in the 1890s and early 1900s. His interest in automatic weapons led to the development of a machine gun in 1895 and several automatic pistols, which ultimately included the .45 M1911A1 Colt. His .30 and .50 machine guns became standard throughout the U.S. military, as did the Browning Automatic Rifle (BAR). He died in Belgium in 1926 while working on the 9mm automatic pistol that would eventually be produced as the Browning High-Power (see pp 206).

GLISENTI

First produced in 1910, the 9mm Glisenti (so-called from its manufacturer, Real Fabbrica d'Armi Glisenti) was the standard sidearm of the Italian Army in World War I. An overly complex firing system, combined with an unusual trigger mechanism, undercut its effectiveness.

ARTILLERY LUGER

Toward the end of World War I, the German Army introduced an interesting Luger variant—the so-called Artillery Model. The Artillery Luger had an 8in/20cm barrel instead of the standard model's 4in/10cm barrel, and was intended for use as a carbine with a wooden shoulder stock and a 32-round drum magazine (see p 195). As the name implies it was originally issued to gun crews as a defensive weapon, but it proved useful in the hands of trench-raiding infantry units.

COLT .45

"Tough, reliable, and packing a punch," in the words of firearms historian Craig Philip, "[Colt .45's] have endeared themselves to soldiers of all nations." At least 3 million of these pistols have been produced in the U.S., and an unknown number made under license (or simply copied) worldwide since its introduction in 1911. The original "government" model was slightly modified, based on combat experience in World War I, to become the M1911A1, which remained in U.S. military service until the mid-1980s. The weapon's main drawbacks were its heavy weight (2.5lb/1.1kg) and the fact that as a double-action weapon, it had to be carried with the slide pulled back in order to be ready to fire the first round quickly—something that could lead to accidental discharge in the hands of an inexperienced user.

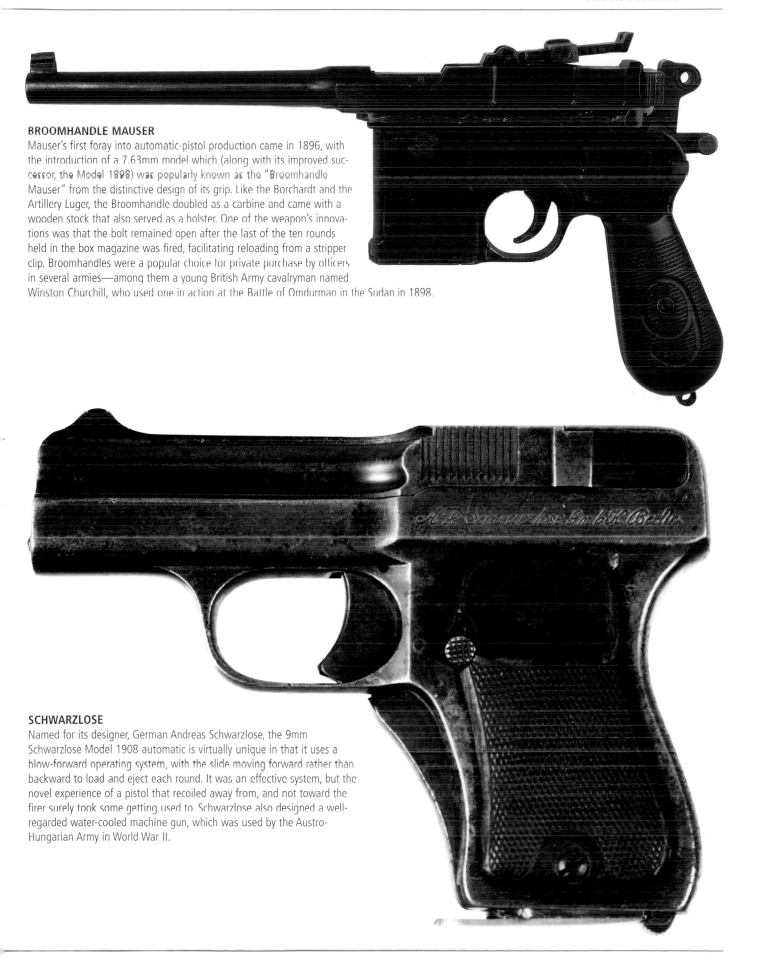

BROOMHANDLE MAUSER

Mauser's first foray into automatic-pistol production came in 1896, with the introduction of a 7.63mm model which (along with its improved successor, the Model 1898) was popularly known as the "Broomhandle Mauser" from the distinctive design of its grip. Like the Borchardt and the Artillery Luger, the Broomhandle doubled as a carbine and came with a wooden stock that also served as a holster. One of the weapon's innovations was that the bolt remained open after the last of the ten rounds held in the box magazine was fired, facilitating reloading from a stripper clip. Broomhandles were a popular choice for private purchase by officers in several armies—among them a young British Army cavalryman named Winston Churchill, who used one in action at the Battle of Omdurman in the Sudan in 1898.

SCHWARZLOSE

Named for its designer, German Andreas Schwarzlose, the 9mm Schwarzlose Model 1908 automatic is virtually unique in that it uses a blow-forward operating system, with the slide moving forward rather than backward to load and eject each round. It was an effective system, but the novel experience of a pistol that recoiled away from, and not toward the firer surely took some getting used to. Schwarzlose also designed a well-regarded water-cooled machine gun, which was used by the Austro-Hungarian Army in World War II.

PERSONAL DEFENSE WEAPONS

Despite advances in public safety, such as the introduction of organized police forces, crime remained a major problem in Europe and the Americas in the nineteenth century. The rise of industrialization led to the massive growth of cities—and also the rise of an urban criminal underclass operating individually or in gangs—while bandits were still a threat in rural, isolated areas. As a result, some people armed themselves with small, easily concealable firearms for defense against robbers and the like—although the same type of weapon was frequently used by criminals themselves. With "gun control" more or less nonexistent at the time, such weapons were readily available for anyone—on either side of the law—who could afford them.

THE PERSONAL PISTOL

These weapons fall into several categories. Besides derringers (see pp 128–29), there were the so-called "pocket pistols," which, as the name implies, were meant to be carried clandestinely on the owner's person. Typically, these were short-barreled revolvers firing very small caliber rounds, often specially manufactured for a particular model of pistol. In order to be as compact as possible, many of these pistols had folding triggers and/or a completely enclosed hammer to reduce the danger of accidental discharge. The pocket-pistol concept continued in the twentieth century with the introduction of compact small-caliber automatics (see pp 196–197).

A subset of these weapons were "Lady's pistols" or "muff pistols," very small guns intended for use by women, which could be concealed in a handbag or in the fur muffs many women of the era wore as hand-warmers.

A more unusual category of weapon was the "palm" or "squeezer" pistols introduced in the late nineteenth century. These eschewed conventional pistol design in favor of a horizontally oriented weapon that could be concealed in the user's palm, with a "squeeze" firing mechanism replacing the standard trigger. The best-known models include the Belgian/French Le Merveilleux and Gauloise series and the American "Chicago Protector."

WALKING WEAPONS

While canes and walking sticks concealing dagger or sword blades were commonplace by the nineteenth century, the introduction of the percussion-cap firing system in the 1810s and 1820s made "cane guns" a practical weapon. In 1823, British gunsmith John Day patented a mechanism in which a downward pull on a hammer, concealed in the cane, dropped a trigger; thereafter, "Day's Patent" cane guns became the industry standard.

According to firearms historian Charles Edward Chapel, nineteenth-century cane guns were "made in large quantities for naturalists, gamekeepers, and poachers." Later in the century, cane guns firing the new fully enclosed metallic cartridge came into use, and while most cane guns of either firing system were single-shot, some cane revolvers were reportedly manufactured.

LADY'S PISTOL
Another example of the so-called "Lady's Pistol," this .22 revolver has a folding trigger and pearl-coated grips.

BELGIAN PALM PISTOL

This rare Belgian five-shot revolver has a grip designed to fit between the thumb and index finger like a wedge. In addition to the eccentric design, the pistol's folding trigger and double-action hammer are made of gold.

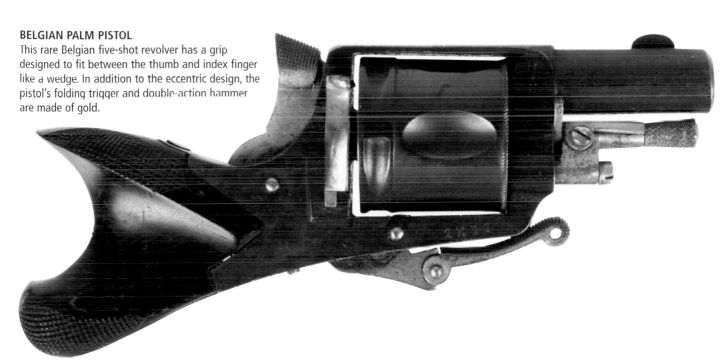

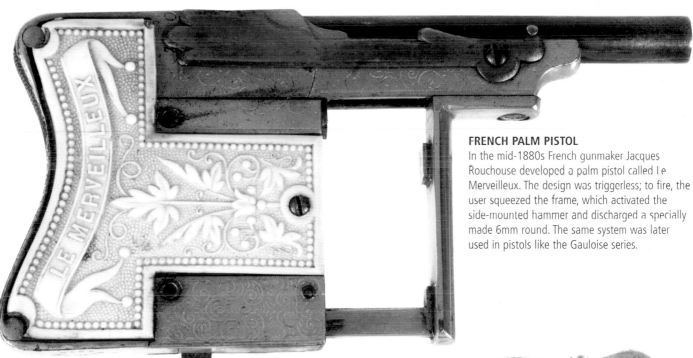

FRENCH PALM PISTOL

In the mid-1880s French gunmaker Jacques Rouchouse developed a palm pistol called Le Merveilleux. The design was triggerless; to fire, the user squeezed the frame, which activated the side-mounted hammer and discharged a specially made 6mm round. The same system was later used in pistols like the Gauloise series.

PROTECTOR PALM PISTOL

In 1882, French gunsmith Jacques Turbiaux patented a pistol designed to fit snugly in the palm; the cartridges (either ten 6mm rounds or seven 8mm) were contained in a horizontal radial cylinder. The design was licensed in the U.S. (firing a special short .32 round) by the Minneapolis Arms Company, and, later, by the Chicago Firearms Company, which marketed it as the "Chicago Protector."

BICYCLE PISTOL

The development of the modern "safety" bicycle in the 1880s touched off a craze for cycling in Europe and North America. Then as now, dogs did not always appreciate the presence of these vehicles on their territory. This .22 pistol, made in France around 1900, was intended for use by bicyclists to frighten dogs; it can fire both blanks and live rounds.

BABY REVOLVER

Starting in the late 1800s, Philadelphia gunmaker Henry Kolb produced a series of ultra-compact, hammerless "Baby" revolvers. This .22 folding-trigger model is nickel-plated with pearl grips.

COACHING CARBINE

This nineteenth-century British percussion "coaching carbine"—so called because it would have been carried by a stagecoach driver or guard to ward off highwaymen—is double-barreled and incorporates a short spring bayonet.

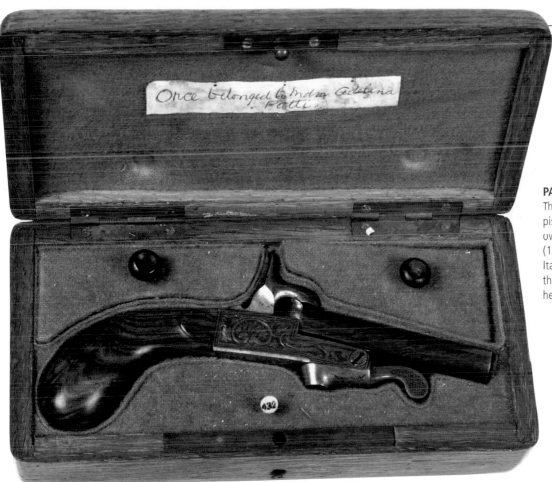

PATTI PINFIRE REVOLVER
This single-shot, .30 pin-fire pistol with a folding trigger was owned by Adelina Patti (1843–1919). Born in Spain to Italian parents, Patti was one of the great operatic sopranos of her era.

MUFF PISTOLS
As the name implies, these Belgian-made, ivory-handled .36 single-shot percussion "muff pistols" were intended to be carried in a lady's hand-warming muff.

WEAPONS OF DECEPTION

LANE CANE GUN

One of the rarest examples of this type of
weapon is the nineteeth-century percussion-
cap British Lane Cane Gun. The upper part of
the cane, which contained the gun, was
detached from the lower part and could be
fired from the shoulder.

UMBRELLA GUN
A nineteenth-century percussion-cap gun disguised as an umbrella. A modern version of the umbrella gun—in this case, firing a projectile coated with the toxic agent Ricin—was used to assassinate a Bulgarian dissident in London in 1978 (see also 212–13).

SWAGGER STICK GUN
A .22 wood-covered swagger-stick gun.

HIKING-STICK GUN
This British gentleman's nineteenth-century hiking stick does double duty with its detachable percussion-cap single shot.

WALKING-STICK GUN
A nineteenth-century English walking-stick gun. The weapon contains a single-shot percussion-cap firing mechanism, a system devised by British gunsmith John Day.

. . . AND A FEW OFFENSIVE WEAPONS

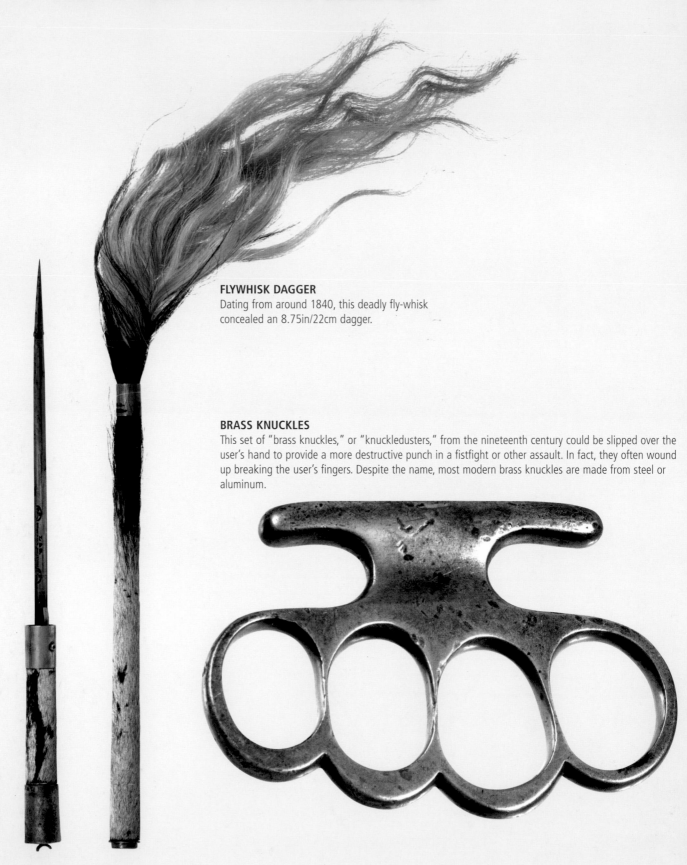

FLYWHISK DAGGER
Dating from around 1840, this deadly fly-whisk
concealed an 8.75in/22cm dagger.

BRASS KNUCKLES
This set of "brass knuckles," or "knuckledusters," from the nineteenth century could be slipped over the
user's hand to provide a more destructive punch in a fistfight or other assault. In fact, they often wound
up breaking the user's fingers. Despite the name, most modern brass knuckles are made from steel or
aluminum.

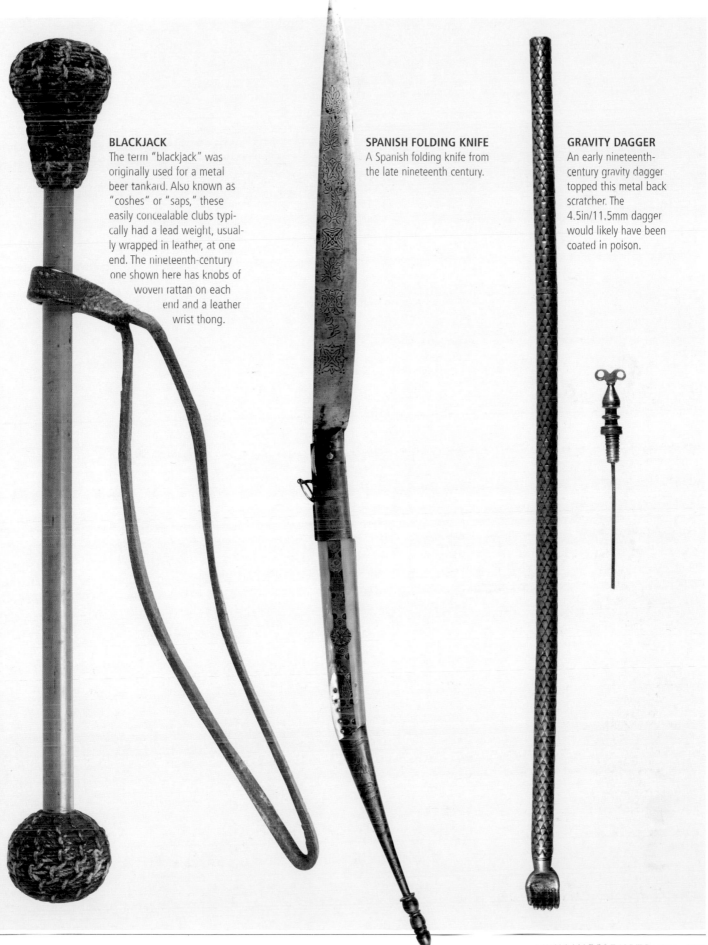

BLACKJACK
The term "blackjack" was originally used for a metal beer tankard. Also known as "coshes" or "saps," these easily concealable clubs typically had a lead weight, usually wrapped in leather, at one end. The nineteenth-century one shown here has knobs of woven rattan on each end and a leather wrist thong.

SPANISH FOLDING KNIFE
A Spanish folding knife from the late nineteenth century.

GRAVITY DAGGER
An early nineteenth-century gravity dagger topped this metal back scratcher. The 4.5in/11.5mm dagger would likely have been coated in poison.

COMBINATION WEAPONS

Weapons that combine a firearm with a blade or a club—or all three—have a pedigree that goes back to the sixteenth century. Until the advent of practical repeating firearms toward the middle of the nineteenth century, guns (unless they were multiple-barreled) could only fire one shot before reloading, therefore, giving the user an additional means of dispatching an opponent (or defending himself against said opponent) was a concern of weapons-makers. The introduction of repeating arms didn't completely end this trend; in the late nineteenth century, there was a vogue for revolver/dagger or knife combinations, and the famous (or infamous) French "Apache" managed to combine a revolver, a knife blade, and a set of brass knuckles in a single weapon. Combination weapons in our own time include "drillings" (a double-barreled shotgun with a rifle barrel—usually of European manufacture); combination guns (one shotgun barrel, one rifle barrel), and the survival guns (incorporating a small-caliber rifle and a shotgun) developed by the air forces of several nations as hunting weapons for downed aircrew stranded in remote areas awaiting rescue.

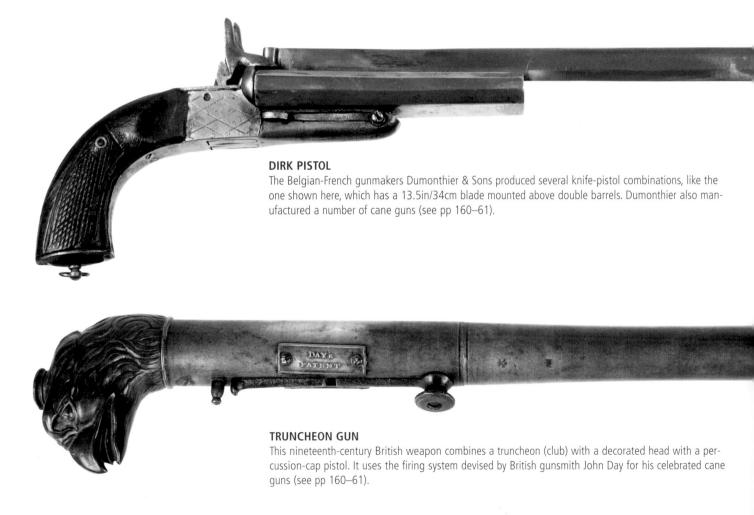

DIRK PISTOL
The Belgian-French gunmakers Dumonthier & Sons produced several knife-pistol combinations, like the one shown here, which has a 13.5in/34cm blade mounted above double barrels. Dumonthier also manufactured a number of cane guns (see pp 160–61).

TRUNCHEON GUN
This nineteenth-century British weapon combines a truncheon (club) with a decorated head with a percussion-cap pistol. It uses the firing system devised by British gunsmith John Day for his celebrated cane guns (see pp 160–61).

DAGGER PISTOL
While disguised as a dagger, this Japanese weapon is actually a single-shot percussion-cap pistol.

BATTLE-AX-GUN
Made in India around 1830, this weapon combines a battle-ax and a percussion-cap gun.

KNIFE PISTOL
The London firm of Unwin & Rodgers, a pioneer in knife-pistol combinations, made this pocket-knife pistol in the early 1870s. It incorporates a .36, muzzle-loading, single-shot pistol and two folding blades.

TURKISH GUN-SHIELD
Engraved across its entire surface and partly inlayed with gold and silver, this shield—16in/41cm in diameter—incorporates a percussion-cap gun in a wooden mount on the reverse side, with a 5in/13cm protruding barrel. Pulling a string discharged the gun.

INDIAN SHIELD WITH PISTOLS
The innocuous-looking "aged" shield hides four barrels behind its bosses, which swivel away to shoot a deadly deluge of bullets. It dates from the nineteenth century and is composed of hand-hammered steel.

ETHIOPIAN SHIELD
Some Persian shields have spikes in their center to use in combat. The one barrel protruding from the middle of this shield looks like a spike at a distance. Only at close (shooting) range is it recognizable as a gun barrel.

KNIFE REVOLVER
Another European combination weapon features a six-shot, double-action revolver with folding, curved-blade knife.

APACHE
One of the rarest and yet most famous combination weapons of the nineteenth century was the "Apache," so-called because it was supposedly used by Parisian gangsters who took the name of the warlike Native American nation. (Firearms historian Charles Edward Chapel considered its name "a gross libel on American Apache Indians.") The "Apache" combined a revolver (usually 7mm pinfire, apparently), a folding blade of about 3.5in/9cm, and a "brass knuckle" grip (see p 162). Given the shortness of the blade and the fact that the pistol component didn't even have a barrel, it's effectiveness as either a firearm or a knife is pretty doubtful.

INDIAN COMBO
Talk about multitasking: This nineteenth-century weapon—custom-made for an Indian prince—incorporates a sword; a shield; a single-shot, percussion-cap pistol; and a 12in/30.5cm needle dagger. It was made of steel with gold inlay and brass embellishments.

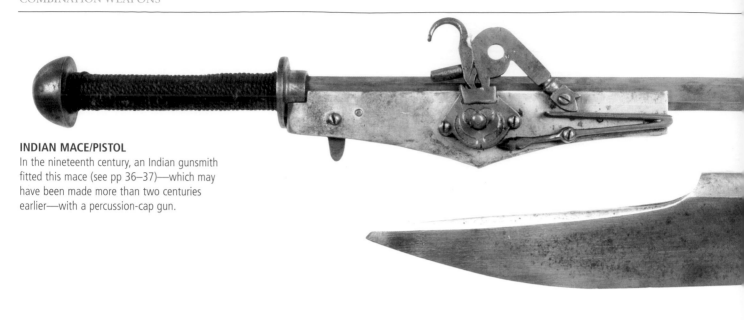

INDIAN MACE/PISTOL

In the nineteenth century, an Indian gunsmith fitted this mace (see pp 36–37)—which may have been made more than two centuries earlier—with a percussion-cap gun.

NINETEENTH-CENTURY COMBO

Another unusual nineteenth-century multi-use weapon—this one of European origin—includes a knife blade, single-shot pistol, and a shaft reinforced with metal for use as a club.

COMBO PISTOL DAGGER

This Belgian pistol (in formidable .80) includes not one but two knife blades—a 6.5in/16.5cm straight blade that slides forward from the frame, and an 8in/20cm curved blade concealed in the buttstock. In addition, the trigger guard is lengthened and reinforced to parry the sword or knife-thrust of an attacker.

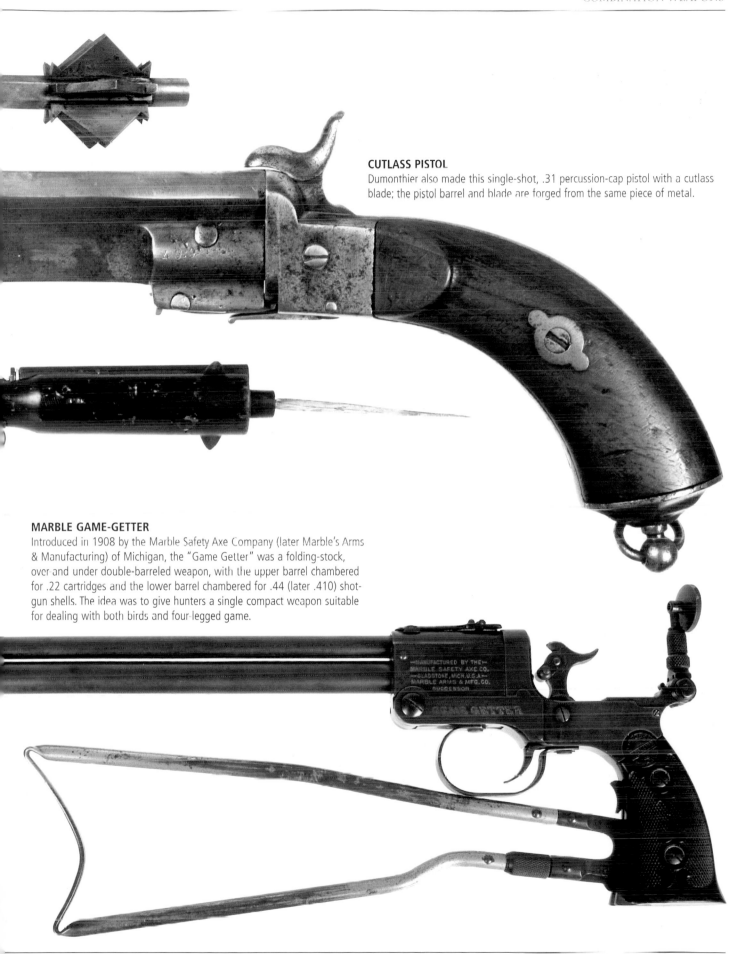

CUTLASS PISTOL

Dumonthier also made this single-shot, .31 percussion-cap pistol with a cutlass blade; the pistol barrel and blade are forged from the same piece of metal.

MARBLE GAME-GETTER

Introduced in 1908 by the Marble Safety Axe Company (later Marble's Arms & Manufacturing) of Michigan, the "Game Getter" was a folding-stock, over-and under double-barreled weapon, with the upper barrel chambered for .22 cartridges and the lower barrel chambered for .44 (later .410) shotgun shells. The idea was to give hunters a single compact weapon suitable for dealing with both birds and four-legged game.

Alarm, Trap, and Special-Purpose Guns

Not all guns are made to kill. From the introduction of gunpowder, various firearms have been used for purposes like signaling, timekeeping, and sounding alarms. The number of these special-purpose guns grew after the introduction of the percussion cap in the first half of the nineteenth century. These pages present some interesting examples from the era.

ALARM AND TRAP GUNS

The alarm gun developed to give homeowners a means of warding off burglars. Usually they were attached to windows or doors; when an intruder tried to open these, a trip wire would activate a percussion cap and fire a powder charge, or in later versions, fire a blank cartridge, alerting the homeowner and, presumably, sending the intruder fleeing. One variation consisted of a small-caliber, blank-firing pistol attached via a screw to a door or window frame, which would discharge when the door or window was opened.

Trap guns—also known as spring guns—were most commonly deployed in rural areas against poachers. Like many alarm guns, they were activated by trip wires, but unlike alarm guns, some of them were intended to fire bullets or shot instead of powder charges or blanks.

LINE-THROWING AND SIGNAL GUNS

At sea it was often necessary for one ship to get a line onto the deck of another, whether to take a damaged vessel in tow or to send across messages or supplies. This led to the development of line-throwing guns, like the pistol version shown on page 105. Coast Guards and lifeboatmen also used line-throwing cannon—like the famous U.S. Lyle Gun, used from the late nineteenth century until the 1950s—to fire lines onto wrecked ships in order to bring passengers and crew safely ashore.

Before the introduction of radio, it was customary for both merchant vessels and warships to announce their arrival in port by firing a signal guns, and it was also often necessary for ships to signal to one another with guns when fog and other weather conditions made visual signaling with flags impossible. Because firing a ship's "big guns" for such purposes was impractical, many ships carried small signal cannons like the one shown on page 170.

WALLIS ALARM GUN
This nineteenth-century alarm gun was manufactured by the Hull, England, gunsmithing firm of John Wallis. The hammer was cocked by a double-ended trip bar; when this bar was tripped by an intruder, the device set off a percussion cap.

NAYLOR TRAP GUN

Another English gunsmith, Isaac Naylor, patented this "Alarm Gun or Reporter and Detector" in 1836. It comprised a steel block with vertical chambers that were loaded with gunpowder; a percussion-cap firing mechanism was activated by the leaf-spring striker at the bottom of the device when triggered by a trip wire. The horizontal hole bored through the block allowed the device to be firmly anchored to the ground with stakes. Various models of the gun have between one and six barrels.

LINE-THROWING PISTOL

A Royal Navy percussion cap line throwing pistol from around 1860. A small line was attached to the brass rod in the barrel and fired from one ship to another using a blank cartridge; once the small line was secured, it would be used to pull across a thicker rope or cable.

NINETEENTH-CENTURY NAVAL CANNON

This nineteenth-century naval signal cannon was used for both signaling and saluting. Similar small cannon were also used for timekeeping—by firing to mark noon, for example—on land. The British Royal Navy started the custom of firing cannon salutes, and being the most formidable presence at sea, compelled ships of other nations to fire salutes first, after which the English ship would respond in kind.

GREENER'S HUMANE CATTLE KILLER

The venerable English gunmaker W W Greener—set up in 1855, later absorbing his late father's business (founded in 1829)—made this interesting device. Marketed as "Greener's Humane Cattle Killer," it was designed to do just that—quickly kill cattle or put down a horse injured beyond hope of recovery. The user unscrewed the cap at the top, inserted a .310 cartridge, replaced the cap, and placed the wide end against the horse's forehead with the notch pointing upward, keeping the barrel in line with the spinal column, so that the bullet will enter the medulla, killing the horse instantly. These were issued to veterinarians accompanying British Army cavalry units in World War I. W W Greener continues to make high-quality arms.

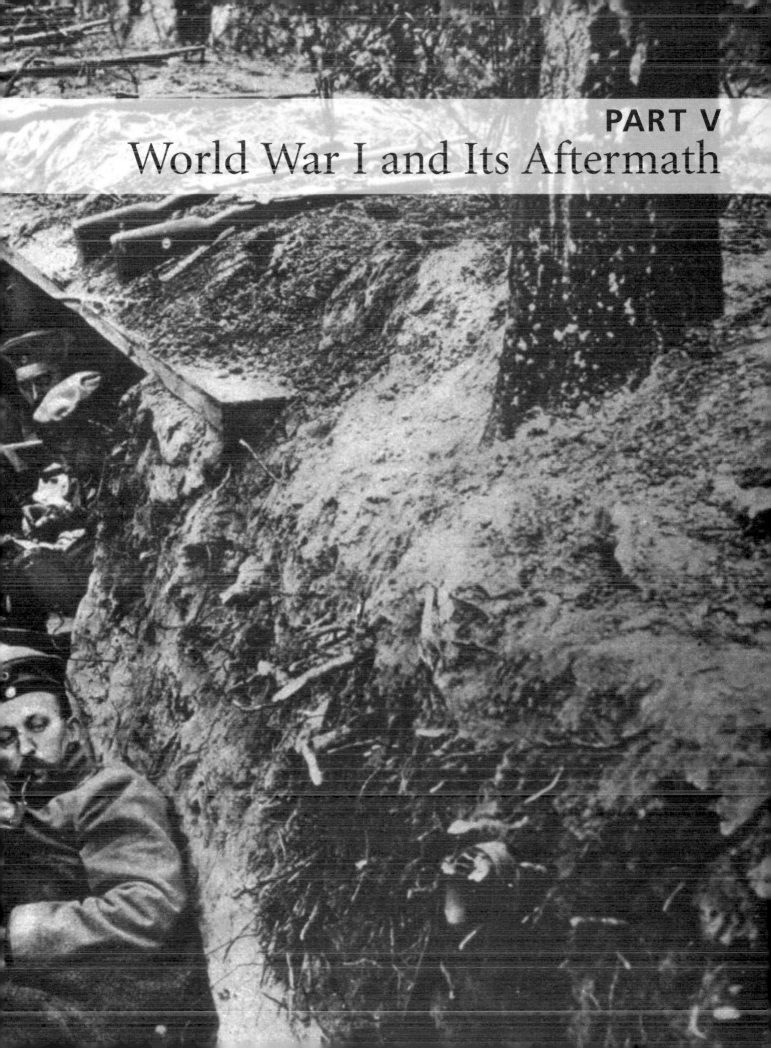

PART V

World War I and Its Aftermath

"But that he has not taken with him his sword red with blood as he intended,—that he has left us alive,—that we wrested the weapon from his hands,—that he has left the citizens safe and the city standing, what great and overwhelming grief must you think that this is to him!"

—Cicero, "The Second Oration Against Catiline," 63 BCE

World War I (1914–18) saw the convergence of the weapons technologies that had developed over the previous century or so—with horrific results for soldiers in all the armies involved. The bolt-action rifle was by now the standard infantryman's weapon, but this war would be dominated not by the rifle but by heavy, crew-served machine guns and rapid-firing artillery delivering heavy explosive and shrapnel shells. The early battlefields of the Western Front proved so deadly that both sides dug in, until a continuous line of trenches snaked across Belgium and France.

World War I also saw the introduction of new weapons like tanks, aircraft, flamethrowers, and—perhaps most terrifying—poison gas. The success of the machine gun, and the need for a weapon that would be more effective in trench fighting than conventional rifles, led armies to experiment with automatic weapons that could be carried into combat by individuals, including automatic rifles and submachine guns, although these innovations arrived too late to make much of a difference.

EDGED WEAPONS OF WORLD WAR I

World War I was a conflict of mass firepower, with machine guns and artillery dealing death at long distances. But the war also saw infantrymen engaged in episodes of desperate close-quarters combat—particularly in the trenches of the Western Front in World War I. Even in modern warfare, edged weapons found a place.

TRENCH KNIVES

By the outbreak of the "Great War," swords were mostly considered ceremonial weapons in European armies—except for sabers, which were still issued to cavalrymen. The mounted forces of the warring armies didn't have much opportunity to wield their sabers.

Although the first clash between the British and German forces—at the Battle of Mons, in August 1914—was a cavalry action, the war on the Western Front in France and Belgium quickly settled into static trench warfare in which cavalry played little part. (The British Army, however, kept large reserves of cavalry in hopes that it could exploit breaches in the German lines.)

Every infantrymen had a bayonet for his rifle—hence the classic images of soldiers going "over the top" and advancing, bayonets fixed, into the "no man's land" that separated the opposing trenches. Even if the World War I infantryman survived a hail of machine-gun fire to reach the enemy's lines, however, using the bayonet was an awkward business in the close confines of a trench. So soldiers increasingly turned to knives in hand-to-hand fights, and several armies developed purpose-built "trench knives" or "trench daggers" like those shown on these pages.

World War I soldiers also improvised edged weapons to meet trench-fighting conditions—weapons that would have been recognizable to medieval warriors. Some sharpened the edges of spades to a bladelike sharpness. Others attached knives to poles to create twentieth-century versions of the pike (see p 40) or halberd (see pp 40–41).

GERMAN SABER
A German cavalry saber from the World War I era.

GERMAN COMBAT KNIFE

The compact *grabendoch* (trench dagger) was widely issued to front-line German troops during World War I. This model has a blade of about 5.75in/14.5cm and an overall length of about 10in/25cm.

US 1917 TRENCH KNIFE

In 1917, the U.S. Army developed a fighting knife (shown with its leather scabbard) designed especially for close combat. It was a triple-threat weapon, featuring a triangular stabbing blade, a handle that doubled as a set of "brass knuckles," and a heavy "skull crusher" pommel cap.

US 1918 TRENCH KNIFE

The original 1917 U.S. trench knife was found to be too fragile and replaced with model shown here, which had a handle of solid brass.

PISTOLS OF WORLD WAR I

In World War I, pistols were carried chiefly by officers and NCOs. They remained a standard cavalry weapon, as they'd been for centuries, but mounted troops played little role in World War I. Still, pistols were prized by frontline infantrymen for use in close combat; they also were carried by tank crews, aircrew, and support troops as a defensive weapon in conditions that made the use of a rifle impractical.

THE REVOLVER

By the time World War I began in 1914 the automatic pistol (see pp 152–55) was finally winning acceptance among the world's armed forces. Switzerland and Germany, for example, had adopted the 9mm Luger, while the U.S. (which would enter the war in 1917) adopted the Colt .45 automatic in 1911. Many military officers, however, believed (with some justification) that automatics, which are far more complicated mechanically than revolvers, weren't reliable or rugged enough to withstand the rigors of muddy, dusty, and damp combat conditions. Throughout the war, the British Army remained strongly devoted to the revolvers made by the Birmingham firm of Webley & Scott, which first entered service in the 1880s; the French used the Lebel revolver, and the Russians, the Nagant—although pistols of any kind were in short supply in the under-equipped Russian Army. Also, most automatics of the era were chambered for the 7.65mm or 9mm cartridge, which supposedly had less "stopping power" than heavier .38 or .45/.455 revolver rounds—.45/.455 being equivalent of 11mm.

BERGMANN-BAYARD M1910
Designed by Danish gunmaker Theodore Bergmann (see p 152) and his associates, the Bergmann-Bayard M1910 was a 9mm automatic that could take either a six- or ten-round magazine. Besides being the official Danish sidearm, it was adopted by the armies of Belgium, Greece, and Spain. They were also widely used by the Danish resistance movement during the German occupation of that country in World War II.

GERMAN REVOLVER
Despite the adoption of the Luger, many German cavalrymen of World War I carried six-shot, .44 revolvers like the one shown here. The ring on the butt accommodated a lanyard that secured the pistol to the trooper's clothing or gear.

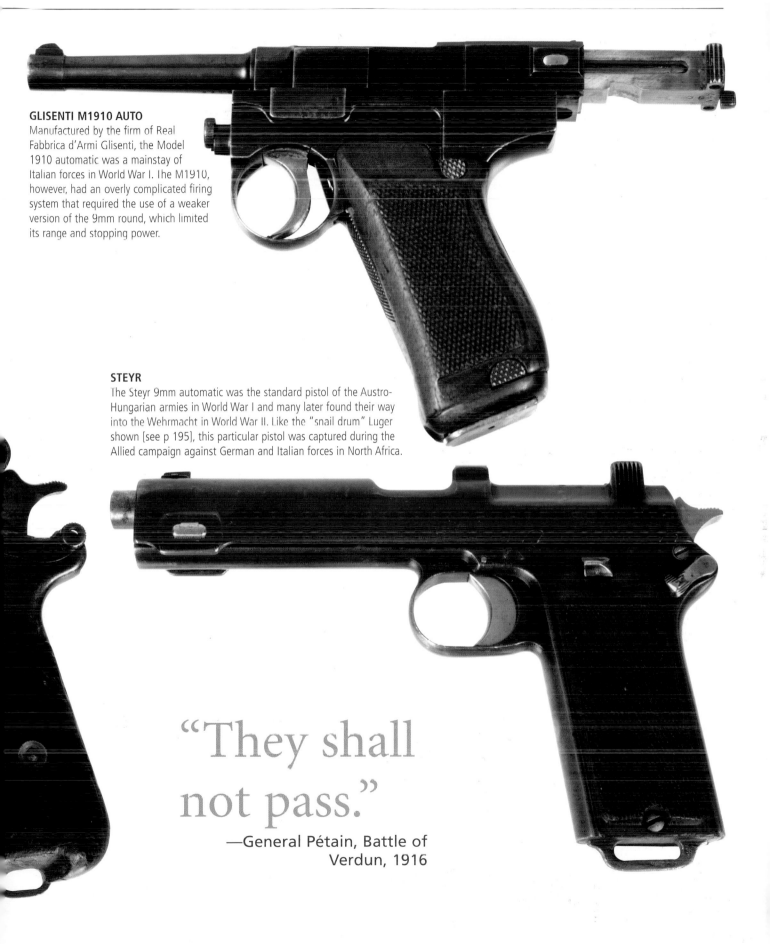

GLISENTI M1910 AUTO
Manufactured by the firm of Real Fabbrica d'Armi Glisenti, the Model 1910 automatic was a mainstay of Italian forces in World War I. The M1910, however, had an overly complicated firing system that required the use of a weaker version of the 9mm round, which limited its range and stopping power.

STEYR
The Steyr 9mm automatic was the standard pistol of the Austro-Hungarian armies in World War I and many later found their way into the Wehrmacht in World War II. Like the "snail drum" Luger shown [see p 195], this particular pistol was captured during the Allied campaign against German and Italian forces in North Africa.

"They shall not pass."

—General Pétain, Battle of Verdun, 1916

Infantry Rifles of World War I

From the turn of the twentieth century, military rifle technology advanced at a slower pace than that of other weapons. The World War I infantryman in most armies went into battle carrying a rifle with a design pedigree dating back to the mid-nineteenth century.

IF AIN'T BROKE …

There were valid reasons for this relative conservatism. Bolt-action rifles were sturdy, and mechanically simple, and accurate over long distances—typically up to 500–600yd/1650–1980 meters. The main trend in rifle development before World War I was simply to make infantry rifles shorter and lighter, blurring the nineteenth-century distinction between rifle and carbine: Examples include the U.S. Springfield M1903, the British SMLE (Short Magazine Lee-Enfield) and the German KAR-98.

Although a well-trained soldier could get off about 15 shots per minute with World War I–era bolt-action rifles, weapons designers were already working on semiautomatic rifles to increase the volume of infantry firepower. (Operating by means of recoil or from the energy of the gas created as a fired cartridge left the barrel, semiautomatic rifles—also known as autoloading rifles—fire once for every pull of the trigger.)

SEMIAUTOMATICS ARRIVE

From the mid-1890s onward, the military establishments of Denmark, Mexico, Germany, Russia, and Italy experimented with semiautomatic rifles, but none saw widespread use. Experimentation continued, but adoption of the semiautomatic rifle was slowed by the same concerns over replacement of revolvers with automatic pistols (see p 152)—the relative complexity of semiautomatic rifles compared to bolt-action rifles, and the fact that most semiautomatics fired a lighter, shorter cartridge. In addition, officers worried that troops armed with rapid-fire rifles would expend their ammunition too quickly.

KAR-98

The 7.92mm KAR-98 (for karabiner, model 1998) was the standard German infantry rifle in both world wars. It used the classic forward-locking Mauser bolt action, weighed 8.5lb/3.9kg, and had an integral 5-round box magazine.

EDDYSTONE ENFIELD

The U.S. entered World War I in April 1917 with an arms industry woefully unprepared to equip a large army. Because of difficulties in expanding production of the standard U.S. Army rifle, the M1903 Springfield, the army also adopted a rifle based on the British Enfield, because the latter weapon was already in production in the U.S. under contract. The result was the U.S. Rifle Model 1917—basically, an Enfield with an action and magazine modified for the U.S .30 cartridges.

"INDIAN PATTERN" BAYONET

Many early SMLEs were issued with an impractically long and cumbersome sword-style bayonet. Historian Pierre Berton notes that during World War I, Canadian troops considered this particular model of bayonet useless for anything except toasting bread over campfires.

MKII BAYONET

This spike-type bayonet was made for use with one of the SMLE's successors, the SMLE Mark IV, during World War II. It was manufactured by the U.S. firm of Stevens-Savage under contract with the British government.

ENFIELD

With a design incorporating lessons learned in the Boer War (1899–1902), the first version of the .303 SMLE (Short Magazine Lee-Enfield), the Mark III, entered service with the British Army in 1907. The SMLE's action gave it a high rate of fire relative to other rifles of the time, and it had a 10-round magazine. When German troops came under British fire early in World War I, the British put up such a sustained, rapid fire that the Germans believed they were under attack by machine guns.

US GAS MASK

Poison gas was one of World War I's special horrors. Both the French and the German armies used irritant gases (i.e., tear gas) early in the war, but gas warfare entered a more deadly phase during the Battle of Ypres in April 1915, when the Germans wafted chlorine gas toward British trenches. Soon both sides used gases, mainly delivered by artillery shells. Some gases (like mustard gas) disabled victims, others (like phosgene) were often immediately fatal. Early countermeasures were crude   such as holding urine-soaked cotton wadding over the nose and mouth—but as the war went on, increasingly effective gas masks, or "respirators," were developed. The one shown here was issued to U.S. troops.

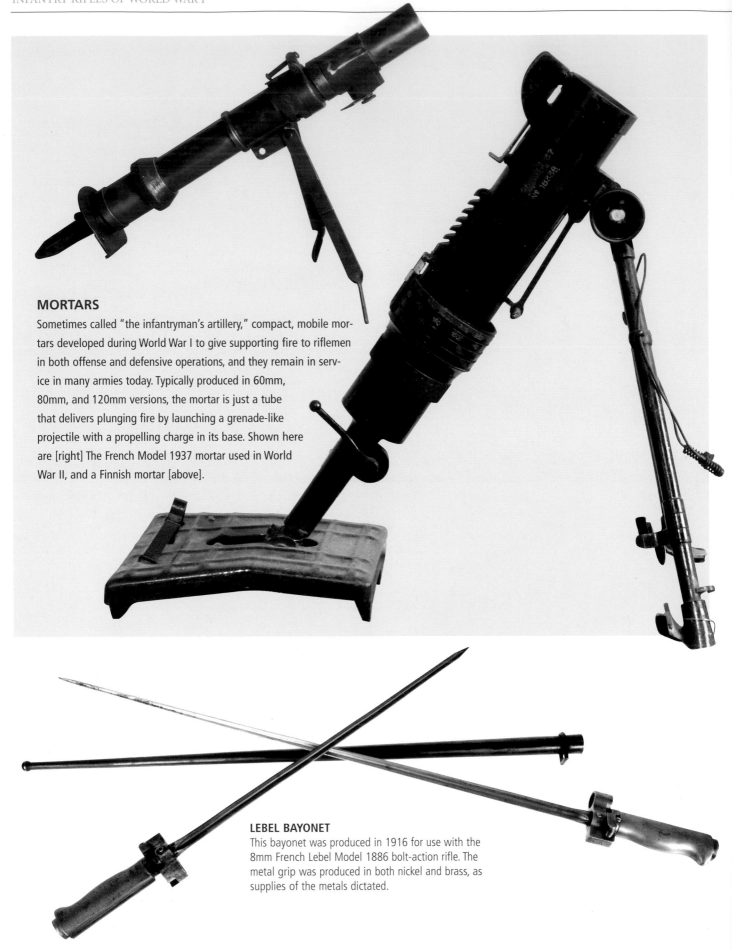

MORTARS

Sometimes called "the infantryman's artillery," compact, mobile mortars developed during World War I to give supporting fire to riflemen in both offense and defensive operations, and they remain in service in many armies today. Typically produced in 60mm, 80mm, and 120mm versions, the mortar is just a tube that delivers plunging fire by launching a grenade-like projectile with a propelling charge in its base. Shown here are [right] The French Model 1937 mortar used in World War II, and a Finnish mortar [above].

LEBEL BAYONET

This bayonet was produced in 1916 for use with the 8mm French Lebel Model 1886 bolt-action rifle. The metal grip was produced in both nickel and brass, as supplies of the metals dictated.

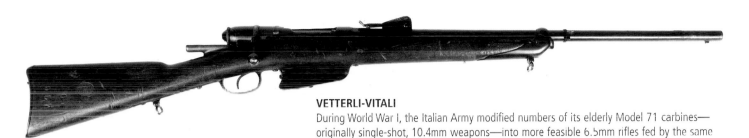

VETTERLI-VITALI

During World War I, the Italian Army modified numbers of its elderly Model 71 carbines—originally single-shot, 10.4mm weapons—into more feasible 6.5mm rifles fed by the same 6-round magazine used by the Mannlicher-Carcano M1891.

JAPANESE PARATROOP RIFLE

Because the standard 7.7mm Arisaka rifle was too long for use in airborne operations, the Japanese military developed a special version for paratroops that could be broken down into two pieces for the jump and then reassembled on landing. Relatively few saw service.

MOSIN-NAGANT M91/30/59

Drawing on design elements provided by the Russian Colonel Sergei Mosin and Belgian Leon Nagant, the 7.62mm, bolt-action Mosin-Nagant would, in various models and upgrades, remain the standard Russian (and later Soviet) infantry rifle from the early 1890s until around 1950.

RUSSIAN CARBINE M1944

The Mosin-Nagant Carbine M944, introduced toward the end of World War II, was the final iteration of the Mosin-Nagant series. Its most distinctive feature was an integral bayonet that folded into the stock.

MANNLICHER-CARCANO

Although they bear the name of the Austro-German gun designer Ferdinand Ritter von Mannlicher, the Mannlicher-Carcano series of 6.5mm carbines and rifles—the mainstay of the Italian armed forces from 1891 through World War II—were actually based on a Mauser design. (The "Carcano" designation is for Salvatore Carcano, a designer at the Italian government arsenal at Turin). The Model 1941 rifle is shown here. The Mannlicher-Carcano gained postwar notoriety in 1963, when Lee Harvey Oswald used a ML carbine he'd purchased through the mail to assassinate U.S. president John F. Kennedy.

MACHINE GUNS OF WORLD WAR I

The concept of an automatic weapon—one that would fire continuously for as long as the operator pulled back the trigger—goes back to at least 1718, when Englishmen James Puckle proposed a multi-cylinder "defence gun." Several manually operated rapid-fire guns were introduced in the mid-nineteenth century. Some, like the U.S. Gatling gun (see p 145) were relatively successful. Others, like the French Mitrailleuse, were not. The first modern machine gun, the Maxim gun, appeared in 1885 (see sidebar). First used in large numbers in the Russo-Japanese War (1904–05), the machine gun changed warfare forever during World War I, and it remains a principal weapon of the world's arsenals in the twenty-first century.

THE BIRTH OF THE MACHINE GUN

Although it had competition from weapons like the British Gardner gun and the Swedish Nordenfeldt gun, the Maxim design was adopted by a number of nations from the 1880s through the early 1900s. Appearing at the high point of European imperialism, the Maxim and other rapid-fire guns proved useful in slaughtering indigenous peoples in colonial conflicts, prompting British writer Hilaire Belloc to rhyme sardonically: "Whatever happens, we have got/The Maxim gun, and they have not."

Then came World War I. Though the British Army had been among the first to adopt the machine gun, it went into action underequipped with the weapon and underestimating its effects, while the French were convinced that "the spirit of the attack" would overcome automatic fire. The German Army did not labor under these misapprehensions, however, and the Allies suffered accordingly—but would rapidly catch up in the firepower sweepstakes.

As many historians have noted, most brilliantly John Ellis in his *The Social History of the Machine Gun*, the devastation wrought by the machine gun in World War I had a psychological as well as a physical aspect. The machine gun reduced killing to an industrial process. It represented the nexus of the Industrial Revolution and the age of mass warfare. Future British Prime Minister Winston Churchill—who spent ninety days as an infantry officer in the trenches of the Western Front—was certainly thinking of the machine gun when he wrote, in a postwar memoir, "War, which used to be cruel and magnificent, has now become cruel and squalid . . ."

MARLIN MACHINE GUN

When the U.S. entered World War I in April 1917, the U.S. Army contracted Marlin Arms to produce a version of the .30 Colt-Browning Model 1895 machine gun, which was already in use by the Navy. Designed by the great John Browning (see p 153), the gun had a big disadvantage in infantry combat: The gas system used a piston that moved back and forth below the barrel, so it could be fired only from a fairly high tripod mount—thus exposing the crew to enemy fire. Because of the piston's tendency to hit the ground below, troops nicknamed it the "potato-digger."

LEWIS LIGHT MACHINE GUN

The British Army went into World War I using a couple of American machine-gun designs, including the Lewis Light Machine Gun. Developed by U.S. Army officer Noah Lewis in 1911, the .303, gas-operated weapon was fed by a tubular 50-round top-mounted magazine, and it had a distinctive "shroud" to cool the barrel. It was widely used to arm Allied aircraft, and a .30 version was developed for U.S. forces.

FRENCH CHAUCHET

One of World War I's worst weapons, France's Chauchat automatic rifle was poorly made from sub-standard components, and it was fed by 8mm Lebel rifle cartridges from a crescent-shaped magazine, an inaccurate and unreliable system for an automatic weapon. When U.S. troops arrived on the Western Front, they were equipped with large numbers of this weapon re-chambered for the American .30 round. In addition to its inherent faults, most of these guns were mechanically clapped-out from years of service. American soldiers and marines—who called the weapon the "Cho-Cho"—considered it worse than useless, and they usually were left behind before going into action.

COLT VICKERS

Shortly before World War I, the British Army adopted the Vickers gun as its standard heavy machine gun. A .303 water-cooled gun based on the basic Maxim design, the weapon's biggest drawback was its weight—83lb/37.7kg with its tripod. It typically required a crew of six to carry and operate.

GERMAN SPANDAU MAXIM

Officially the Maxim LMG 08/15, the "Spandau" got its nickname from one of Imperial Germany's arsenals. The 7.92mm, water-cooled, belt-fed weapon was the standard armament for German aircraft from 1915 on, after the development of the "interrupter gear," which synchronized the weapon's firing rate with the revolution of the aircraft's propeller, allowing the gun to shoot safely through the plane's propeller arc.

SIR HIRAM MAXIM

Born in Maine in 1840, Hiram Maxim became a prolific inventor at an early age, patenting—among other items—the proverbial "better mousetrap." While attending an industrial exhibition in Paris in 1881, a friend told him that if he really wanted to make a fortune, he should "invent something that will enable these Europeans to cut each other's throats with greater facility." Maxim took these words to heart, and a few years later he unveiled the gun that would bear his name. Fed by a continuous belt of ammunition (initially .45, later .303), the Maxim gun was recoil-operated; the operator cocked and fired the weapon, and the recoil ejected the spent cartridge and chambered a new round. Because the rapid rate of fire—up to 600 rounds per minute—could melt the barrel, he surrounded it with a jacket filled with water. (Later "air-cooled" machine guns would use a perforated metal jacket.) The Maxim design was soon adopted by several nations, including Britain, and reportedly, turn-of-the-twentieth century Maxims were being used by the Chinese Army in the Korean War more than a half-century later. Maxim took British citizenship and, in 1901, was knighted for his services.

TRENCH WARFARE

In 1897, a Polish-Jewish financier named Ivan Bloch (c. 1832–1902) published a book titled *The War of the Future*. Bloch contended that given the combination of mass conscript armies and weapons like machine guns and quick-firing artillery firing explosive shells, any European conflict would degenerate into a war of attrition fought by soldiers burrowing into the earth for protection. His theory was ignored or scoffed at. Not much more than a decade after his death, he would be proved a prophet. Even after the horrors of World War II and the nuclear knife-edge of the Cold War, the misery and deadliness of the trench warfare of World War I haunts the Western world into the twenty-first century.

THE WESTERN FRONT

Trench warfare was not new in 1914. During the American Civil War (1861–65), the effectiveness of the rifled musket (see pp xx) was such that both sides learned the value of "digging in." Indeed, photographs of the Union Army's lines around Petersburg, Virginia—the gateway to the Confederate capital at Richmond—in 1864–65 are eerily similar to photographs of the Western Front in France and Belgium fifty years later.

Observers from European armies failed to learn any lessons from that conflict. When World War I broke out in Europe in August 1914, the French Army still held to the doctrine of *"L'Attaque! Toujours l'attaque!"*("The attack—always the attack!"), believing that a spirited offense over open ground would always overwhelm the enemy. In the opening months of the conflict, the French managed to hold the Germans attackers on the Marne River and save Paris from capture, but their tactics cost hundreds of thousands of lives.

Thereafter the French and their British allies established a line of trenches that stretched nearly 500 miles from the English Channel to the Swiss border, separated from the German trenches by a "no-man's-land" that in places was no more than a few hundred feet or even less.

LIFE AND DEATH IN THE TRENCHES

These trenches ranged from mere scratched-out ditches to (especially on the largely defensive German side) elaborate positions with bunkers well below ground to give protection from shellfire. In general, though, trench lines consisted of forward trenches directly facing the enemy, backed by a couple of lines of support trenches, connected to each other and to the rear by communication trenches. Beds of barbed wire protected the forward trenches, which also had extensions known as saps for placement of machine guns, snipers, and observation posts to keep tabs on the enemy.

For soldiers in all armies, life in the trenches was miserable, so much so that whenever possible units were rotated to rear areas after a few days or weeks on the front line. They had to endure cold, wet, lice, and rats—the last often bloated from feeding on corpses. Uninterrupted sleep was impossible thanks to snipers and artillery barrages. Even in the quiet periods between major offensives, there was a steady stream of casualties from conditions like "trench foot" (caused by prolonged immersion of the feet in the water that inevitably collected in the bottom of trenches) and among men sent into "no-man's-land" each night to install or repair barbed wire, or on combat patrols against enemy positions to seize prisoners for questioning. The British referred to these attritional casualties as "normal wastage." And besides these miseries, there was the ever present threat of gas (see p 181), and the psychological injuries—dubbed "shell shock"—as men broke down from hardship, the strain of combat, and particularly, the shattering effects of artillery bombardment.

WEAPONS OF TRENCH WARFARE

For hundreds of years, infantry had generally been the decisive factor on European battlefields, but in World War I artillery achieved preeminence. At the Third Battle of Ypres in 1917, for example, British artillery fired a staggering 4.7 million shells over three weeks. The intent, in this as in many other battles, was to "soften" the enemy in preparation for infantry assault across no-man's-land. However, these bombardments rarely achieved their purpose. Dug deep into the ground, the Germans were usual able to emerge with their machine guns intact and ready to scour the advancing Allied infantry. On the first day of the First Battle of the Somme—July 1, 1916—for example, British forces suffered 58,000 casualties, one-third of them deaths. By the time the offensive halted four months later, the British had lost 420,000 men in all—for a gain of 7.5km/12mi.

In an effort to break the deadlock on the Western Front, the British developed a new weapon—the tank, a tracked, armored "land battleship." While tanks had some success, especially at the Battle of Cambrai (November 20–December 7, 1917), they didn't prove a decisive factor in the war. For their part, the Germans sought to break the deadlock by developing tactics based around small groups of *strosstruppen* (literally, "storm troops") armed with new weapons like flamethrowers and submachine guns (see pp 208–09).

Despite these innovations, some weapons of trench warfare were throwbacks to the past. Personal armor reappeared in the form of steel helmets; raiding parties carried improvised pole arms (see pp 40–41), clubs, and edged weapons; and the hand grenade—whose use had declined after the eighteenth century—once again became an important part of the infantryman's personal arsenal.

In the end, attrition prevailed. In the spring of 1918, the Germans launched a series of offensives aimed at knocking out the British and French before large numbers of American troops (the U.S. had entered the war a year earlier) arrived in France. They narrowly failed. The guns finally fell silent at 11:00 a.m. on November 11, 1918—by which time the trenches of the Western Front had become graves for millions of young men.

GUNS OF THE AMERICAN ROARING TWENTIES

In January 1920, Prohibition—a federal ban on the "manufacture, sale, or transportation" of alcohol—went into effect in the United States. Intended to stop the crime and social ills associated with drinking, this "noble experiment" backfired badly. People still wanted to drink, "bootleggers" were willing to make or smuggle alcohol, and organized crime, sniffing rich profits, stepped in to control the trade in illicit hooch. Throughout the 1920s and beyond, gangsters fought each other and the authorities using a variety of powerful weapons, forcing law-enforcement agencies to catch up in the firepower stakes.

THE TOMMY GUN

The most iconic weapon of the 1920s is surely the Thompson Submachine Gun. Much to the embarrassment of its inventor, John T. Thompson (see sidebar), who had developed it for military use, the weapon was eagerly taken up by gangsters in Chicago and other cities and put to deadly use in their battles with rival gangs and with the authorities. (Given the lax gun-control laws of the era, obtaining weapons—even automatic weapons—was not difficult for criminals.)

The Thompson soon earned a variety of nicknames, including the "Tommy Gun," the "Chicago typewriter," and the "chopper." Perhaps the Thompson's most notorious application came in the "St. Valentine's Day Massacre" of 1929, when members of Al Capone's gang murdered seven associates of a rival concern in a Chicago garage. The power of the Thompson's .45 ACP rounds at close range was such that several of the victim's bodies were reportedly cut nearly in half.

PISTOLS IN POCKETS, BANDITS ON WHEELS

The success of the Thompson in outlaw hands led many law-enforcement agencies, including the FBI, to finally purchase the weapon; the Thompson would be part of the "G-Men's" arsenal for decades. The FBI also made use of the BAR (see p 207). Most local police forces, however, remained armed solely with revolvers and shotguns—giving the lawmen a distinctive disadvantage when gangsters came to town.

Another weapons development of the 1920s was the widespread adoption of "pocket pistols" by criminals. These were small automatic pistols, usually in .22 or .25 caliber, which, as the name implies, could be easily concealed in a coat pocket, ankle holster, or tucked behind the belt in the small of the back. They were handy weapons in case a bootlegging deal went bad, or in last-ditch struggles to escape the police.

Prohibition ended in 1933, but the Great Depression saw the rise of a new breed of outlaw: The "motorized bandits" who roamed the roads of the Midwest and Southwest commiting crime. Such felons included the Barker Gang, John Dillinger, "Pretty Boy" Floyd, and Bonnie Parker and Clyde Barrow. These outlaws also made use of the Thompson, sawed-off shotguns, and even the BAR, the latter sometimes in cut-down form.

MITRAILLEUSE
This highly unusual gun, dubbed a "window revolver" was made in France as a defensive weapon; it was fitted to a window or barricade, and the firer, under cover, pulled a string attached to the lever to fire and advance each of the 24 cylinders. By some accounts, Al Capone's gang mounted the gun on the bows of the motorboats used to bring in illegal booze from Canada in case they encountered U.S. Customs patrols or other authorities. This would have been impractical under these circumstances, as the weapon could only be aimed by steering the boat directly at the target.

COLT POLICE POSITIVE
By the 1920s many U.S. policemen and private armed guards carried .32 or .38 Colt "Police Positive" revolvers. The name came from a new safety feature, introduced in 1905, which separated the hammer from the firing pin, thus reducing the chances of accidental discharge. This particular .38 was manufactured for use by security guards of Wells Fargo & Co.

LILIPUT PISTOL

The Liliput series of automatic pistols made by Waffenfabrik August Menz in Germany was aptly named—this one measures 3.5 in./8.9cm long; to keep the weapon as small as possible, Menz chambered it for the rare 4.25mm round. (Other, slightly larger Liliput models used a 6.35mm round.) The 1927 4.25mm is shown here.

J. T. THOMPSON

Born in Kentucky in 1860, John Taliaferro Thompson graduated from West Point and served as an artillery officer before joining the U.S. Army's Ordnance Department. During his long tenure, Thompson played a key role in the development of the Springfield M1903 rifle and the Colt M1911 pistol. During World War I, Thompson became convinced that the Allies needed a handheld automatic weapon—which he dubbed a "trench broom"—to break the stalemate on the Western Front, and he set up a firm, the Auto-Ordnance Company, to manufacture such a gun. The result was the Thompson Submachine Gun. Unfortunately, the gun went into production too late to see service, leaving Auto-Ordnance with a large inventory. Thompson tried to sell the weapon to police forces, with only modest success. As a result, he lost control of Auto-Ordnance. Thompson died in 1940, just as the Thompson came into its own as an Allied weapon in a new world war.

GAS BILLY CLUB

A real rarity: Federal Laboratories Inc. of Pittsburgh, Pennsylvania, produced this combination billy club/tear-gas launcher for police use in the mid-1920s.

PARKER BROTHERS SHOTGUN

In the prosperous 1920s, many Americans adopted skeet shooting and fowl hunting as a hobby. Parker Brothers of Meriden, Connecticut, made this 20-gauge shotgun in 1928. Made especially for women shooters, it is lightweight (6lb/2.7kg) and has a lighter trigger pull than the standard model.

THOMPSON

The Thompson submachine used a delayed-blowback operation developed by U.S. Navy officer John Blish. It fired the same .45 ACP cartridge as the Colt M1911 pistol and fed either from a 50-round drum magazine or a 20 (later 30)-round box magazine. Hollywood forever linked the "Tommy Gun" with U.S. gang wars of the 1920s in the public mind, but the weapon also first saw military service during the decade. The Irish Republican Army (IRA) in the Irish Civil War of the early 1920s also used the Thompson; in 1928, the U.S. Navy adopted the gun as the M1928A1 (the model shown here), and marines used it to fight a leftist insurgency in Nicaragua. It was later adopted by the U.S. Army and remained the standard U.S. submachine well into World War II, in the M1A1 model, which simplified some aspects of the action and eliminated the forward grip and the capacity to take the drum magazine. An excellent weapon, the Thompson's chief drawbacks were its weight (over 10lb/4.5kg) and its manufacturing cost.

"Wars may be fought with weapons, but they are won by men. It is the spirit of men who follow and of the man who leads that gains the victory."

—General George S. Patton

To a great extent, World War II (1939–45) was fought with weapons that had their antecedents in World War I. Automatic pistols, already in widespread use during the earlier conflict, replaced the revolver as the standard military sidearm. Submachine guns—from the U.S. Thompson to the German MP40 "Schmeisser" to the cheap and simple Ppsh 41 used by the Soviet Red Army—joined the infantry's arsenal. The years preceding the war also saw various nations experimenting with semi-automatic, or self-loading, rifles to replace bolt-action models, but only the U.S. Army made such a weapon its standard rifle during the war itself, in the form of the M1 Garand.

During the war, Germany developed the MP44 Sturmgewher ("assault rifle"), an innovative weapon that combined the rapid-fire capabilities of the submachine gun with the range and "stopping power" of the rifle. The MP44 is the direct ancestor of the assault rifles that became the dominant infantry weapon of the postwar world, the outstanding examples being the AK47 (first produced in the Soviet Union, but manufactured worldwide in huge numbers and in several variations) and the U.S. M16.

Edged Weapons of World War II

In World War II, edged weapons were used most widely in the Allied struggle to push back the tide of Japanese conquest in the Pacific. The Japanese military's code of Bushido placed great emphasis on close-in fighting, and U.S. troops fighting on the Pacific islands often faced Japanese Banzai charges—wild onrushes of infantry led by officers brandishing swords, which were inevitably referred to as "Samurai swords" by their American opponents. (In fact, some Japanese did carry swords that had been passed down in their families for generations.) Japanese troops were also expert at infiltrating American positions at night, often leading to grim hand-to-hand fights in which the Marine Corps fighting knife, the legendary Ka-Bar, proved its worth.

Knives were also utilized in all theaters of the war by Commandos and other special forces, and by operatives of agencies such as the U.S. OSS and the British SOE (see pp 212–13) for assassinations and "silent elimination" of sentries. Undoubtedly the most famous of these weapons was the Sykes-Fairbairn Commando Knife.

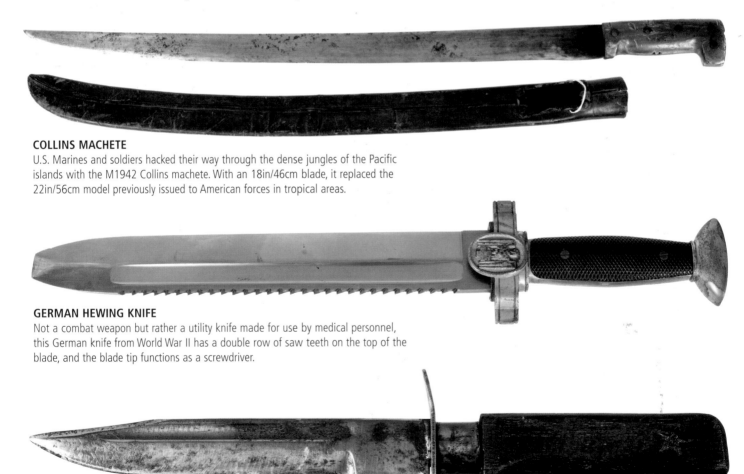

COLLINS MACHETE
U.S. Marines and soldiers hacked their way through the dense jungles of the Pacific islands with the M1942 Collins machete. With an 18in/46cm blade, it replaced the 22in/56cm model previously issued to American forces in tropical areas.

GERMAN HEWING KNIFE
Not a combat weapon but rather a utility knife made for use by medical personnel, this German knife from World War II has a double row of saw teeth on the top of the blade, and the blade tip functions as a screwdriver.

RUSSIAN FIGHTING KNIFE
A Russian fighting knife of World War II. Like most Soviet weapons, Red Army knives were simple, sturdy, and designed to be manufactured cheaply and in large quantities.

SYKES-FAIRBAIRN

One of the most famous knives of World War II, the Sykes-Fairbairn Commando Knife was widely used by U.S. and American special forces. Developed by two experts in hand to hand combat (see sidebar) it was a lightweight, stainless steel weapon. The slender 7.5 in/19mc blade was designed especially to slip between the ribs of an opponent.

W. E. FAIRBAIRN AND ERIC SYKES

While serving as a police officer in Shanghai, China, in the early 1900s, William Ewart Fairbairn became one of the first Westerners to achieve proficiency in Asian martial arts. (Ironically, in light of later events, he initially trained with a Japanese instructor.) Fairbairn eventually rose to command the Shanghai Municipal Police, and together with his colleague Eric Sykes, began training his officers in hybrid hand-to-hand fighting techniques they named the "Defendu System." With the coming of World War II Sykes and Fairbairn were recalled to Britain, where they began teaching their system to the newly formed Commandos. During this time, the duo designed the famous dagger-style knife that bears their names. With the U.S. entry into the war, Fairbairn left for America to train the OSS; Sykes stayed on to work with SOE and SIS (Secret Intelligence Service).

KA-BAR

Officially the "USN Fighting Knife, Mark 2" but universally known as the Ka-Bar after an advertising slogan of its manufacturer, the Union Cutlery Co., the Ka-Bar was the official fighting knife of the U.S. Marine Corps in World War. Its famously tough construction made it an excellent utility knife as well as a fighting weapon.

"Ka-Bar was there."

—advertising slogan

AXIS PISTOLS

With little room for improvement in revolver design, the interwar years saw automatics become the standard sidearm in most armies. The Soviet Union adopted the Tokarev, which the great weapons writer Ian Hogg described as a "[Colt] M1911 with a distinctive Russian accent." In Japan, the Nambu series of automatics (named for Colonel Nambu Kirijo, the nation's foremost weapons designer), chambered for 8mm, came into use. The Walther P38 gradually replaced the Luger in the Wehrmacht (German Army) during World War II.

CZ27 AUTO
A refinement of a German design, the Ceska Zbrojovoka Model 1927 (CZ27) was a straight blowback-operated 9mm with a 9-round magazine. Following its occupation of Czechoslovakia, Germany diverted the production of that nation's excellent arms industry, including Ceska Zbrojovoka, for its own use.

NAMBU M94
Many firearms experts consider the notorious Japanese Nambu Type 94 automatic to be the worst military pistol of modern times. The cocking mechanism was so poorly designed that the weapon could fire accidentally if any pressure was put on it. In addition, the majority of these pistols were manufactured toward the end World War II, when Allied bombing was battering Japan's arms industries, so materials and workmanship were particularly poor.

NAMBU M14
The Nambu Type 14 was so-called because it was first produced in 1925, the fourteenth year in the reign of the Emperor Yoshito—a naming convention used for some other Japanese military weapons. The 8mm automatic was the principal Japanese military pistol of World War II, but because Japanese officers were required to personally purchase their sidearms, a variety of pistols saw service.

LUGER WITH DRUM MAGAZINE

Although the Walther P38 largely replaced the Luger as the standard German service pistol, the latter still saw much service in World War II. This particular pistol—fitted with a 32-round drum magazine—was taken from a German general following the Allied capture of the North African city of Tunis in May 1943. The so-called "snail drum" magazine was never popular because it had a tendency to jam.

WALTHER P38

A military adaptation of the PP (Polizei Pistole, or Police Pistol) series of pistols developed by Carl Walther Waffenfabrik in the 1920s, the 9mm P38 was adopted by the German Wehrmacht in the 1930s to replace the more expensive and complicated Luger. The P38's action was designed so that as long as the safety was on, it could be carried while cocked and ready to fire when the safety was disengaged—a highly desirable feature in a service pistol.

BERETTA M1934 AUTO

The blowback-operated 9mm Beretta M1934 was Italy's standard sidearm in its wars in Africa in the 1930s and in World War II. The M1934 was mainly army-issue; a 7.65mm version, the M1935, was used principally by the Italian navy and air force.

THE HOUSE OF BERETTA

In 1526 the Venetian Republic contracted with gunsmith Bartoleomo Beretta of Gardone for a quantity of arquebuses. That deal was the start of a gunmaking dynasty that has endured for nearly half a millennium; the modern firm of Fabbrica d'Armi Pietro Beretta is still largely owned and run by Bartolemo's descendants. The firm's reputation for high quality and excellence in design has made it one of the world's foremost manufacturers of weapons for both military, police, and sporting use. While it makes every kind of gun from shotguns to assault rifles, Beretta's pistols are held in especially high regard. This was dramatically underscored by the U.S. Army's 1985 adoption of the 9mm Beretta M92SB/92F as its standard sidearm, replacing the venerable Colt .45 M1911.

ALLIED PISTOLS

U.S. forces continued to carry the Colt M1911—and would do so for four decades after the war's end. The British, however, retained their great devotion to Webley revolvers in World War II, although quantities of the Browning High Power 9mm automatic (see p 153) were issued to British forces.

WEBLEY MARK IV
Introduced in 1899, the Webley Mark IV revolver remained popular with British forces—especially the aircrew of the Royal Air Force—during World War II. Originally .455, World War II–era Mark IV's were more commonly of .38 caliber. The pistol here is shown in subdued "wartime" finish.

WEBLEY MARK VI
This variant of the Webley Mark VI (introduced in 1916) is chambered for the .22 round and fitted with a special cylinder. It was used to train British troops in pistol shooting during World War II. (The use of the .22 cartridge allowed firing on relatively compact shooting ranges.)

SWEDISH M40 PISTOL

When the outbreak of World War II led Germany to suspend export of the Walther HP pistol, which neutral Sweden had just adopted as its service pistol, the Swedish government licensed a 1935 design from Finnish designer Almo Lahti. The 9mm M40, as it was known in Swedish service, looked like a Luger but used a firing system closer to that of a Bergmann-Bayard, with an added kick to ensure proper action movement in cold temperatures.

TOKAREV

Developed by Feodor Tokarev, a former Czarist officer turned Soviet gun designer, the Tokarev pistol was introduced in the late 1920s and adopted as the standard Red Army sidearm a few years later. Known as the TT (from "Tula-Tokarev," Tula being one of the principal Soviet arsenals), the pistol's firing system was essentially a copy of the one used in John Browning's Colt M1911 .45, chambered for the 7.62 round. The original model, the TT30, was later replaced by the TT-33 (shown here).

WEBLEY 7.65 AUTO

While Webley & Scott was best known for revolvers, it produced several fine automatics over the years. This 7.65mm model was one of fifty especially made for the City of London Police (who traditionally do not carry firearms) for use in case of invasion during the dark days of 1939–41, when Britain fought Nazi Germany virtually alone.

WORLD WAR II RIFLES

When World War II broke out only one nation, the U.S., had adopted a semiautomatic rifle—the M1 Garand (see sidebar)—as its standard infantry arm. The tempo of rifle design quickened, however, when the militaries of other nations realized that in modern warfare, a high rate of fire at short range was often more important than long-range accuracy.

In 1942, Germany developed the 7.92mm Fallschirmgewehr (Paratroop rifle) for its airborne forces, which could fire in both single-shot and fully automatic modes. Two years later came the MP44, another 7.92 selective-fire weapon meant to combine the functions of the rifle, submachine gun, and light machine gun. A truly revolutionary gun, the MP44's alternate designation, Sturmgewehr, would provide the name for an entirely new class of weapon—the assault rifle.

M1 CARBINE
In the run-up to World War II, the U.S. decided to develop an "intermediate" weapon for use by officers and NCOs, armored crews, truck drivers, and support personnel—one that would be more compact than the M1 Garand rifle but more effective in combat than the M1911 pistol. The result was the M1 carbine, a lightweight (5.5lb/25kg), semiautomatic weapon firing a special .30 cartridge. The M1 was followed by the M2, which was capable of full-auto as well as semi-auto fire, and a folding-stock version of the M1 (the M1A1, shown here) was developed for airborne troops. Although more than 6 million such carbines were issued before production ceased in the 1950s, the combat verdict was mixed; the weapon proved handy in street fighting in Europe and in jungle fighting in the Pacific, but many thought that it was too delicate and that the pistol-strength .30 carbine cartridge was too weak.

JAPANESE TYPE 38
Introduced in 1905—the thirty-eigth year of the Emperor Meiji's reign, and thus named the Type 38—this 6.5 bolt-action rifle was the standard Japanese service rifle until the introduction of the Type 99 thirty-four years later. It was also produced in a carbine version.

JAPANESE TYPE 99 RIFLE
Firing a more powerful round (7.7mm) than the earlier 6.5 Type 38 Arisaka rifle, the Japanese Type 99 rifle first entered service in 1939. The Type 99's most distinctive features are an integral wire monopod and a set of rear sights that (very optimistically) were intended for use against aircraft.

JOHN C. GARAND

Born in Quebec in 1888, John Cantius Garand (pictured at left) moved, as a child, to New England with his family, where he worked in textile mills and machine shops. His passion was for weapons design, howev-er, and during World War I he submitted a design for a light machine gun to the U.S. Army. It was adopted, but put into production too late to see service. His obvious talents led to a position as an engineer with the U.S. government arsenal at Springfield, Massachusetts.

There, in the early 1930s, he developed a gas-operated, 8-shot, .30 semiautomatic rifle that beat out competitors to win adoption by the U.S. Army in 1936. (The Marine Corps also adopted the rifle, but shortages led the marines to fight their first battles of World War II with bolt-action M1903 Springfields.) The M1 Garand gave U.S. forces a big advantage in firepower during that conflict; General George S. Patton described the rifle as "the greatest battle implement ever devised."

The M1 Garand remained the standard U.S. infantry weapon through the Korean War (1950–53), and the rifle that replaced it in the mid–1950s, the M14, was essentially a selective-fire version of the M1. As a government employee, Garand earned no royalties on his design, though almost 6 million were eventually produced. A resolution to grant Garand a special bonus of $100,000 failed to pass Congress. He died in Massachusetts in 1974.

1169 ENTRENCHING TOOL BAYONET (BRITISH)
Issued to British troops in World War II, this entrenching tool combined a spade and a pick for digging foxholes; with a spike bayonet fixed to the handle, it could be used to probe for land mines.

M1 GARAND
Despite its undoubted success on the battlefield, the M1 Garand was not without its drawbacks. The rifle's magazine fed only from an eight-round stripper clip, so in combat it could not be topped off by inserting individual rounds into the magazine. And when the clip was emptied, it was ejected upward with a distinctive clang! sound that could betray the firer's location to the enemy.

MANNLICHER-CARCANO CARBINE/GRENADE LAUNCHER
A true rarity from World War II, this weapon was a combination 6-shot carbine and grenade launcher. While most infantry rifles of the World Wars era could fire grenades from a cup fitted into the barrel, the gun had a permanently attached grenade launcher on its right side.

CEREMONIAL WEAPONS OF THE WORLD WAR ERAS

By the turn of the twentieth century, the sword had ceased to have any real usefulness on the battlefield (in the Western world at least) and was increasingly relegated to a ceremonial role, remaining—as it had for many centuries—a symbol of the officer's authority. Other purely ceremonial weapons that endured into the twentieth century include the officer's swagger stick and the field marshal's baton. Another custom that endured into the era of the World Wars was the presentation of ceremonial weapons—usually richly decorated swords or pistols—to honor victorious commanders.

TOTALITARIAN SYMBOLS

Both Fascist dictator Benito Mussolini, who seized power in Italy in 1922, and Adolph Hitler, head of the Nazi Party that gained control of Germany in 1933, had an intuitive understanding of popular psychology and the uses of propaganda. Along with mass rallies, rousing films, and other propaganda elements, both Fascist Italy and Nazi Germany used the symbolism of weaponry as a tool to cultivate fervent militaristic spirit in their citizens and to bind them more closely to an all-powerful state.

One such practice was the widespread distribution of elaborate ceremonial blades, especially daggers. In Nazi Germany, each branch of the military, paramilitary groups, party organizations like the Hitlerjugend (Hitler Youth), and even civilian organizations like police and firefighting formations had its own unique knives or daggers to be worn with dress uniform. Often these weapons were engraved with "patriotic" mottos—such as the Hitler Youth knives, which bore the inscription Blut und Ehre ("Blood and Honor").

While the alliance that eventually defeated Italy and Germany—the Soviet Union, the U.S., and Great Britain—did not fetishize the blade, their leaders also, on occasion, recognize its role as a symbol of courage and martial prowess. During the Teheran Conference in November 1943, for example, British Prime Minister Winston Churchill presented Soviet leader Josef Stalin with a magnificent custom-made presentation sword—the "Sword of Stalingrad"—on behalf of King George VI and the British people in commemoration of the Soviet victory in that epic battle.

SWAGGER STICK
Officers and sometimes NCOs of various armies (and the U.S. Marine Corps) often carried swagger sticks like the one shown here. Typically about 2ft/61cm or less in length, they were short canes, often covered in leather and metal-tipped. The swagger stick's origin is obscure; they may have derived from the "pacing sticks" used to space out soldiers in marching ranks—or to mete out corporal punishment. By the twentieth century the item became merely a symbol of rank.

MUSSOLINI SWORD
This Shotel—the traditional curved sword of Ethiopia—was presented to Benito Mussolini following Italy's conquest of Ethiopia (or Abyssinia, as it was alternatively known at the time) in 1936. The dictator was in fact an enthusiastic swordsman who liked to fence and who reportedly fought duels as a young man.

GERMAN ARMY OFFICER'S SWORD

With a single-edged 32.25/82 cm blade, the Heer Mannschaftsabel (officer's sword) was the standard dress sword of the German Army from around the turn of the twentieth century through World War II. Most were manufactured by firms in the Westpahlian city of Solingen, a city renowned for its fine edged weapons since the late fourteenth century.

GOERING BATON

The baton is the traditional symbol of the field marshal, the highest military rank in many countries. This baton is topped with a bust of Feldmarschall Hermann Goering, head of the German Luftwaffe (air force) and one of Adolph Hitler's principal deputies. The exceptionally vain Goering treasured his collection of highly decorated batons.

NAZI LABOR CORPS KNIFE

Nazi Germany organized the German Labor Service (the Reichsarbeitsdienst, or RAD) in 1934 to provide labor for public-works projects; the organization later became an auxiliary service of the Wehrmacht. RAD officers carried a smaller, decorated version of the hewer knife issued to enlisted laborers. The stag-handled version shown here was made by the famous Eickhorn firm of Solingen.

LUFTWAFFE/ARMY DAGGERS
These daggers were worn by officers of the Luftwaffe [left, the 1937 Model] and Wehrmacht [right]. An officer's dagger of the German Kriegsmarine (Navy). Some naval daggers had a pommel decorated with both the eagle of Imperial Germany and the Nazi swastika.

LUFTWAFFE SWORD
Made in Solingen, this Luftwaffe officer's dress sword bears the Nazi swastika on both its pommel and the base of its hilt. It is shown here with its scabbard.

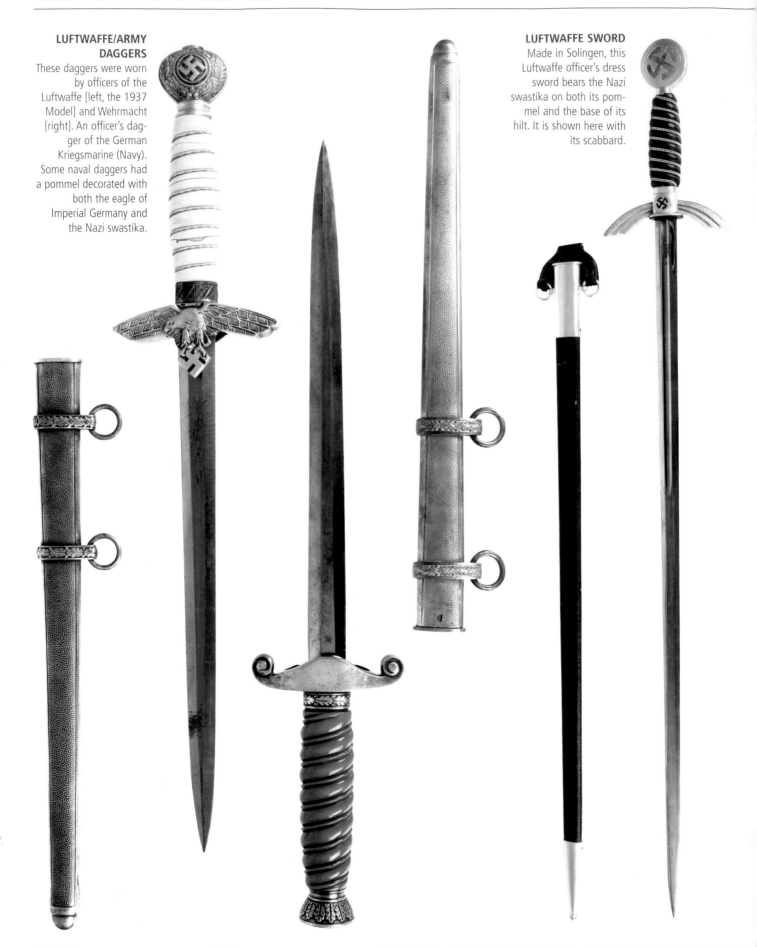

HIMMLER RIFLE

This Schuetzen rifle was custom-made for Heinrich Himmler, head of the Schutzstaffel (SS), the troops of the Nazi party, and one of the most powerful Nazi leaders. Patterned on a traditional German hunting rifle, the lever-action weapon fired a 7.7mm cartridge.

SA DAGGER

Bearing the inscription "Alles for Deutschland" ("All for Germany") on the blade, the dagger shown here was worn by members of the Sturmabteilung (SA), the Nazi Party's paramilitary security force.

GERMAN POLICE BAYONET

The hilt of this German Police bayonet is in the form of an Eagle, symbol of the Weimar Republic, Germany's government from the end of World War I until the establishment of the Third Reich in 1933.

ITALIAN FASCIST PARTY KNIFE

Only members of Italy's Fascist Party, in power from 1922 until the overthrow of dictator Benito Mussolini during World War II, possessed this blade. It is shown with its steel scabbard.

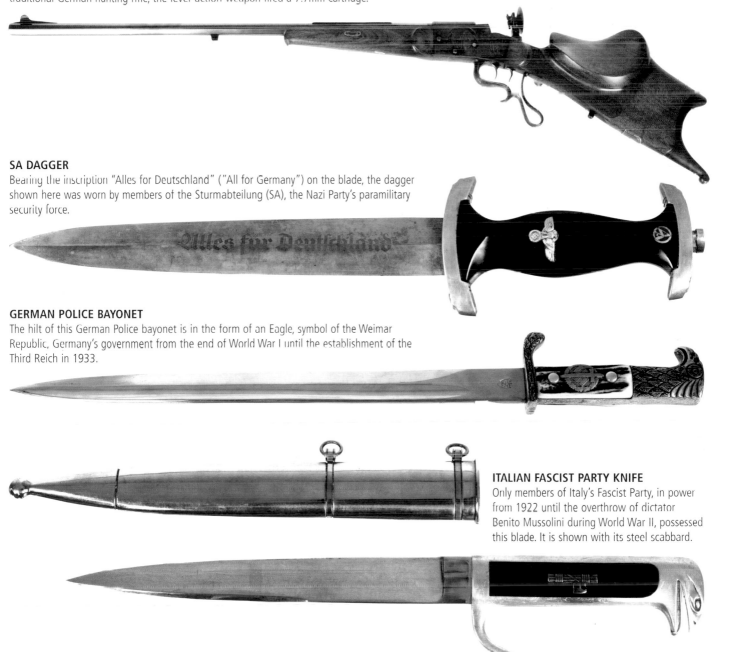

US OFFICER SWORD

The U.S. Army adopted the saber shown here as the official ceremonial sword for officers and senior NCOs in 1902.

MACHINE GUNS OF WORLD WAR II

Besides their infantry application, World War I also saw machine guns fitted to aircraft (and used against them from the ground), armored cars, and tanks. In the interwar years, weapons designers developed even more powerful machine guns, like John Browning's .50 M2, which fired a cartridge the size of an old-fashioned Coca-Cola bottle. Even before World War I ended, however, several nations sought to package the punch of the machine gun in a weapon that could be carried by an individual infantryman.

By World War II, these included the British Bren gun and the U.S. BAR (Browning Automatic Rifle). These weapons were typically magazine-fed, but based on their experience in World War I, the German Wehrmacht made a belt-fed light machine gun, the 7.92mm MG42, the foundation of its infantry squad in World War II. The concept of the "squad automatic weapon" evolved, postwar, into guns like the U.S. military's Vietnam-era M60 and the contemporary M249, the latter based on a Belgian design.

JAPANESE AIRCRAFT CANNON
While the British Royal Air Force (RAF) and the U.S. Army Air Forces (USAAF) armed their fighters and bombers mostly with machine guns, the air forces of other nations preferred automatic cannons, usually 20mm weapons firing explosive shells rather than bullets. Such as this 20mm Japanese aircraft cannon.

GERMAN MG42
One of World War II's most effective weapons, the 7.92mm, belt-fed German MG34 and its wartime replacement, the MG42, were distinguished by their versatility. Equipped with a bipod, they went into action in an infantry support role. Tripod-mounted, they proved an excellent defensive weapon; and they could be fitted on tanks and other vehicles as well. The MG series' high rate of fire—up to 1200 rounds per minute—and their distinctive sound led Allied troops to nick-name the weapon "Hitler's Zipper."

BROWNING M2

During World War I, John Browning designed the .30 machine gun shown here for aircraft use; designated the M2, it didn't arrive in time to see wartime service. The weapon was used by the U.S. Army Air Corps (later the U.S. Army Air Forces) into the early days of World War II, when it was largely replaced by the formidable .50 M2.

BROWNING AUTOMATIC RIFLE

Another Browning design, the gas-operated, .30 Browning Automatic Rifle (BAR) was introduced in 1918, too late to see more than limited service in World War I. It would remain in U.S. service, with some modifications, through the Korean War (1950–53). In most respects an excellent weapon, capable of both fully automatic fire and, in the hands of an experienced user, single shots. Disadvantages included its weight (19.5lb/8.9kg) and its magazine capacity of only 20 rounds—low for a full-auto weapon.

"Why does the soul always require a machine-gun?"

—E.M. Foster, from "What Has Germany Done to the Germans?" 1940

Submachine Guns of World War II

As World War I ground to a bloody stalemate on the Western Front, soldiers of the warring nations began to acknowledge the inadequacies of the standard infantry rifle—its length, weight, and above all its relatively slow rate of fire. As a result—and inspired by the success of the machine gun (see pp 182–83, 206–07)—weapons designers developed the submachine gun. This infantryman's firearm sacrificed the rifle's long-range accuracy in favor of a smaller weapon that could be fired from the hip or shoulder, and which could unleash a rapid volume of fire in close combat. Refined in the interwar years, the submachine gun figured prominently in World War II, and even today—when the assault rifle has largely subsumed its functions—submachine guns retain a role in antiterrorism and other specialized operations.

THE SUBMACHINE GUN'S ORIGINS

The Italian Army introduced a prototypical submachine gun in 1915, but pride of place in the weapon's development really goes to Germany, which, three years later, adopted the Bergmann MP18/1 designed by Hugo Schmeisser. The blowback-operated weapon fired a slightly modified version of the 9mm parabellum round used in the Luger pistol. The MP18/1 originally used the 32-round "snail drum" magazine also developed for the Luger, but postwar versions used a side-mounted box magazine. The MP18/1 arrived too late and in too few numbers to change Germany's fortunes on the Western Front. Around the same time the Bergmann was being developed, U.S. Army colonel J.T. Thompson designed the now-legendary gun that bears his name but by the time the first Thompsons were ready for shipping, the Armistice had been signed.

WORLD WAR II AND AFTER

Most nations adopted some form of submachine gun before the advent of World War II, although military conservatives often derided the weapon as "cheap and nasty" and lamented its relative lack of accuracy and "stopping power" (most submachine guns fired a pistol-strength cartridge rather than a rifle round, the latter being too powerful for the submachine gun's firing system.) The weapon proved its worth, however, in all theaters of World War II, especially in street-fighting in Europe and in close-quarter battle in the Pacific islands.

The Soviet Union especially took to the weapon, producing millions of PPSh41/42/43 models, and even equipping whole battalions with them. While technically crude compared to German submachine guns like the MP40, the PPSh series (short for *Pistolet Pullemet Sh*pagin) were rugged and reliable in the brutal conditions of the Eastern Front, easy to use even by minimally trained Red Army soldiers, and could be produced quickly and cheaply. Chinese copies of the Russian design, like the Type 50, saw extensive service in the Korean War (1950–53), in which U.S. troops dubbed them "burp guns" from their distinctive sound.

STEN

Simple and cheap to manufacture and easy to use, the STEN submachine gun and its numerous variants were a mainstay of British and Commonwealth forces throughout World War II. Its name derived from the initials of its designers, R.V. Shepard and H.J. Turpin, combined with those of Britain's Enfield National Arsenal. The 9mm, blowback-operated submachine gun—which fed from a 32-round, side-mounted detachable magazine—saw service everywhere from Normandy to New Guinea. The Australian version was known as the AUSTEN, from "Australian STEN."

FRENCH MAS

The 7.65mm MAS (from Manufacture d'Armes de St. Etienne) Model 1938 submachine gun was the French army's principal World War II submachine gun. It was an unusual weapon in that the trigger had to be pushed forward to put the weapon in safety mode and the bolt recoiled into a tube inside the buttstock.

REISING

The U.S. .45 Reising gun (named for its designer, Eugene Reising) was a selective-fire, delayed blowback-operation weapon used by the U.S. Marine Corps early in World War II. Issued in a full-length, wooden-stock version as well as the folding wire-stock model shown here, the Reising's locked-breech firing system was susceptible to fouling from dirt and moisture, so it proved ineffective and unpopular in the jungle campaigns on Guadalcanal and other islands.

MP40

Although popularly known as the "Schmeisser," this German submachine gun, officially the MP (Machinenpistole) Model 1940, was not in fact developed by the great German weapons designer Hugo Schmeisser. More than 1 million were manufactured for Wehrmacht use during World War II, and the 9mm, blowback-operated, metal-and-plastic MP40 is generally considered the first standard-issue infantry weapon to use no wood in its construction. Its excellent reputation is reinforced by the fact that many Allied troops used captured MP40s in preference to their own issue submachine guns.

MP44

Officially the MP (Machinenpistole) Model 1944, aka the Sturmgewehr (Assault Rifle) Model 1944, this gun represented the cutting edge of small-arms technology as World War II headed to its bloody close. Gas-operated, the selective-fire weapon used a short (kurtz) version of the standard 7.92 German cartridge, feeding from a detachable 30-round magazine. (Although designated "44," the first models were issued in 1943.) The Soviet AK-47 design (see p 216), the world's most popular assault rifle, is a direct descendant. The MP44 shown here was issued with a special curved barrel—useful for shooting around corners in street fighting.

SPECIALIZED WEAPONS OF WORLD WAR II

The special battlefield conditions of World War II required specialized infantry weapons. The appearance of the tank as a major battlefield presence led to the development of rocket-propelled weapons to allow infantrymen to deal with enemy armor. In the brutal conflict between the Soviet Union and Nazi Germany on the Eastern Front, both armies fielded sniper units armed with specially adapted rifles. While World War II saw the widespread use of radios for communication, the venerable flare pistol continued to be used for signaling when radio silence had to be observed. A grimmer type of weapon were the brutal devices used in Nazi Germany's POW and concentration camps.

SNIPERS

Many World War II armies made use of snipers to kill at long ranges. Most of these shooters used conventional bolt-action service rifles or civilian hunting rifles fitted with telescopic scopes. The Soviet Red Army especially took to sniping; the "highest-scoring" snipers (some of them women) became national celebrities. The most famous Soviet sniper, Vasily Grigoryevich Zaitsev (1915–1991), had 225 confirmed kills. During the Battle of Stalingrad, Zaitsev reportedly killed one of the Wehrmacht's top snipers, who had been sent to the city specifically to hunt Zaitsev down. This duel was the basis for David L. Robbins's 1999 novel *War of the Rats* and the 2001 movie *Enemy at the Gates*. Zaitsev and his fellow snipers used the standard Mosin-Nagant (see p 183), which remained in service in the Soviet Union and its satellites until the 1960s.

ANTI-TANK WEAPONS

During World War I and in the inter-war years, the principal antitank weapon was the antitank rifle—high-powered weapons firing heavy, armor-piercing rounds. The best-known weapons of this type are the British Army's .55 Boys and the German 13.2mm Mauser Panzerbusche. As tank armor was made thicker after the outbreak of World War II, antitank rifles proved increasingly ineffective. The U.S. Army was the first to develop a rocket-powered antitank weapon. Introduced in 1942, the M1A1 "Bazooka" was a shoulder-mounted tube, operated by a two-man team, that fired a 2.36in/60mm HEAT (High Explosive Anti-Tank) projectile. (The Bazooka got its nickname because it looked like a spoof musical instrument played by a popular comedian.) The Germans copied the weapon—upgrading its caliber to 3.5in/88mm—as the Panzerschreck. The Wehrmacht also used large numbers of a simple, one-shot rocket-launcher, the Panzerfaust, while the British Army adopted the rather unique PIAT.

GERMAN SNIPER RIFLE

During World War II, the German Wehrmacht adapted pre-war Mauser rifles, made originally as civilian hunting and target weapons, for use by snipers. The 8mm Mauser shown here is fitted with a Hensolt single-post telescopic sight. An American officer took this particular rifle from a dead German sniper during the Battle of the Bulge in the winter of 1944–45.

GERMAN FLARE PISTOL
Made of zinc, this World War II Walther German flare pistol (leuchtpistol) could fire both flares or tear-gas cartridges. The breech opens by means of a downward pull on the trigger guard.

DOUBLE-BARREL GERMAN FLARE PISTOL
Flares were used not only for signaling on the ground, but also from the air—for example, to alert ground crews to be prepared for on-board casualties before landing, or to indicate changes in formation while in flight. Shown here is a double-barreled flare pistol used by the Luftwaffe, Nazi Germany's air force. A "hammerless" design, the weapon cocks when broken open for loading, applying the safety automatically when the barrels return to firing position.

RUBBER TRUNCHEON
This type of rubber truncheon was used by both the German secret police (the Gestapo) and the SS (the Schultzstaffel, special Nazi Party forces) during World War II. This type of weapon was known as a "cosh" or "billy club" in British and American terminology, respectively.

WHIP
Based on the classic "cat o' nine tails," this whip was used by guards at German concentration and prisoner-of-war (POW) camps. A Polish POW seized this one when his camp was liberated in the waning days of World War II.

PIAT
First used in combat in 1943, the British Army's PIAT (Personal Infantry Anti-Tank Projector) was an unusual weapon in that it used a spring loaded firing system to ignite a relatively small propulsion charge, which in turn sent a HEAT (High-Explosive Anti-Tank) round to a maximum of 330ft/100m. The PIAT's advantage was that, unlike the U.S. bazooka, it did not spew a sheet of flame upon firing, revealing the user's position to the enemy. For the same reason, the PIAT was safe to use in tight spaces in a non-antitank role—house-to-house fighting, for example. Its disadvantages were its heavy weight (34lb/15kg) and the inability of the 3lb/1.4kg HEAT round to penetrate the frontal armor of some German panzer (tank) models.

WEAPONS OF ESPIONAGE

Some of the most innovative and intriguing weapons are those intended for use by spies, assassins, intelligence agents, and guerrilla fighters. Because concealment is obviously of paramount importance for their users, many of these weapons (including most of the items shown on these pages) are disguised as ordinary objects. While some specialized espionage weapons were made in the nineteenth and early twentieth centuries, their real heyday was during World War II and the decades of Cold War that followed.

OSS AND SOE

In June 1942, six months after its entry into World War II, the United States set up the Office of Strategic Services (OSS), an agency whose missions included not only gathering intelligence, but carrying out sabotage and aiding resistance movements in areas occupied by the Axis powers (Germany, Italy, and Japan), in close cooperation with its British counterpart, the Special Operations Executive (SOE).

Drawing many of its operatives from Ivy League universities and other bastions of the East Coast "establishment" (detractors claimed its initials stood for "Oh So Social"), the OSS used a variety of unusual weapons in its clandestine operations, many developed by the National Defense Resource Council (NDRC), like the famous "Liberator" single-shot pistol (see sidebar), or borrowed from the British, like the Sykes-Fairbairn Commando Knife (see p 193).

THE COLD WAR

When World War II gave way to the Cold War, the OSS gave way to the Central Intelligence Agency (CIA). The CIA continued the use of one the most effective OSS weapons, the .22 Hi-Standard automatic pistol. With a design similar to the civilian Colt Woodsmen pistol, the Hi-Standard was equipped with a silencer developed by Bell Telephone Laboratories. In keeping with the agency's doctrine of "plausible deniability" in covert operations, the Hi-Standards in the CIA's arsenal were manufactured without any markings that would indicate their American origin. The CIA also developed its share of unusual weapons; reportedly, the agency worked up an exploding seashell in an unsuccessful effort to kill Cuban dictator Fidel Castro, an avid skin-diver.

The KGB, the postwar version of the Soviet Secret Police, had its own arsenal of unusual weapons, including a 4.5mm gun disguised as a lipstick (issued to female agents, it was nicknamed "the Kiss of Death"); an umbrella firing poison pellets, used to assassinate Bulgarian dissident Georgi Malenkov in London in 1978; and perhaps most bizarre, the "rektal" knife—a dagger designed to be concealed in that particular body cavity.

GAS GUN

Patented in 1932 as a "disabling gas firing weapon" by the Lake Erie Chemical Corporation of Ohio, this pen-shaped device was designed to discharge tear gas. Although intended for use by law-enforcement agencies, similar devices discharging more deadly chemical compounds have been used in espionage by various secret services.

DART AND DAGGER

Two OSS/SOE weapons of World War II: The dart (above) could be fired by a pistol-style crossbow using rubber bands, while the easily concealable wrist dagger was widely issued to Allied operatives.

MIGHTIER THAN THE SWORD

This German pen gun from World War II fired a .22 round. The weapon was cocked by pulling back on the top and fired by pressing a small button on the side.

LOZENGE-CASE GUN

An agent of Italy's Fascist government reportedly used this pistol, disguised as a tin of throat lozenges, to assassinate an American intelligence operative in Switzerland during World War II. (As a neutral nation, Switzerland was a hotbed of espionage and intrigue throughout the conflict.) To fire the weapon, the assassin opened the lid and pressed on one of the "lozenges," which served as a trigger.

DEADLY TOOLS

The tire gauge and screwdriver shown here are replicas of actual weapons produced for Allied operatives in World War II. Each is a single-shot .22 pistol.

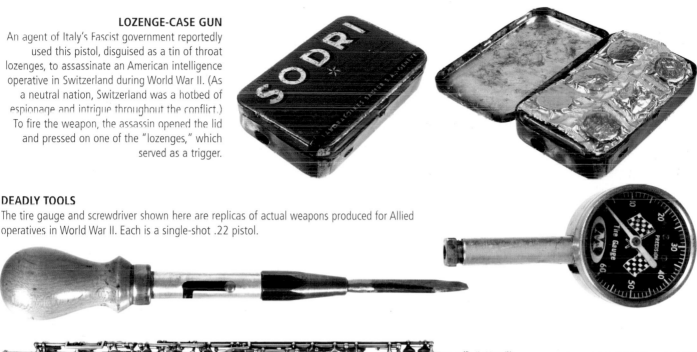

DEADLY MUSIC

Made in 1965, this fully functional silver flute was adapted to fire a .22 round. A brass screw on one of the keys functions as a trigger.

THE LIBERATOR

Although not produced especially for the OSS, the "Liberator" pistol has—rightly or wrongly—long been associated with that organization. The Liberator was simplicity itself: A single-shot pistol firing a .45 ACP round through a smoothbore barrel. Made of 23 pieces of stamped metal, it came in a cardboard box with ten cartridges (five of which could be stored in a compartment in the grip), a wooden rod for ejecting spent cartridges, and wordless, comic strip-style sheet with assembly instructions. About a million of these guns were made by the Guide Lamp Division of the General Motors Corporation in 1942. The weapon was nicknamed "the Woolworth gun" after the discount store where all items sold for five or ten cents. (The actual unit cost was about U.S. $2.00.)

With an effective range of about six feet, the Liberator was really a weapon designed to allow the user (if he or she were brave and lucky) to obtain better weapons. This gun was apparently intended for mass distribution to resistance fighters in Axis-occupied Europe and Asia, the idea being that they would be used on stragglers and sentries, whose weapons would then be captured and added to the guerrilla group's arsenal.

Just how many Liberators actually saw service, and where, and how effectively are questions fiercely debated by firearms historians. While they may have been originally intended mainly for distribution in Nazi-occupied Europe, there's not much evidence many were actually used there, but guerrillas fighting Japanese forces in the Philippines apparently used some Liberators to good effect.

In the early 1960s, the CIA revived the idea of a no-frills, single-shot pistol in the form of the so-called "deer gun," a 9mm weapon the U.S. distributed to anticommunist guerillas in Southeast Asia.

CHEMICAL AND
BIOLOGICAL WARFARE

The use of chemical and biological agents in warfare—whether against enemy forces, animals, or civilian populations—stretches back to antiquity. Despite the fear that they inspire, these weapons have proved difficult to use effectively, then and now, because spores (like those that cause Anthrax) and toxins (like botulin, which causes botulism), and other agents often disperse unpredictably and can be just as deadly to the "attackers" as to the "defenders." Still, the possibility of a chemical or biological attack by a terrorist group or "rogue state"— with the at least theoretical possibility of millions of deaths—is a terrifying prospect in the twenty-first century.

EARLY BIOLOGICAL WARFARE

Arrows and other projectiles dipped in poison from the venom of snakes and other reptiles, or from plants, were likely the first chemical weapons. Their use in hunting and warfare continued into modern times—among the indigenous peoples of the South American rainforest, for example, who used arrowheads coated with the plant derived curare, which causes respiratory paralysis. People have also long known that introducing excrement into a wound can lead to infection and death: In the twentieth century, Vietnamese guerrillas used excrement-smeared "punji spikes" and other "booby traps" against their French and later American opponents.

Probably the first recorded use of germ warfare on a large scale in the Western world came during the Peloponnesian War between the Greek city-states of Athens and Sparta in the fifth century BCE. The historian Thucydides (c. 460–404 BCE) reported how "pestilence" killed many Athenians around 430 BCE, an outbreak he ascribed to the Spartans poisoning wells. (Modern research, however, has raised the possibility that the pestilence was actually a variation of the Ebola virus, unintentionally brought by the Athenians themselves from Africa.) Later, during the struggle for supremacy in the Mediterranean between Rome and Carthage, sailors of the Carthaginian navy (c. 247–183 BCE) was said to have hurled jars of poisonous snakes on the decks of Roman warships.

There are plenty of medieval accounts of attackers using catapults to hurl the dead bodies of diseased humans, horses, or other animals into castles or fortified towns to spread disease. Many historians believe that this tactic introduced the devastating bubonic plague into Europe when ships carrying traders from Kaffa—a Venetian trading post in what is now Ukraine, which had been besieged by the Turks—arrived in Italy in 1347. They brought with them rats bearing fleas infected with the plague; the resulting "Black Death" killed between a quarter and a third of Europe's population.

MODERN TIMES

One of the most notorious episodes of deliberate biological warfare came in the aftermath of the French and Indian War (1754–63; known as the Seven Years War in Europe), which gave Britain control of most of North America. When the Native American leader Pontiac led a revolt against the new British overlords, the British commander at Fort Pitt (now Pittsburgh, Pennsylvania), Sir Jeffrey Amherst, arranged for blankets used by smallpox patients at the base to be given to local Native Americans. Coincidentally or not, a smallpox epidemic quickly spread throughout the region.

The use of biological weapons during the world wars and, especially, the Cold War remains shrouded in controversy. In World War I, German agents are known to have tried to introduce anthrax among cavalry horses in Romania. (World War I also saw the use of chemical warfare, in the form of gases, by both sides—see p 187).

In World War II, a secret unit of the Japanese Army, Unit 731, attempted to spread diseases like cholera and plague among Chinese civilians—besides conducting gruesome experiments on Chinese and Allied prisoners. While the facts are in dispute, some historians believe Unit 731's activities caused hundreds of thousands of deaths in China. They may also have inspired both the U.S. and the Soviet Union to step up their own research into biological warfare. In the Cold War, both sides continued this research and stockpile biological agents like anthrax and Ricin (an extremely deadly poison derived from the castor bean). In 1972, concern over the dangers of germ warfare led to an international treaty forbidding their manufacture and use; by the 1980s, more than 100 nations had signed the document, although it's suspected in some quarters that research continues secretly in many nations.

In the 1980s, Iraqi dictator Saddam Hussein used chemical weapons against its own minority Kurdish population and, probably, against Iranian troops in the Iran-Iraq War (1980–88). In one documented episode, as many as 5,000 Kurds may have died in a single chemical attack in 1988. Fear that Iraq was developing "weapons of mass destruction," including biological agents, was a major justification for the invasion of that nation in 2003 by the United States and some of its allies.

Because they are relatively inexpensive to produce, chemical and biological weapons are sometimes called the "poor man's weapons" and as such they are attractive to terrorists organizations. On March 20, 1995, for example, members a Japanese religious cult, Aum Shinrikyo, released the nerve agent Sarin into the Tokyo subway system, killing twelve people and injuring more than 6,000. And in late 2001, five people in the U.S. died after receiving mail laced with anthrax bacteria. The case remains unsolved and may have no connection to international terrorism, but the episode rattled the nerves of a nation already shaken by the attacks of September 11, 2001.

POST–WORLD WAR II WEAPONS

The most significant development in firearms in the decades after World War II was the incredible proliferation of the assault rifle, especially the AK47. Critics have charged that the widespread availability of these cheap but deadly weapons fuels ongoing civil, political, and ethnic conflict in the world's poorest regions, such as sub-Saharan Africa. Recent decades have seen civilian and military engineers experimenting with "caseless" ammunition and even rocket propulsion to replace conventional ammunition and firing systems, but most contemporary firearms remain based (albeit in highly evolved forms) on designs and systems introduced decades ago or even in the nineteenth century. As the events of September 11, 2001, showed, in the twenty-first century, even the simplest weapons—box-cutters and ceramic knifes—can still be used to devastating effect.

INFANTRY WEAPONS

The most successful infantry weapon of the post–World War II era is the AK47 assault rifle, often called the Kalashnikov after its chief designer (see sidebar). Simple construction with few moving parts made this rifle easy to maintain and use even by relatively untrained troops or guerrilla fighters. The AK47 remains ubiquitous in the twenty-first century, with as many as 100 million of the weapon and its variants produced as of this writing.

The postwar years saw the armies of most nations adopt selective-fire assault rifles, most (like the Belgian FN FAL, introduced in 1950 and adopted by more than 50 nations) chambered for the 7.62mm round. An exception was the U.S., which adopted the 5.56mm M16, based on the Armalite rifle designed by Eugene Stoner, in the mid-1960s. In recent years, many armies have adopted rifles using smaller cartridges, often in "bullpup" designs that place the magazine and action behind the trigger guard. Just as the assault rifle was an outgrowth of the World War II German Sturmgewehr (see pp 198–99), the belt-fed squad automatic weapons now used by many armies are an evolution of the German MG42 (see p 206).

HANDGUNS

Pistol design lagged somewhat until the 1970s, when the rise of terrorism led to the development of a new generation of automatics, most chambered for 9mm.

Intended to meet the needs of law-enforcement agencies and antiterrorist military units, these pistols could be carried safely, used in close confines (like airplane passenger cabins) with minimal danger to hostages or bystanders, and had a high magazine capacity.

One of the first pistols to meet these criteria was Germany's Heckler & Koch VP70, also the first pistol made with plastic in its construction. In 1983 the Austrian firm Glock AG introduced the first of its extremely successful Glock series of automatics, with magazine capacities of up to 19 rounds. Glocks are composed mostly of plastic, which led to fears they could pass through metal detectors, but these fears have proven unfounded.

AK47
Perhaps the AK47's greatest virtue is its reliability under tough combat conditions: During the Vietnam War, Vietcong guerrillas reportedly retrieved AK47s hidden for days in muddy rice paddies, but which fired perfectly. In contrast, the U.S. M16—while a technically superior and, in some respects, more lethal rifle—has to be kept meticulously clean to avoid jamming. The model shown here is a Chinese version.

WESTON MINIATURE

Although Tom Weston is perhaps the best-known twentieth-century maker of miniature guns, the details of his life are sketchy. The Mexico City resident was apparently a leading collector and seller of antique firearms when, in the 1930s, he engaged Mexican craftsmen to make tiny but fully functioning guns. These unique weapons, produced mainly in the 1950s and 1960s, are prized by collectors of firearms curiosa. Shown here is a 2mm "Reforma" single-shot pistol.

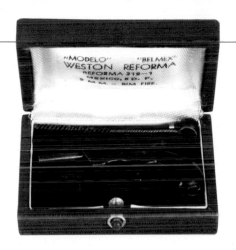

GYROJET PISTOL

Americans Robert Mainhardt and Art Biehl developed one of the most unusual and innovative firearms of recent decades, the Gyrojet pistol, in the early 1960s. The Gyrojet was actually a pistol-scale rocket launcher, firing a 12mm (later 13mm) projectile burning a solid propellant. MBA Associates, the company Mainhardt and Biehl set up to manufacture the weapon, also produced a carbine version. According to some sources, the U.S. military became interested in the Gyrojet concept because it seemed to promise a "jam-free," recoilless infantry weapon, but it proved impractical in tests under combat conditions. Gyrojet weapons never found much of a civilian buyership because of the expensive ammunition.

M. T. KALASHNIKOV

Born in Kurya, Siberia, in 1919, Mikhail Timofeyevich Kalashnikov had no formal technical education, instead, receiving hands-on training as a railway "technical clerk." Seriously wounded in 1941 while serving as a tank commander with the Red Army, Kalashnikov began working on weapons designs during his convalescence. He designed a couple of submachine guns, but as the Red Army already had successful submachine guns in production (see pp 208–09), they weren't adopted. Kalashnikov then turned his talents toward the development of a weapon known, in Soviet terminology, as an "Automat"—the same assault-rifle concept pioneered by the Germans with the MP44 (see p 209). (The German weapons designer Hugo Schmeisser and some of his associates, who had been captured and pressed into Soviet service at the end of World War II, may have contributed to Kalashnikov's work; this is still debated.) In 1947 the Automat Kalashnikov (AK) Model 47, debuted, and the Red Army adopted the weapon in 1951. Kalashnikov rose to the post of chief weapons designer for the Soviet military, produced other weapons (such as the 5.54mm AK-74), won every award possible in the Soviet Union and, later, the Russian Federation. In 2004, he endorsed his own brand of vodka. He is still alive at this writing.

WINCHESTER MODEL 70
Produced in a variety of calibers (from .22 to .458 magnum) and configurations from 1936 to the present day, the bolt-action Winchester Model 70 is considered one of the finest sporting rifles of all times.

SKS CARBINE
During World War II, Soviet weapons designer Sergei Simonov worked to develop a semiautomatic rifle firing a "short" version of the standard 7.62mm Soviet round. The result was the SKS-45 carbine, a gas-operated weapon that fed from a 10-round box magazine and featured an integral bayonet that folded into the forestock. The SKS was a highly successful weapon and it was produced in large numbers in China and other nations until it was largely replaced by the AK47.

FENCING EPEES
The swordfighting tradition continues in the sport of fencing, which began to coalesce in its modern form with the first modern Olympic Games at Athens, Greece, in 1896. The sport makes use of three types of swords—the Epée, the foil, and the saber. Epées (like the mid-twentieth-century American models shown here) are based on European dueling swords of the seventeenth and eighteenth centuries, and have a 35in/90cm blade.

Appendices

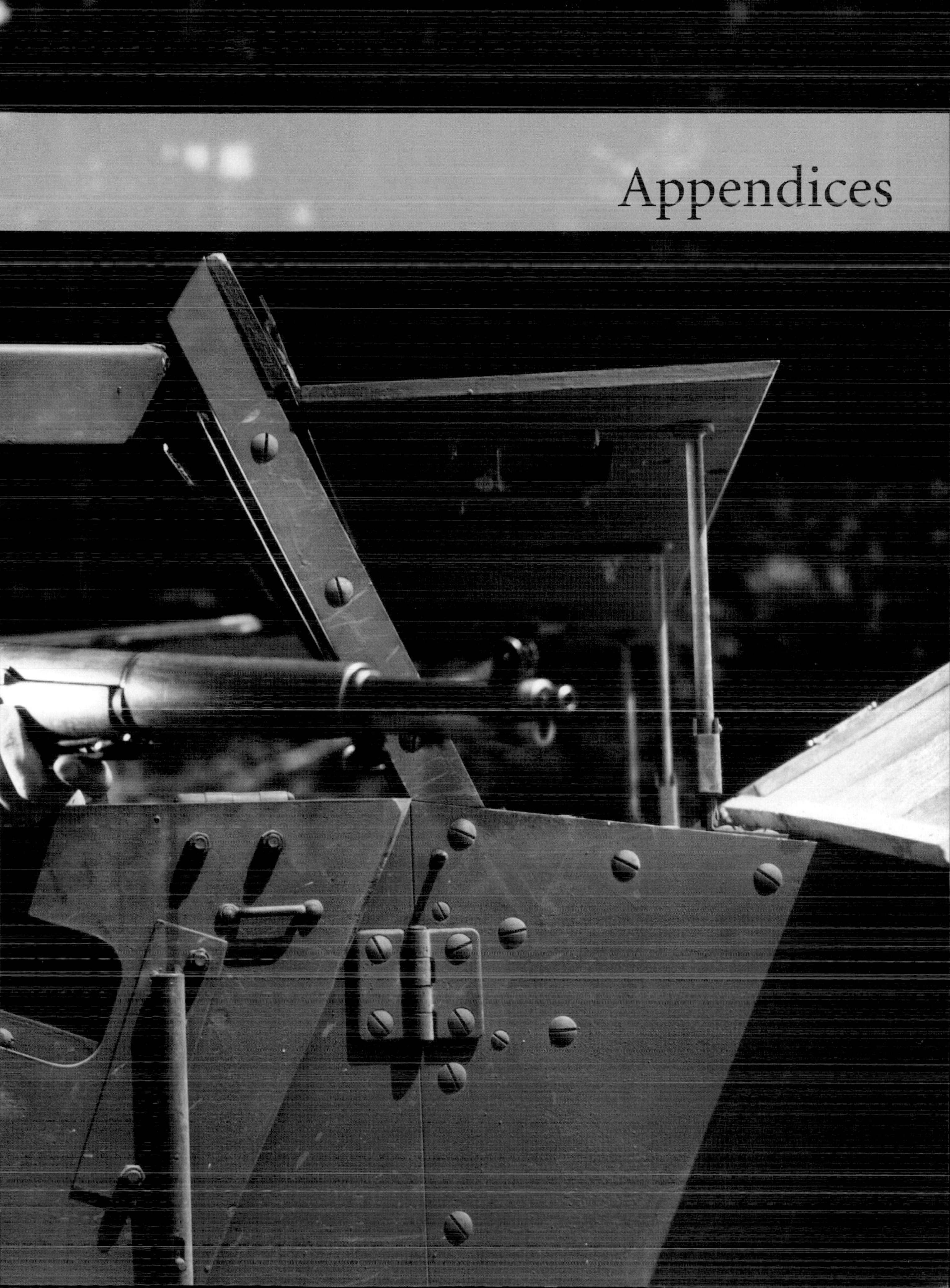

Glossary

a

action Generally speaking, the overall firing mechanism of a gun

atlatl A spear-throwing device

araquebus Shoulder-fired matchlock musket

assegai A South African throwing spear, most famously used by Zulu warriors

b

bagh nakh Indian claw daggers with three to five curved blades

ball A synonym for bullet

blunderbuss A short, smoothbore musket (occasionally a pistol) with a flared muzzle

bolt In reference to crossbows, a short dartlike projectile, also known as a quarrel

bolt-action A gun (typically a rifle) whose action is operated by manipulating a bolt, either by drawing it back ("straight pull") or on a rotational axis

bore *See* gauge

buckshot Lead pellets fired by shotguns

butt, or buttstock The part of a gun braced against the shoulder for firing

c

calacula A Fijian club with a saw-toothed blade

caliber The diameter of a cartridge, expressed in fractions of an inch (e.g., .38, .45) or millimeter (e.g., 7.62mm, 9mm)

carbine A short-barreled, compact musket or rifle, originally carried by mounted troops or, in modern times, by soldiers whose primary jobs (vehicle crews, for example) made it impractical to carry a full-size rifle

cartridge The cased combination of bullet, powder, and primer used in modern firearms; prior to the introduction of the metallic cartridge in the nineteenth century, the term referred to bullet and powder wrapped in paper for ease of loading muzzle-loading weapons

centerfire A type of cartridge with the *primer* sealed in a cavity in the center of its base

chain mail Personal armor made of many links of iron or steel riveted together

chamber The part of a gun in which the cartridge is seated before firing

chassepot Nineteenth-century French bolt-action rifle

chukonu Chinese repeating crossbow

clip A metal strip holding a number of cartridges for insertion into a gun

composite bow A bow using bone or other material to reinforce wood.

crossbow Type of bow using laterally fixed "limbs"

crossguard *See* guard

d

dagger Short knife used for stabbing

Darra guns Guns produced by the gunsmiths of Darra Adem Khel (then part of India, now part of Pakistan)

Deringer The original weapons made by Henry Deringer; the imitation was spelled with an additional *r*

derringer Short, extremely compact and concealable pistol

dha hymyung A Burmese dagger

dha lwe A Burmese sword

dhal A Persian shield

double-action A pistol (either revolver or automatic) in which a single, long trigger pull both fires the weapon and brings a cartridge into the chamber in readiness for firing. *See also* single-action

dyak Sword used by the Dyak people of Borneo

f

fighting knife, or combat knife Edged weapon intended for use in combat rather than as a tool

firing pin The part of a gun's firing mechanism that strikes the cartridge's primer

flintlock Gun-firing system utilizing a piece of flint striking against a piece of steel to strike sparks for ignition

fu pa (Chinese "tiger fork") Three-pronged head metal head on a shaft

g

gas-operated Term used to describe a gun that taps excess gas from the weapon to operate the action

Gatling gun A multi-barreled gun fed from a hopper, developed during the American Civil War and still in use in an eletctrically operated version

guard Vertical projections on a sword or knife, separating the hilt from the blade. Also known as *crossguard*

gauge For shotguns, the equivalent of the term "caliber," in this case expressed as fractions of a pound, e.g., 12-gauge; synonymous with bore

grabendoch German term for "trench dagger"

grip General term for the handle of a sword or knife

h

handgun Originally used to refer to any firearm that could be carried and used by an individual; in modern usage it refers solely to pistols

hilt The portion of a sword grasped by the user, usually consisting of the guard, grip, and pommel

hoplite Armed artillery soldier of Ancient Greece

howdah pistol A powerful British pistol used by elephant riders to fend off tigers

j

jambiya An Arabian curved dagger that was mostly decorative it was but also an effective fighting knife

jian A Chinese short sword

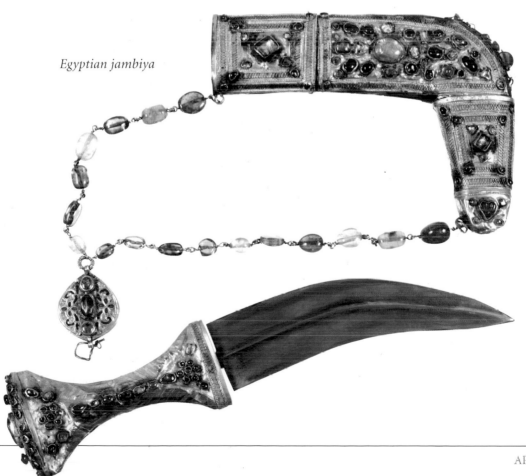

Egyptian jambiya

k

katana Traditional sword of the Japanese samurai

kindjal A curved double-edged fighting knife of the Cossacks

koftgari A form of decoration consisting of gold-inlaid steel

kora The national sword of Nepal

kris, or *keris* A traditional knife of Malaysia and Indonesia

kuba Deadly weapon of the Kuba people from West Africa

kukri, or *khukuri* A Nepalese fighting knife

kulah khud Indo-Persian helmet

l

lever-action A gun that uses a lever, pushed downward and then upward by the firer, to load and eject cartridges

luk Bend in a kris

m

magazine The part of a gun containing cartridges in readiness for firing; in rifles, the magazine is often charged (loaded) by a clip

main-gauche A dagger held in the left hand, used in conjunction with a sword in European swordfighting during the Renaissance

Mameluke sword A curved sword used by the slave-soldiers of Islamic armies, its pattern later adopted for ceremonial use in the West

matchlock Early firearms which used a slow-burning match to provide ignition

mere *See* patu

musket Generally, a smoothbore, shoulder-fired infantry weapon, in use in the West up until the widespread introduction of rifles in the mid-nineteenth century

musketoon A short-barreled musket

muzzle The opening of a gun's barrel

muzzle-loading Used to refer to a gun that loads by the muzzle

n

nimcha A curved, North African blade of varying lengths

p

pallask A double-edged sword designed to penetrate the chain-mail armor worn by mounted soldiers of the Ottoman Empire

Nepalese kukri

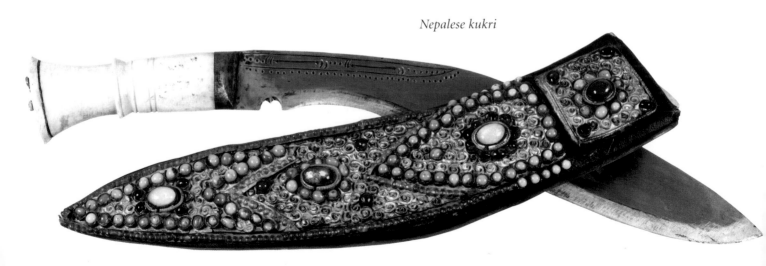

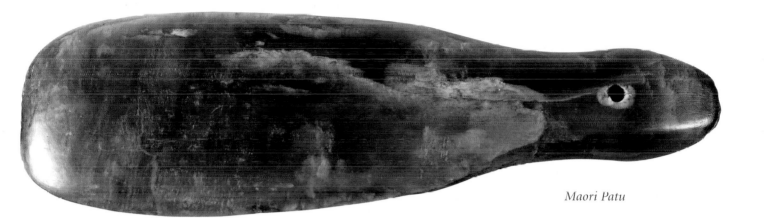

Maori Patu

partisan *See* patu

patu A short-handled war club that was the principal weapon of the Maori people of New Zealand; also known as a *partizan*

percussion cap A capsule containing a fulminating agent

pesh-kabz A curved Persian knife used to penetrate chain-mail armor

piha kaetta A traditional knife of Sri Lanka (now Ceylon); mainly a ceremonial weapon

pinfire An early type of self-contained cartridge, no longer in common use

plate armor Personal armor made of overlapping plates of iron or steel

pommel The often knoblike projection atop a sword or knife

primer The part of a cartridge which, when struck by the firing pin, ignites and fires the main charge

pump-action A gun whose action is operated by a sliding mechanism, usually mounted below the barrel

q

quarrel *See* bolt

quillion Sword separator between blade and hilt that can be either straight or curved; *see* guard

quiver A container for arrows

r

receiver Generally speaking, the part of a gun incorporating the action, as distinct from the stock and barrel

recoil The backward pressure exerted when a gun is fired

recoil-operated A type of semi or fully automatic gun that uses recoil to operate the action

rifling The process of boring cylindrical grooves into a gun barrel to stabilize the bullet in flight, thus increasing accuracy

rimfire A type of cartridge in which the primer is evenly distributed around the rear of the base

round Synonym for cartridge, usually used to refer to magazine capacity, e.g., twenty-round.

s

saber, or sabre Curved sword typically used by cavalry

safety The part of a gun's action designed to prevent accidental firing

salampusa An iron-bladed sword used by the warriors of the Salampasu people of Africa

scabbard Receptacle for carrying a sword

scimitar Catch-all term for curved-bladed swords of Middle Eastern origin

self-loading Used to refer to guns that will fire once with each trigger pull without the need to reload; synonymous with semi-automatic

German wheel-lock rifle

semi-automatic *See* self-loading

snaphance, snaphaunce A type of lock, an ancestor of the flintlock

sheath Receptacle for carrying a knife

shotgun Smoothbore, shoulder-fired weapon, typically firing buckshot; most commonly used in hunting but also in combat

single-action A revolver which has to be manually cocked before each shot; single-action automatics require cocking only before the first shot is fired; *see also* double-action

smoothbore A gun with an unrifled barrel. *See* rifling

sodegarami The Japanese sleeve grabber was used by police to immobilize criminals

stock Any part of a gun which is gripped with the hand before firing, e.g., forestock; *see also* butt

t

torador An matchlock musket that was used in India for hundreds of years

tanto A Japanese dagger utilized by the Samurai

thumbscrew A torture device that compressed the thumb or other fingers using a screw

trebuchet Medieval catapult

trigger The part of a gun's action pulled back by the firer's finger to discharge the weapon

tulwar, or talwar All-steel Indian curved saber

u

umKhonto South African spear

w

wheel lock Firing mechanism that used the friction of a spring-powered metal wheel against iron or flint for ignition

y

yari A Japanese straight-headed spear

yataghan A major blade weapon of the Ottoman Empire from the fifteenth through the nineteenth centuries

z

zweihänder The longest sword of the European Renaissance; from the German for "two-hander"

BIBLIOGRAPHY

Agoston, Gabor, and David Morgan. *Guns for the Sultan: Military Power and the Weapons Industry in the Ottoman Empire*. New York: Cambridge University Press, 2005.

Ahearn, Bill. *Muskets of the Revolution and the French & Indian Wars*. Woonsocket, RI: Andrew Mowbray Publications, 2005.

Akehurst, Richard. *The World of Guns*. London: Hamlyn, 1972.

Anglim, Simon, et al. *Fighting Techniques of the Ancient World (3000 B.C. to A.D. 500): Equipment, Combat Skills, and Tactics*. New York: Thomas Dunne Books, 2003.

Armour, Richard. *It All Started with Stones and Clubs: Being a Short History of War and Weaponry from Earliest Times to the Present, Noting the Gratifying Progress Made by Man Since His First Crude, Small-Scale Efforts to Do Away with Those Who Disagreed with Him*. New York: McGraw-Hill, 1967.

Berk, Joseph. *Gatling Gun: 19th-century Machine Gun to 21st-century Vulcan*. Boulder, CO: Paladin Press, 1991.

Bezdek, Richard H. *American Swords and Sword Makers*. Boulder, CO: Paladin Press, 1994.

Blackmore, Howard L. *Hunting Weapons: From the Middle Ages to the Twentieth Century*. Mineola, NY: Dover Publications, 2000.

Boorman, Dean K. *History of Winchester Firearms*. Guilford, CT: The Lyons Press, 2001.

Breuer, William B. *Secret Weapons of World War II*. New York: Wiley, 2002.

Bruce, Robert. *German Automatic Weapons of World War II*. Marlborough, UK: Crowood Press, 1998.

Canby, Courtlandt. *A History of Weaponry*. New York: Hawthorne Books, 1963.

Canfield, Bruce N. *U.S. Infantry Weapons of World War II*. Woonsocket, RI: Andrew Mowbray Publications, 1996.

Chapel, Charles Edward. *The Gun Collector's Handbook of Values* (eighth rev. ed.). New York: Coward-McCann, 1968.

Collier, James Lincoln. *Gunpowder and Weaponry*. New York: Benchmark Books, 2004.

Finnish mortar

Tibetan ritual dagger

Craig, Philip. *The World's Great Small Arms*. London: Amber Books, 1993.

Daugherty III, Leo. *Fighting Techniques of a Japanese Infantryman 1941–1945: Training, Techniques and Weapons*. Staplehurst, UK: Spellmount Publishers, 2002.

David, Nicolle. *Mughul India 1504–1761*. Oxford, UK: Osprey, 1993.

Diagram Group. *Weapons: An International Encyclopedia from 5000 B.C. to A.D. 2000*. New York: St. Martin's Griffin, 1991.

Draeger, Donn F. *The Weapons and Fighting Arts of Indonesia*. North Clarendon, VT: Tuttle Publishing, 2001.

Dupur, Tervor Nevitt. *The Evolution of Weapons and Warfare*. Cambridge, MA: Da Capo Press, 1990.

Fleming, David. *Weapons of the Waffen SS*. St. Paul, MN: MBI Publishing Company, 2003.

Gommans, Joseph. *Mughal Warfare: Indian Frontiers and Highroads to Empire 1500–1700*. New York: Routledge, 2003.

Hall, Bert S. *Weapons and Warfare in Renaissance Europe: Gunpowder, Technology, and Tactics*. Baltimore, MD: Johns Hopkins University Press, 2001.

Healy, Mark, and Angus McBride. *The Ancient Assyrians*. Oxford, UK: Osprey, 1992.

Hogg, Ian. *The Guinness Encyclopedia of Weaponry*. Enfield, Middlesex, UK: Guinness Publishing, 1992.

———. *Handguns & Rifles: The Finest Weapons from Around the World*. Guilford, CT: The Lyons Press, 2003.

Hogg, Ian, and John Walter. *Pistols of the World* (fourth ed.). Iola, WI: Krause Publications, 2004.

Hogg, Ian, and John Weeks. *Military Small Arms of the 20th Century* (seventh ed.) Iola, WI: Krause Publications, 2000.

Holmes, Richard. *Britain at War: Famous British Battles from Hastings to Normandy, 1066–1944*. Irvington, NY: Hylas Publishing, 2004.

Hutton, Alfred. *The Sword and the Centuries*. Boulder, CO: Paladin Press, 2002.

Kelly, Jack. *Gunpowder: Alchemy, Bombards, and Pyrotechnics—The History of the Explosive That Changed the World*. New York: Basic Books, 2004.

Izuka, Kunio. *Weapons of the Samurai*. London: Chrysalis Books, 2001.

Kern, Paul Bentley. *Ancient Siege Warfare*. Indianapolis: Indiana University Press, 1999.

Marcot, Roy. *The History of Remington Firearms: The History of One of the World's Most Famous Gun Makers*. Guilford, CT: The Lyons Press, 2005.

McChristian, Douglas C. *The U.S. Army in the West, 1870–1880: Uniforms, Weapons, and Equipment*. Oklahoma City: University of Oklahoma Press, 2000.

McNab, Chris. *The Great Book of Guns: An Illustrated History of Military, Sporting, and Antique Firearms*. San Diego, CA: Thunder Bay Press, 2004.

Medieval Siege Weapons: Western Europe AD 585–1385. Oxford, UK: Osprey, 2002.

Miller, David, ed. *The Illustrated Book of Guns*. London: Salamander Books, 2000.

———, ed. *Illustrated Directory of Twentieth-Century Guns*. St. Paul, MN: MBI Publishing Company, 2003.

Nagayama, Kokan. *The Connoisseur's Book of Japanese Swords*. Translated from the Japanese by Kenji Mishina. Tokyo: Kodansha International, 1998.

Nicholson, Helen. *Medieval Warfare*. New York: Palgrave Macmillan, 2004.

Nicolle, David, and Christa Hook. *Italian Militiaman 1260–1392*. Oxford, UK: Osprey, 1999.

O'Connell, Richard, and John Batchelor. *Soul of the Sword: An Illustrated History of Weaponry and Warfare from Prehistory to the Present*. New York: Free Press, 2002.

Partridge, Robert B. *Fighting Pharaohs: Weapons and Warfare in Ancient Egypt*. Clearwater, FL: Peartree Books, 2002.

Poyer, Joe. *U.S. Winchester Trench and Riot Guns and Other U.S. Combat Shotguns: For Collectors Only*. Tustin, CA: North Cape Publications, 1992.

Pritchard Jr., Russ A. *Civil War Weapons and Equipment*. Guilford, CT: The Lyons Press, 2003.

Pyhrr, Stuart W., Donald J. LoRocca, and Morihiro Ogawa. *Arms and Armor: Notable Acquisitions 1991–2002*. New York: Metropolitan Museum of Art, 2003.

Ricketts, Howard. *Firearms*. London: Octopus Books, 1972.

Sato, Kanzan. *The Japanese Sword: A Comprehensive Guide*. Translated from the Japanese by Joe Earle. Tokyo: Kodansha America, 1983.

Stratton, Charles R. *British Enfield Rifles, Vol. 4, the Pattern 1914 and U.S. Model 1917 Enfield Rifles*. Tustin, CA: North Cape Publications, 2000.

Thompson, Logan. *Ancient Weapons in Britain*. South Yorkshire, UK: Pen and Sword, 2005.

Tunis, Edwin. *Weapons: A Pictorial History*. Baltimore, MD: The Johns Hopkins University Press, 1999.

Turnbull, Stephen, and Wayne Reynolds. *Siege Weapons of the Far East: AD 960–1644*. Oxford, UK: Osprey, 2002.

Van Zonneveld, Albert G. *Traditional Weapons of the Indonesian Archipelago*. Amsterdam: KITLV Press (Royal Netherlands Academy of Arts and Sciences), 2002.

Walter, John. *The Luger Story: The Standard History of the World's Most Famous Handgun*. London: Greenhill Books, 2001.

Warry, John Gibson. *Warfare in the Classical World: An Illustrated Encyclopedia of Weapons, Warriors, and Warfare in the Ancient Civilizations of Greece and Rome*. New York: St. Martin's Press, 1981.

Watts, Steven. *Practicing Primitive: A Handbook of Aboriginal Skills*. Layton, Utah: Gibbs Smith, 2005.

Weir, William. *Fifty Weapons That Changed Warfare*. Franklin Lakes, NJ: New Page Books, 2005.

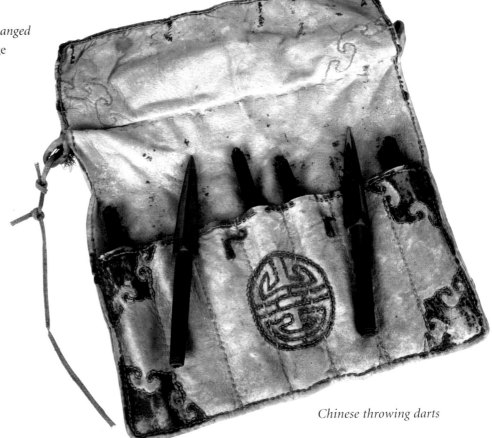

Chinese throwing darts

ABOUT THE BERMAN MUSEUM

Since the Berman Museum of World History opened its doors to the public in April of 1996, thousands of visitors have enjoyed its unique and varied collection of art, historical objects, and weapons. Located in Anniston, Alabama—in the Appalachian foothills—and next door to the seventy-five-year-old Smithsonian-affiliated Anniston Museum of Natural History, the Berman Museum's reputation and collection have grown exponentially since its inception. The Berman Museum's holdings number 8,500 objects, with 3,000 items related to world history exhibited in its galleries. Objects from around the world include such items as a rare air rifle from Austria, military insignia from German and Italy, a scimitar from the Middle East, and graphically carved kris holders from Indonesia. The Museum attracts both a global and regional audience. All who visit can appreciate the historic significance of the collection and gain greater awareness and respect of other cultures.

Its five galleries—Deadly Beauty, American West, World War I, World War II, and Arts of Asia—exhibit items span a 3,500-year period. A focal point of the Deadly Beauty gallery is the elaborate Royal Persian Scimitar, circa 1550, created for Abbas the Great, King of Persia. The American West gallery covers approximately 200 years (ca. 1700 to 1900), emphasizing the United State's political, economic, social and cultural structures, and their influences on settling the West.

The World War galleries use objects from the Museum collection to explore the causes and conditions of both wars, the historical significance of the countries involved, and the resulting political, economic, cultural and social changes brought about by each war. A rare piece of equipment in the World War I gallery is the Tanker's Splinter Goggles, used by tank personnel to protect their eyes and faces from metal splinters from machine-gun fire. Exhibited in the World War II gallery is the M1942 "Liberator" Pistol, as well as a large collection of Adolf Hitler's tea and coffee service, purported to have come from the last bunker that the Führer occupied. The Arts of Asia exhibit features an extensive and ever-growing collection of Asian textiles, ceramics, sculpture, jade, and metal.

The Berman Museum of World History is home to the vast and eclectic collection of Colonel Farley L. Berman and his wife, Germaine. Farley Berman, a lifelong resident of Anniston, Alabama, served in the European theater during World War II, and in the occupation force afterward. There he met Germaine, a French national. They were married and spent the next fifty years traveling the world acquiring historic weapons and artifacts, paintings, bronzes, and other works of art. Berman's self-trained collector's eye recognized the importance of items that were perhaps seen as ordinary, and he made it his mission to preserve a few. The Bermans established contacts—and a reputation—in numerous auction houses and among antique dealers in Europe and America.

The Bermans freely shared their collection with the public long before the City of Anniston constructed the Museum facility. Hundreds of military dignitaries and others were invited to their home for personal tours of their collection. Colonel Berman could best be described as a colorful storyteller and was notorious for firing blank rounds from his collection of spy weapons when guests least expected. He advised aspiring collectors to purchase good reference books, spend some years reading, and visit museums before acquiring.

During the early 1990s, several large museums expressed interest in receiving the Bermans' collection. They were disappointed when Germaine proposed that the collection remain in Anniston. Colonel and Mrs. Berman's collection stands as the core of Berman Museum. Since the Museum's opening, many have recognized its importance and have contributed their own personal treasures to this impressive collection.

INDEX

a

Abbas I, 10–11, 91
Adams, Robert, 134, 147
Adams revolvers, 140, 147
adze, 94
African swords, 90
    ceremonial, 94
    Kuban, 94
    Masai seme, 55
    Salampasu, 95
aircraft cannon, Japanese, 206
air rifle, 112
AK47 (Automat Kalashnikov), 47, 193, 209, 216,
    217
Akehurst, Richard, 102, 114
alarm guns, 170
    Naylor, 171
    Wallis, 170
Alexander II, Czar, 144
Allen, C. B., 135
Allen, Ethan, 126
Allen & Thurber, 126
Allen & Wheelock, 137
Allied pistols of World War II, 198–199
    Swedish M40, 199
    Tokarev, 199
    Webley 7.65 auto, 199
    Webley Mark IV, 198
    Webley Mark VI, 198
American blunderbuss, 103
American Civil War, 138–139
    Confederate weapons, 142–143
    experimentation and innovation, 139
    tactics and technology, 139
    Union weapons, 140–141
American West, weapons of the, 144–147
    across the mountains, 144
    Adams revolver, 147
    Belle Star revolver, 147
    Colt Lightning rifle, 145
    Elephalet Remington, 147
    Maximilian rifle, 145
    on the frontier, 144
    Oliver Winchester, 145
    push dagger, 146
    Remington rifle, 147
    Sharps, 146
    Winchester 66, 144, 145
    Winchester 73, 146
    Winchester Model 1866, *see* Winchester 66
Amherst, Sir Jeffrey, 215
anthrax, 214, 215
Apache, 167
Argentine Mauser, 151
Arisaka rifle, 183, 200
Armalite rifle, 216
armor, 46–49
    helmets, 46–47
    hoplites to knights, 46
    non-metal, 46
    shields, 48–49

Spanish, 48
arrowhead, Persian, 20
arrows:
    African, 28
    African quiver, 29
    flaming, 27
    Japanese signal, 29
artillery, 31, 65, 70
    Napoleonic, 111
Asian blades, 62–63
Asian swords, 90–99
    Chinese, 90, 98–99
    Damascus steel, 92
    dha lwe, 95
    dyak, 93
    history of, 90
    Indian ritual, 92
    Japanese, 90, 96–97, 194
    kora, 93
    Mughal, 92
    Persian, 91, 92
    Tibetan, 93
    tulwar, 92
assegai, 40, 44
atlatl, 15, 16, 19
AUSTEN, 208
Australasian weapons, 24–25
Australopithecus, 16
automatic pistols, 152–155
    Bermann, 152, 153
    Borchardt, 152
    Broomhandle Mauser, 155
    Browning, 152, 153
    Colt .45, 154
    Glisente, 154
    Luger, 152, 153, 154
    Schwarzlose, 155
Auto-Ordinance Company, 189
ax heads:
    African ceremonial, 45
    African copper, 45
    Bronze Age, 21
    stone, 19
    Turkish, 8
Axis pistols of World War II, 196–197
    Bertta M1934 automatic, 197
    CZ27 automatic, 196
    Luger with drum magazine, 197
    Nambu automatics, 196
    Walther P38, 197
ax-pistols:
    Balkan, 78–79
    German, 79

b

baby revolver, 158
Bacon, Roger, 8
bagh nakh, 59
Baker, Ezekiel, 10
Baker rifle, 110
Barker Gang, 188

battle-ax-gun, 165
battle axes, 40
    African, 45
    Chinese, 43
    Indian, 44
    Indo-Persian lance head, 42
Battle of Morat gun, 71
Bayeux Tapestry, 36
bayonet, 110
    with Argentine Mauser, 151
    Austrian steel, 143
    with French Musket, 75
    German police, 205
    "Indian Pattern," 180
    Lebel, 182
    MKII, 181
    with Mosin-Nagant, 150
    with SMLE, 150, 181
    with Swedish Mauser, 151
Beaumont-Adams, 134
Beaumont "Mousqueton," 149
Belgian carbine, 148
Belgian pistols, 105
    auto 7966, 178
    dueling, 101
    palm, 157
Belle Star revolver, 147
Belloc, Hilaire, 184
Bell Telephone Laboratories, 212
belt pistols, 78
    Spanish, 83
Berdan, Hiram, 139
Beretta, House of, 197
Beretta M1934 automatic pistol, 197
Bergmann, Theodor, 152
Bergmann-Bayard M1910, 178
Bergmann Model 1894, 153
Berman, Colonel Farley, 91
Berthier carbine, 149
Berton, Pierre, 180
Bhagavad-Gita, The, 34
bicycle pistol, 158
Biehl, Art, 217
biological warfare, 214–215
blackjack, 163
black powder, 64–67
Blish, John, 189
Bloch, Ivan, 186
blunderbuss, 102–103
    American, 103
    Euro, 103
    French, 103
    Indian, 74, 103
    on the road and off, 102
    Spanish, 118
    as the "thunder-box," 102
    trap gun, 102
    Turkish, 103
boarding ax, British naval, 105
bola, 18
bolt-action magazine rifles, 148–151
    Beaumont "Mousqueton," 149

Belgian carbine, 149
Berthier carbine, 149
chassepot, 148
Gewehr, 150
Krag, 148
Mausers, 149, 151
Mosin-Nagant, 150
needle-gun, 148
SMLE, 150
"Torino," 150
Vetterli, 150
Bonnie and Clyde, 10, 118
Booth, John Wilkes, 126
Borchardt, Hugo, 152
Borchardt pistol, 152
botulism, 214
Boutet, Nicholas, 119
Boutet pistol, 119
Bowie, Jim and Rezin, 143
Bowie knife, 143
bows, 26–29
    African, 27
    Central American Indian, 29
    Indo-Persian, 29
bracelet, fighting, 57
brass knuckles, 162
Bren gun, 206
British swords:
    1897, 125
    general's, 120, 121
broadsword, Scottish, 87
Bronze Age, 20–21
Brooklyn Arms Company, 136
Broomhandle Mauser, 155
"Brown Bess," 110
Browning, John M., 152, 153, 184, 199, 206, 207
Browning Automatic Rifle (BAR), 153, 186,
    206, 207
Browning High-Power, 153, 198
Browning M2, 206, 207
Burnside carbine, 139
Burr, Aaron, 101

C

camel gun, 74
cane guns, 156
    hiking-stick, 161
    Lane, 160
    walking-stick, 161
cannon bar pistol, 82
cannon igniter, 75
cannons, 65, 67
    bronze artillery, 111
    Japanese aircraft, 206
"cap and ball" weapons, 130, 131, 134
caplocks, see percussion cap weapons
Capone, Al, 188
carbines, see specific carbines
Carcano, Salvatore, 183
Caron, Alphonse, 100
Caron dueling pistols, 100

cartridge-firing revolvers, 134–137
    see also specific revolver
Castro, Fidel, 212
Catherine the Great, 10–11, 91
cellular phone/pistol, 9
ceremonial weapons of World War II, 202–205
    German army officer's sword, 203
    German police bayonet, 205
    Goering baton, 203
    Himmler rifle, 205
    Italian Fascist Party knife, 205
    Luftwaffe/army daggers, 204
    Luftwaffe sword, 204
    Mussolini sword, 202
    Nazi Labor Corps knife, 203
    SA dagger, 205
    swagger stick, 202
    totalitarian symbols, 202
chain mail, 46
Chalcolithic Age, 20–21
Chapel, Charles Edward, 156, 167
Charles the Bold, 71
Charles VII, King, 65
Charlesville musket, 110
Chase, Anton, 132
chassepot, 125, 148, 149
Chassepot, Antoine, 148
chastity belt, 37
Chauchet automatic rifle, 185
chemical warfare, 214–215
Chicago Firearms Co., 157
"Chicago Protector," 156
    palm pistol, 157
Chinese percussion conversion, 118–119
Chinese swords, 90
    double sword, 98
    fang, 98
    helmet breaker, 99
    jian, 98
    short, 98, 99
cholera, 215
Churchill, Winston, 184
CIA (Central Intelligence Agency), 212, 213
Cicero, 174
claw daggers, Indian, 59
claymore, 87
Clermont pistol, 81
clubs:
    Fijian calacula, 24
    Fijian war, 25
    Maori patu, 24
    Northwest Indian, 22
    Plains Indians, 24
    Sioux dance, 24
    Tlingit, 23
coaching carbine, 158
coat pistols, 78
    French, 80
Cochran, J. W., 135
Coehorn mortar, 76
Cogswell & Harrison, 135
Cogswell transition gun, 135
Cold War, 212

Collier, Elisha, 130
Collins machete M1942, 194
Colt, Samuel, 130, 132
Colt-Browning Model 1895 machine gun, 184
Colt M1911 automatic pistol, 152, 153, 154,
    178, 189, 196, 197, 198, 199
Colt revolvers, 130–133
    competitors of, 134–137
    evolution of, 130
    Model 1860, 140
    Model 1873 SAA, 144
    Navy, 131
    new double action, 133
    New Navy, 133
    Paterson, 130, 132
    Pocket Model, 131
    Police Positive, 188
    rifle, 132
Colt Vickers machine gun, 185
combination weapons, 9, 164–169
    Apache, 167
    battle-axe-gun, 165
    combo pistol dagger, 168
    cutlass pistol, 169
    dagger pistol, 165
    dirk pistol, 164
    Ethiopian shield with pistols, 166
    Indian, 167
    Indian mace/pistol, 168
    Indian shield with pistols, 166
    knife pistol, 165
    knife revolver, 167
    Marble game-getter, 169
    19th century combo, 168
    truncheon gun, 164
    Turkish gun-shield, 166
    Twigg, 116
Confederate weapons of the Civil War,
    142–143
    Austrian steel, 143
    carbines, 142
    homemade blade, 143
    imports and imitations, 142
    Jefferson Davis, 142, 143
    LeMat pistol, 143
    starting from scratch, 142
Cornell, Bernard, 77
Cortes, Hernan, 19
crossbows, 26–29, 31
    child's, 28
    Chinese repeating, 27
cross dagger, 37
crowbill, Indo-Persian, 43
Crusades, the, 30–31
    Saracens and, 31
    sieges in the Holy Land, 31
cuirass, 46
Custer, Colonel George Armstrong, 147
cutlass, 105
    see also swords
cutlass pistol, 169
CZ27 automatic pistol, 196

d

dagger pistol, 165
daggers and fighting knives, 50–63
    around the world, 50
    Asian, 62–63
    Bowie, 143
    bronze, 21
    ceremonial, of World War II, 203–205
    Chinese, 63
    Chinese export, 63
    Cossack kindjal, 53
    dagger cane, 50
    dha hmyaung, 95
    flywhisk, 162
    gravity, 163
    Indian, *see* Indian fighting implements
    Indo-Persian, 55
    kukri, 51
    left-handed, 52
    main gauche, 52
    naval dirk, 52
    North African, *see* North African blades
    Persian 3-blade, 56
    push, 146
    Spanish fighting knives, 53
    Spanish folding, 163
    Syrian, 53
    tanto, 96, 97
    in the West, 50
    of World War I, 176–177
    of World War II, 194–195
dags, 72
daisho, 90
Damascus steel, 92
Danish short sword, 87
Darra, 127
dart and dagger, 212
Darwin, Charles, 18
da Vinci, Leonardo, 8–9
Davis, Jefferson, 142
    cased pistols, 143
Day, John, 156
deadly music, 213
deadly tools, 213
death battery, 77
deception, weapons of, 160–161
    hiking-stick gun, 161
    Lane cane gun, 160
    swagger stick gun, 161
    umbrella gun, 161
    walking-stick gun, 161
"deer gun," 213
Deringer, Henry, 126
derringers, 126
    British, 129
    howdah, 129
    ladies case with pistol compartment, 128
    Remington, 128
    turn-over, 129
Deutsch Waffen & Munitions Fabriken
    (DWM), 152

dha hmyaung, 95
dhal, 49
dhal lwe, 95
Diamond, Jared, 85
Dillinger, John, 10, 188
dirk, naval, 52, 105
dirk pistol, 164
dog head pistol, 80
double-action revolvers, 130, 134
double sword, Chinese, 98
dragoon sword, 122
dress pistol, Balkan, 79
dress sword, French, 89
drummer boy rifle, 112
dual-fire pistols, 119
    Spanish, 115
Dublin Castle pistol, 80
duckfoot pistol, 78, 79
dueling pistols, 100–101
    accuracy and reliability, 100
    Belgian, 101
    Caron, 100
    great gunsmiths, 100
    Wogdon, 101
Dumonthier & Sons, 164
dyak, 93

e

East India pistol, 117
Eastwood, Clint, 136
Eddystone Enfield, 180
edged weapons of World War I, 176–177
    German combat knife, 177
    German saber, 177
    U.S. trench knives 1 and 2, 176
edged weapons of World War II, 194–195
    Collins machete, 194
    German hewing knife, 194
    Ka-Bar, 194, 195
    Russian fighting knife, 194
    Sykes-Fairbairn Commando Knife, 194,
        195
Edward III, King, 38, 39
Edward VII, King, 146
Elliott, William, 145
Ellis, John, 184
Enfield Mark III, 181
Enfield rifled musket, 142
entrenching tool bayonet M1169, 201
espionage, weapons of, 212–213
    Cold War, 212
    dart and dagger, 212
    deadly music, 213
    deadly tools, 213
    gas gun, 212
    Liberator pistol, 212, 213
    lozenge-case gun, 213
    OSS and SOE, 212
    pen gun, 212
estoc, 84
Ethiopian shield with pistols, 166

Euro blunderbuss, 103
European swords, 84–89
    bigger and longer, 84
    British cavalry, 113
    French dress, 89
    King's Guard, 113
    King's Own Royal Border Regiment, 88
    Knights of Malta, 87
    landsknecht, 84
    longswords, see longswords
    Louis XIII Royal Guard, 87
    made in Toledo, 85
    Scottish broadsword, 87
    short, see short swords
    as status symbol, 84

f

Fairbairn, W. E., 195
falcata, 85
fang, 98
fencing epees, 219
fighting knives, *see* daggers and fighting knives
finger knife, 59
flails, 37
flare pistols, German, 211
flintlock long guns, 69, 72, 74–77
    African trade guns, 75
    Arab miquelet, 77
    camel gun, 74
    cannon igniter, 75
    conversion to percussion, 118–119
    French musket, 75
    Indian blunderbuss, 74
    volley gun, 77
flintlock pistols, 78–83
    ax-pistols, 78–79
    Balkan dress, 79
    cannon bar, 82
    Clermont, 81
    coat, 80
    conversion to percussion, 118–119
    dog head, 80
    Dublin Castle, 80
    French, 82
    Guard, 81
    Italian, 83
    Persian, 75
    pistol-sword, 79
    revolvers, 130, 132
    Scottish ram horn, 82
    Spanish belt, 83
    square barrel, 81
    tinder lighter, 78
Floyd, "Pretty Boy," 188
flywhisk dagger, 162
FN FAL, 216
Forsyth, Rev. Alexander, 114
fouchard, 41
Franklin, Benjamin, 76
French blunderbuss, 103
French 1845/55 sword, 122

French chassepot sword, 125
French gunner saber, 121
French pepperbox, 127
French pistols, 82
    palm, 157
French Second Empire sword, 123
French small sword, 88, 89
Froissart, Jean, 39
fu pa, Chinese, 41

g

Garand, John C., 201
gas billy club, 189
gas gun, 212
gas mask, U.S., 181
Gatling, Richard Jordan, 141
Gatling gun, 10, 139, 141, 184
General Motors Corporation, 213
George III, King, 80, 105
George VI, King, 202
German army officer's sword, 203
German hewing knife, 194
German MG42 machine gun, 206, 216
German police bayonet, 205
German WWI revolver, 179
Gewehr:
    Model 1871, 149
    Model 1888, 150
    Model 1898, 149
Girandoni, Bartolomeo, 112
glaive, 41
Glisenti, 154
    M1910 auto, 179
Glock AG, 216
Goering, Hermann, 203
Goering baton, 203
Grattius, 85
gravity dagger, 163
great sword, 86
Greek fire, 104
Greener, W. W., 171
Greener's Humane Cattle Killer, 171
greenstone celt, 17
grenade launcher, 105
grenades, 9
Guard pistols, 81
gunpowder:
    castles under siege, 65
    fireworks to firearms, 65
Guns, Germs, and Steel (Diamond), 85
gun-shield, Turkish, 166
Gyrojet pistol, 217

h

halberd, 40
    English, 40
    Swiss, 41
Halstaffe of Regent Street, 178
Hamilton, Alexander, 101

hand cannons, 65
    to matchlocks, 70–71
    Spanish, 71
Handel, G. W., 84
handgonne, French, 71
handheld firearms, 64–67, 69
    see also specific firearms
Hannibal, 108
Hanson, Victor Davis, 22
Harper's Ferry musket, 114–115
Hawken, Jacob, 144
Hawken, Samuel, 144
HEAT (High Explosive Anti-Tank) projectile,
    210, 211
Hecker & Koch, 149
    VP70, 216
helmet breaker, 99
helmets, 46
    English, 47
    Indo-Persian, 47
    Italian parade, 46
Henry, Benjamin Tyler, 140, 145
Henry rifle, 140, 144, 145
Henry V, King, 39
Henry VII, King, 37
Henry VIII, King, 104
hiking-stick gun, 161
Himmler, Heinrich, 205
Himmler rifle, 205
Hi-Standard automatic, 212
Hitler, Adolf, 202, 203
Hogg, Ian, 196
holster pistols, 78, 112, 117
howdah pistol, 129
Hundred Years War, 26, 38–39
hunting sword, 124
Hus, Jan, 36
Hussein, Saddam, 215

i

Indian blunderbuss, 74, 103
Indian combo, 167
Indian fighting implements, 58–61
    claw daggers, 59
    finger knife, 59
    kris, 60–61
    piha kaetta, 59
    throwing knife, 58
    wrist knife, 58
Indian mace/pistol, 168
"Indian Pattern" bayonet, 180
Indian percussion conversion, 118–119
Indian ritual sword, 92
Indian shield with pistols, 166
infantry rifles of World War I, 180–183
    bolt action, 180
    Eddystone Enfield, 180
    Enfield, 181
    Japanese paratroop, 183
    KAR 98, 180
    Mannlicher-Carcano, 183

mortars, 182
Mosin-Nagant M91/30/59, 183
Russian carbine M1944, 183
semiautomatics, 180
Vetterli-Vitali, 183
infantry rifles of World War II:
    British entrenching tool bayonet M1169,
        201
    Japanese Type 38, 200
    Japanese Type 99, 200
    Mannlicher-Carcano carbine/grenade
        launcher, 201
    M1 carbine, 200
    M1 Garand, 201
Iron Age, 20
Italian Fascist Party knife, 205
Italian pistols, 83

j

jambiya, 54
Japanese pistol, 71
Japanese rifles:
    Type 38, 200
    Type 99, 200
Japanese swords, 90
    katana, 96, 97
    officers, 97
jian, 98
Joan of Arc, 39
John II, King, 39
Jorgensen, Erik, 149

k

Ka-Bar fighting knife, 194, 195
Kalashnikov, M. T., 217
Kalashnikov rifle, 47, 193, 209, 216, 217
KAR-98, 180
kaskara, 90
katana, 90, 92
    18th century, 96
    officers, 97
Keegan, John, 39
Kennedy, John F., 183
Kentucky rifle, 73
Kerr, James, 146
key pistol, 71
KGB, 212
kilic, 90
kindjal, Cossack, 53
King of Siam sword, 125
King's Own Royal Border Regiment sword, 88
knife pistol, 165
knife revolver, 167
Knight's of Malta sword, 87
knives, see daggers and fighting knives
Kolb, Henry, 158
kora, 93
Krag, Ole, 149
Krag Jorgensen, 148, 149

kris, 50, 60–61
    Bali, holder, 6, 61
    scabbard, 60
Kuban sword, 94
kukri, 50, 51
kulah khud, 47

l

Lahti, Almo, 199
Lake Erie Chemical Corporation, 212
Land pattern musket, 110
landsknecht, 84
Lane cane gun, 160
langes schwert, 84
Lebel:
    bayonet, 182
    revolver, 178
Leckie, Andrew, 142
Lee, Robert E., 139, 142
Lee-Metford, 148
left-handed dagger, 52
    main gauche, 52
Lemans family, 73
LeMat, Jean Alexander Francois, 143
LeMat pistol, 143
Le Merveilleux and Gauloise pistols, 156, 157
LePage pistol, 117
Lewis, Light Machine Gun, 185
Lewis, Noah, 185
Lewis and Clark, 103
"Liberator" pistol, 212, 213
Liliput pistol, 189
Lincoln, Abraham, 126, 141
Lindley, Robert, 8–12
line-throwing guns, 170
    Royal Navy pistol, 171
lipstick gun, 212
Lloyd, Thomas, 117
London Armoury Co., 146
longbow, 26, 30, 31
longswords, 84
    German, 85
    great sword, 86
    knight's, 84
    Maximilian I pallask, 86
Lorenz rifled musket, 143
Louis XI, King, 65
Louis XIII Royal Guard sword, 87
Louis XIV, King, 88
lozenge-case gun, 213
Ludwig Loewe & Company, 152
Luftwaffe/army daggers, 204
Luftwaffe sword, 204
Luger, Georg, 152
Luger pistol, 152, 153
    Artillery Model, 154
    with drum magazine, 197
Lyle gun, 170

m

M16, 193, 216
M1A1 "Bazooka," 210
maces, 36
    flails, 37
    Indian, 36
    Morgenstern, 37
    Turkish, 36
Machiavelli, Niccolo, 68
machine guns of World War II:
    Browing Automatic Rifle, 207
    Browning M2, 206, 207
    German MG42, 206
    Japanese aircraft cannon, 206
machine guns of World War I, 184–185
    Chauchet, 185
    Colt Vickers, 185
    Lewis Light, 185
    Marlin, 184
    Spandau Maxim, 185
main gauche, 52
Mainhardt, Robert, 217
Malenkov, Georgi, 212
mandau, 93
Manhattan Firearms Co., 147
Mannlicher-Carcano:
    carbine/grenade laucnher, 201
    Model 1941, 183
Manton, John, 100
Manton, Joseph, 100, 114
Marble Arms Manufacturing Co., 169
Marble game-gutter, 169
Mariette pepperbox, 127
Marlin machine gun, 184
Martin Arms, 184
MAS (Manufacture d'Armes de St. Etienne)
    submachine gun, 209
Massachusetts Arms Company, 135
matchlocks, 65, 69
    from hand cannon to, 70–71
    Indian, 70
    Japanese, 71
    successors to, 72
Mauser, Paul, 148
Mauser, Wilhelm, 148
Mausers, 149, 210
    Argentine, 151
    Broomhandle, 155
    Panzerbusche, 210
    Persian, 151
    Swedish, 151
    Turkish, 151
Maxim, Hiram, 109, 152, 185
Maximilian I pallask, 86
Maxim machine gun, 109, 184
    Spandau, 185
Maynard, Edward, 114
Maynard Percussion Tape Primer system, 142
MBA Associates, 217
M1 carbine, 200
Merlin machine gun, 184

Mesolithic Era, 26
M1 Garand, 181, 193, 201
Miller, David, 82
miniature pepperboxes, English, 128
Minié, Claude, 139
Minié ball, 114, 139
Minneapolis Arms Company, 157
miquelot lock, 72
    Arab, 77
Mitrailleave:
    machine gun, 184
    "window revolver," 188
Mongol swords, 90
    Mamekuke saber, 91
Moore, Daniel, 137
Moore's Patent Firearms Company, 137
mortars:
    Coehorn, 76
    French Model 1937, 182
Mosin, Sergei, 183
Mosin-Nagant, 150, 210
    carbine M1944, 183
    M91/30/59, 183
MP 40/44 (Machinepistole), 193, 200, 209
muff pistol, 156, 159
Mughal sword, 92
multiple-barreled pistols, 78, 79
multishot weapons, 9–10
Mussolini, Benito, 202, 205
Mussolini sword, 202

n

Nagant, Leon, 183
Nagant revolver, 178
Nambu automatic pistols, 196
Nambu Kirijo, Colonel, 196
Napoleon I, Emperor, 114
    as general, 110, 111
Napoleonic weapons, 110–113
    air rifle, 112
    artillery, 111
    British cavalry sword, 113
    British pistols, 112
    cavalry, 110
    drummer boy rifle, 112
    infantry, 110
    King's Guard sword, 113
    sword cane, 110–111
    youth saber, 111
Napoleon III, Emperor, 142
Narmer Palette, 36
Native American weapons, 22–25
naval weapons, 104–105
    Belgian pistols, 105
    boarders away, 104
    British boarding ax, 105
    broadsides, 104
    cutlass, 105
    dirk, 105
    Greek fire, 104
    grenade launcher, 105

rail gun, 105
Navy Colt, 131
    New, 133
Naylor, Isaac, 171
Naylor trap gun, 171
Nazi Labor Corps knife, 203
needle-gun, 148
Nelson, Horatio, 104
New Land Pattern pistol, 112
nimcha, 56
nineteenth-century swords, 120–125
    British 1831, 121
    British 1897, 125
    British general's, 120
    British presentation, 123
    Chinese double, 124
    dragoon, 122
    French 1845/55, 122
    French 1886 chassepot, 125
    French gunner, 121
    French Second Empire, 123
    hunting, 124
    King of Siam, 125
    parade, 125
    Prussian general's, 120
    Royal Horse Guard, 123
    U.S. foot artillery, 121
    Wilkinson Sword Company, 120
Nock, Henry, 77, 103
North African blades, 54–57
    African ritual knife, 56
    African sword, 55
    Arabian dagger, 54
    dagger, 56
    fighting bracelet, 57
    fighting knives, 57
    jambiya, 54
    nimcha, 56
    pesh kabz, 55
    scissors dagger, 57
    throwing knife, 57
    yataghan, 55

O

O'Bannon, Presley, 90
Odo, Bishop, 36
organ guns, 77
OSS (Office of Strategic Services), 212, 213
Oswald, Lee Harvey, 183
Ötzi, 21

P

pallask, Maximilian I, 86
palm pistols, 156
    Belgian, 157
    French, 157
    "Protector," 157
Panzerfaust, 210
panzerstecher, 84

parade sword, 125
Parker Brothers shotgun, 189
partisan, 41
Paterson revolver, 130, 132
Patti, Adelina, 159
Patti pinfire revolver, 159
Patton, General George S., 192, 201
"Peacemaker," 132
Pearson, John, 132
Pelissier, Aimable-Jean-Jacques, 103
pen gun, 212
pepperboxes, 126
    English miniature, 128
    French, 127
    Mariette, 127
percussion cap weapons, 114–119
    early, 114
    East India, 117
    flintlock conversions to, 118–119
    Harper's Ferry, 114–115
    Horse Guards, 117
    LePage, 117
    single-shot, 116
    Spanish, 115
    Springfield, 115
    Swiss, 116
    turnover, 117
    Twigg, 116
Persian Mauser, 151
Persian pistol, 75
Persian swords, 90, 92
    scimitar, 91
personal defense weapons, 156–159
    baby revolver, 158
    bicycle pistol, 158
    coaching carbine, 158
    muff pistol, 156, 159
    palm pistols, 156, 157
    Patti pinfire revolver, 159
    personal pistol, 156
    walking weapons, 156
    see also derringers
pesh kabz, 55
pestilence, 215
Philip, Craig, 154
Philip VI, King, 39
PIAT (Personal Infantry Anti-Tank) projector, 210, 211
piha kaetta, 59
pikes, 40, 43
    see also polearms
pistols, 72
    automatic, see automatic pistols
    blunderbuss, 103
    derringers, 126, 128–129
    dueling, 100–101
    pepperboxes, 126–127
    percussion cap, 114–119
    post-World War II, 216, 217
    of World War I, 178–179
    of World War II, 196–199
    see also individual pistols
pistol-sword, 79

plague, 215
Pocket Model Colt, 131
pocket pistols, 156, 188
polearms, 40–45
    Chinese, 41
    Chinese battle-ax, 42
    English, 40, 42
    Indian battle-ax, 44
    Indo-Persian crowbill, 43
    Indo-Persian lance head battle-ax, 42
    Italian, 41
    partisan, 41
    Swiss, 43
    Swiss halberd, 41
    see also spears
post–World War II weapons, 216–219
    AK47, 216, 217
    fencing epees, 219
    Gyrojet pistol, 217
    handguns, 216
    infantry weapons, 216
    SKS carbine, 219
    Weston miniature, 217
    Winchester Model 70, 219
Ppsh 41/42/43, 193, 208
prehistoric and ancient weapons, 12–31
Prince, The (Machiavelli), 68
Prussian general's sword, 120
Puckle, James, 184
pulwar, 90
push dagger, 146

q

"Queen Anne pistols," 82

r

rail gun, 105
ram horn pistols, Scottish, 82
rampart gun, 73
Real Fabbrica d'Armi Glisente, 154, 179
Reising, Eugene, 209
Reising submachine gun, 209
"rektal" knife, 212
Remington, Eliphalet, 147
Remington Arms Co., 147
    Model 1863 Army revolver, 134
    New Army, 136
    Rider magazine pistol, 128
    rifle, 147
Requa-Billinghurst battery gun, 139
revolvers, see specific revolvers
Richard the Lionhearted, 31
"Richmond Sharps," 142
Ricin, 215
rifles:
    bolt action, see bolt-action magazine
        rifles
    Mausers, see Mausers
    of the World Wars, see infantry rifles of

World War I; infantry rifles of World War II
   see also specific rifles
rimfire cartridges, 134, 136
Roaring Twenties, guns of the, 188–189
   Colt Police Positive, 188
   gas billy club, 189
   Liliput pistol, 189
   Mitrailleuse, 188
   Parker Brothers shotgun, 189
   pocket pistols, 188
   Tommy Gun, 188, 189
Robbins, David L., 210
Rouchouse, Jacques, 157
Roughing It (Twain), 126
Royal Company of Archers short sword, 85
Royal Horse Guards:
   pistol, 117
   sword, 123
Royal Persian scimitar, 91
rubber truncheon, 211
Rupert, Prince, 78
Russian fighting knife, 194

S

sabers, 90
   British cavalry, 113
   French gunner, 121
   German WWI, 177
   youth, 110–111
   see also swords
SA dagger, 205
saif, 90
Saladin, 31
Salampasu, 95
"salon" pistol, 116
Saracens, 31
Sarin, 215
Savage-North revolver, 140
Savage Revolving Arms Co., 140
Schmeisser, Hugo, 152, 178, 208, 209, 217
Schmeisser, Louis, 152
Schofield revolvers, 147
Schwarzlose, Andreas, 155
Schwarzlose Model 1908, 155
scimitars, 90
   Royal Persian, 10–11, 91
screw-off pistols, 78
set triggers, 100
Shaka, 44
shamshir, 90
Sharps, Christian, 140, 144, 146
Sharps carbines, 139, 142, 144
   "Big Fifty," 146
sharpshooter's glasses, 146
Shaw, Joshua, 114
Shepard, R. V., 208
shields:
   Ethiopian, with pistols, 166
   French, 49
   Indian, with pistols, 166

Indo-Persian, 49
Italian, 48
spike, 48
Turkish gun-shield, 166
short swords, 21
   Chinese, 98, 99
   cutlass, 105
   Danish, 87
   French, 88, 89
   Royal Company of Archers, 85
Shotel swords, 125, 202
shuangian, 98
siege guns, 65
signal guns, 170
   Chinese, 70
   nineteenth-century naval, 171
Simonov, Sergei, 219
single-action pistols, 128, 130, 134
single-shot percussion cap pistol, 116
"Six-Shooter," 132
SKS carbine, 219
sleeve grabber, 41
Slocum, 136
Smith, Horace, 134, 136
Smith & Wesson, 134, 136
   "Military & Police" revolver, 136
   Model 3 revolver, 136
   No. 2 revolver, 137
SMLE (Short Magazine Lee Enfield), 149, 150, 180
   MKII bayonet for, 181
   MKIII, 181
smoothbore firearms, 71, 110, 115
snaphance lock, 72
sniper rifle, German, 210
Social History of the Machine Gun, The (Ellis), 184
sodegarami, 41
SOE (Special Operations Executive), 212
spadone, 84
Spandau Maxim machine gun, 185
Spanish blunderbuss, 118
Spanish folding knife, 163
spearhead, Mycenaean, 20
spears, 40
   Amazon, 23
   atlatls and, 15, 16, 19
   Japanese, 40, 44
   Stone Age, 16
   Zulu, 40, 44
specialized weapons of World War II, 210–211
   anti-tank weapons, 210, 211
   flare pistols, 211
   PIAT, 210, 211
   rubber truncheon, 211
   snipers, 210
   whip, 211
Spencer, Christopher, 140, 141, 144
Spencer carbine, 139, 141, 144
Springfield:
   Model 1903, 148, 149, 180, 181, 189
   Model 1835 musket, 115
   Model 1861 musket, 140, 141

"trap-door," 144
spring guns, 170
square barrel pistol, 81
squeezer pistols, 156
Stalin, Josef, 202
Starr revolver, 140
steatite hoe, 17
STEN gun, 208
Stevens-Savage, 181
Steyr automatic, 179
stiletto, 50
Stoner, Eugene, 216
stone weapons, 14–17
Sturmgewehr MP44, 200, 216
submachine guns of World War II, 208–209
   French MAS, 209
   MP40, 209
   MP44, 209
   origins of, 208
   Reising, 209
   STEN, 208
   WWII and after, 208
sundial gun, 76
swagger, stick, 202
swagger stick gun, 161
Swedish Mauser, 151
Swedish M40 pistol, 199
Swiss percussion cap pistol, 116
sword cane, Napoleon's, 110–111
swords:
   African, *see African swords*
   Asian, *see Asian swords*
   European, *see European swords*
   nineteenth-century, *see nineteenth-century swords*
   pistol-, 79
   World War II ceremonial, 202–205
Sykes, Eric, 195
Sykes-Fairbairn Commando Knife, 194, 195, 212

t

tabouka, 90
tanto, 62, 96, 97
Terni carbine/grenade launcher, 201
Texas Paterson, 130
Thompson, John T., 188, 189, 208
Thompson sub-machine gun, 10, 188, 189, 193, 208
throwing knives:
   African, 57
   Indian, 58
Thucydides, 215
thumbscrews, 37
Tibetan sword, 93
tinder lighter, 78
"tip-up" revolvers, 137
Tokarev, Feodor, 199
Tokarev pistol, 196, 199
Torador, Indian, 70
"Torino," 150

transition from hunter-gatherer to agriculture, 16
trap gun, 102, 170
  Naylor, 171
traveler's pistols, 78
trench warfare, 186–187
  life and death during, 187
  weapons of, 187
  Western front, 187
truncheon gun, 164
tuck, 84
Tula-Tokarev, 199
tulwar, 90, 92, 113
Turbiaux, Jacques, 157
Turkish blunderbuss, 103
Turkish Mauser, 151
turn-off pistols, 78
turn-over pistols, 78, 117, 129
Turpin, H. J., 208
Turret pistol, 135
Twain, Mark, 126
Twigg, John, 116
Type 50 "burp gun," 208

u

umbrella gun, 161, 212
Union Cutlery Company, 195
Union weapons of the Civil War, 140–141
  carbines and pistols, 140
  Gatling gun, 141
  Spencer carbine, 141
  Springfield rifled musket, 140, 141
U.S. foot-artillery sword, 121
Unwin & Rodgers, 165
Urban II, Pope, 30

v

van Coehorn, Menno, 76
Vetterli, Friedrich, 148
Vetterli infantry rifle, 150
Vetterli-Vitali, 183
Virgil, 14
volley gun, 77
von Dreyse, Nikolaus, 148
von Mannlicher, Ferdinand Ritter, 183

w

Waffenfabrik August Menz, 189
wakezashi, 90
Walker, Samuel, 132
Walker Colt, 132
walking-stick gun, 161
Wallis, John, 170
Wallis alarm gun, 170
Walther P38, 196, 197
War of the Future, The (Bloch), 186
Washington, George, 100

Webly & Scott automatic, 199
Webly & Scott revolvers, 178, 198
Wesson, Daniel, 134, 136
Wesson, Edwin, 136
Westinghouse Corporation, 150
Weston, Tom, 217
Weston "Reformer" miniature gun, 217
wheel-lock, 72
  German, musket, 73
  German, pistol, 74
  German, rifle, 72
  rampart gun, 73
whip, 211
White, Rollin, 134
Whitney, Eli, Jr., 132
Whitworth rifle, 139
Wilhelm II, Kaiser, 124
Wilkinson Sword Company, 120
William the Silent, 72
Wilson, Daniel, 137
Winchester, Oliver, 136, 145
Winchester, Sarah Pardee, 145
Winchester, William, 145
Winchester Repeating Arms Company, 153
  Model 70, 219
  Model 1866, 144, 145
  Model 1873, 144, 145, 146
windbuchse, 112
WKC (Weyersberg, Kirschbaum, & Company), 124
Wogdon, Robert, 100, 101
Wogdon pistols, 101
World War I, 175
  edged weapons of, 176–177
  infantry rifles of, see infantry rifles of World War I
  pistols of, 178–179
  U.S. gas mask, 181
World War II, 193
  Allied pistols, 198–199
  Axis pistols, 196–197
  ceremonial weapons, 202–205
  edged weapons of, 194–195
  machine guns, 206–207
  rifles, 200–201
  specialized weapons, 210–211
  submachine guns, 208–209
wrist knife, 58

y

yari, 40, 44
yataghan, 55

z

Zaitsev, Vasily Grigoryevich, 210
zweihänder, 84, 86

ACKNOWLEDGMENTS

Unless otherwise noted, all silhouetted weaponry images are from the Berman Museum of World History, Anniston, Alabama, with the exception of the following:

Colt Peacemaker on page 144 © 2006 Jupiterimages Corporation;

Model 1911 Colt Semi-Automatic on page 154 © 2006 Jupiterimages Corporation;

Broomhandle Mauser on page 155 © 2006 Jupiterimages Corporation;

Greener Humane Cattle Killer on page 171 © copyright Graham N. Greener, 2006;

and the Browning Automatic Rifle (BAR) on page 155 © 2006 Jupiterimages Corporation.

OTHER CREDITS

Art on pages 12–13 © Rohit Seth/Shutterstock

Images on pages 14, 30, 31, 34, and 65 © 2006 Jupiterimages Corporation;

Image of "Warrior with Club" on page 15 by William Henry Jackson (1843–1942) from the World's Transportation Commission Photograph Collection (Library of Congress).

Art on page 31 © Matt Purciel/Shutterstock; art on page 32 © Edward Burns/Shutterstock; art on page 38 © Ingvar Tjostheim/Shutterstock; art on page 39 © James R. Hearn/Shutterstock; art on page 64 © Tim Pleasant/Shutterstock; art on page 108 © Cfan/Shutterstock;

Image on pages 66–67 published by John H. Daniels & Son, Boston, 1903, courtesy of Library of Congress, Washington, D.C.

Art on page 69, "The Fruits of Arbitrary Power, or the Bloody Massacre," originally published in 1770, courtesy of Library of Congress, Washington, D.C.

Photos of Napoleon (p 110), Richard Gatling (p 141), Oliver Winchester (p 145), Eliphant Remington (p 147), John M. Browning (p 153), Sir Hiram Maxim (p 185), J. T. Thompson (p 189), John C. Garand (p 201), and M. T. Kalashnikov (p 217) courtesy of Wikipedia.

Photo of Kaiser Wilhelm on page 124 courtesy of the George Grantham Bain Collection (Library of Congress).

Samuel Colt photo on page 132 courtesy of Cedar Hill Cemetery, Hartford, Connecticut.

Images on pages 138, 139, 175, 186, 214, 219–20 courtesy of Library of Congress, Washington, D.C.

Photo of Jefferson Davis on page 142 courtesy of the Berman Museum of World History, Anniston, Alabama.

Image on pages 172–73 courtesy of George Grantham Bain Collection (Library of Congress).

Images on pages 190–91, 193 by Alfred T. Palmer, 1942 (Library of Congress).

Also:

Many thanks to the staff of the Berman Museum of World History, in Anniston, Alabama, Cheryl Bragg, Executive Director; Dan Spaulding, Curator of Collections; Matt Mumbauer, Registrar; Adam Cleveland, Facilities Manager; Teresa Bradshaw, Office Manager; and especially Robert Lindley, Collections Manager, who proved an invaluable resource. Additional thanks to Tim Moon, Registrar of the Anniston Museum.

Thanks also to Graham Greener, of W. W. Greener, for his assistance in identifying and explaining the workings of a rare Greener implement.

Hylas would also like to thank former COO *f*-stop fitzgerald, who took a week away from his regular Hylas duties to be our staff photographer for this project.